THE INDUSTRIAL SOCIETY
HANDBOOK OF
MANAGEMENT SKILLS

The Industrial Society

The Industrial Society works to develop the full talents and potential of people at work and those seeking work. The aim is to maximise the contribution that organisations and the individuals in them can make to the country's economy. In achieving this, the community as a whole can benefit from increased satisfaction, success and wellbeing.

The Society is a leading training and advisory body. It is independent and self-financing, providing services which include courses and conferences, in-house training and advice, publications, audio-visual training programmes, and a quarterly magazine.

Our staff includes 200 management advisers with wide practical experience in industry, commerce and the public sector.

For further information, please contact the Society's principal office at:

The Industrial Society
Robert Hyde House
48 Bryanston Square
London W1H 7LN
Telephone: 071-262-2401

THE INDUSTRIAL SOCIETY
HANDBOOK
of
MANAGEMENT SKILLS

The Industrial Society

First published 1990 by
The Industrial Society
Robert Hyde House
48 Bryanston Square
London
W1H 7LN
Tel: 071–262–2401

British Library Cataloguing in Publication Data

Industrial Society handbook of management skills.
  1. Management. Techniques
  I. Industrial Society
  658.4

ISBN 0–85290–903–9

Typeset by Columns Design and Production Services Ltd, Reading
Printed and bound in Great Britain by
Butler & Tanner Ltd, Frome and London

Design by Oliver Relfe

Contents

14 THE MANAGEMENT OF HEALTH AND SAFETY   249

List of authors

Each chapter is adapted from the original *Notes For Managers* series and is available separately from The Industrial Society Press. The authors of these chapters are as follows:

1. Colin Chase
2. John Garnett
3. Christine Wright
4. Ruth Watts-Davies
5. Ian Lawson
6. Ian Lawson
7. Winifred Gode
8. Jennifer McKibben
9. William A. Simpson
10. Andrew Forrest
11. Colin Chase
12. Roy Pernet and David Wright
13. Betty Ream
14. Inspectors in the Health and Safety Executive's Accident Prevention Advisory Unit (APAU)
15. Ruth Watts-Davies
16. Jeremy Thorn
17. Derek Coulthard
18. Sandra Horne

FOREWORD

We are entering a highly competitive decade. The Single European Market will bring great opportunities and great challenges for every organisation. Success, or otherwise, will depend upon how managers lead, motivate and involve staff to achieve their common goals.

Most people have to work at being good managers. Even the most committed of us need some help occasionally. It is for this reason that the *Industrial Society Handbook Of Management Skills* has been compiled. It is a practical, down-to-earth reference book for managers who need information as succinctly and simply as possible.

Every manager should be able to make these things *happen*, and it is our actions which speak volumes about our ability to lead others.

ALISTAIR GRAHAM
Director, The Industrial Society

1 THE MANAGER AS A LEADER

Management or leadership?

Leadership is fashionable, and good leaders are recognised as being those in management that really make things happen, rather than those who simply administer. We have witnessed the leadership abilities of those that have turned around giants like ICI, British Steel, Rolls Royce and British Airways, whilst others have achieved much the same but on a smaller scale. These are the smaller business people, and also the leaders of management buyouts. They may not have the national profile of corporate leaders, but their leadership abilities are still vital to their organisation's success in today's international market place.

Yet the efforts of all these top leaders would be to no avail without the applied leadership abilities of *all* those in charge, at every level of their organisations. As a former chairman of British Steel expressed it: 'however grand the driver's intentions, the only thing that matters is where "the rubber meets the road".'

It is therefore vital that we seek to understand leadership so that those in a position of authority (at any level) can be trained in how they achieve results with people.

It is no longer good enough to operate on a basis of ignorance. We live in the age of communication, where we expect to know what is happening; to be part of the action; to have a say in the affairs of the society we live in and the organisation we work in. Somehow, those expectations have to be matched to the requirements of the organisation so that there is a sharing of vision and achievement of common purpose.

Defining leadership

How, then, can we define leadership in order to develop the abilities of those in charge of others? First, we must understand the basis of any manager's job. This can be described as being within three skill areas.

1 *Technical.* A manager must have sufficient technical competence to know what to expect from others and be able to recognise when the job is of the right quality and when it is below standard. It is seldom necessary to be technically excellent, thereby having the ability to carry out the technical context of a job better than any individual team member. This issue will be addressed again later.

2 *Administration.* It is necessary to understand the methods and procedures that are the administrative framework of the organisation. It is then possible both to maintain the standards of these procedures and be a champion for changing those that no longer suit the needs of the current operation. Again, it is not necessary to be the administrative expert.

3 *Achieving results through people.* This is the focus of leadership which begins to stand 'leaders' apart from 'managers'. We do not administer people, nor do we get others to do only those jobs that we don't want to do. As the Chief Executive of British Aerospace put it: 'leadership is the art of getting more from people than they think they are capable of giving'.

Identifying the ability

How then do we identify and develop our leadership abilities? There have traditionally been three different approaches, though there are many 'schools' that can be identified within each. These divisions are:

- qualities or traits
- situational
- functional.

Qualities or traits

Any team will expect its leader to have certain qualities, which invariably will differ with individual perceptions. Numerous lists have been carefully drawn up, particularly by those seeking to identify leadership potential for the armed forces: courage; willpower; initiative; knowledge; integrity; fitness; judgement and team spirit to name a few.

There may be a sense of discomfort about some of these qualities and traits: for example, the level of fitness to be attained, or the amount of initiative required. However, these are the briefest lists of qualities. The Royal Canadian Mounted Police, for example, seek 18 qualities that include humour, honesty, good judgement, and decisiveness.

Clearly, it is dangerous to select leaders solely by virtue of their qualities, because of the different appeal and interpretations of such things as 'humour' or 'honesty'. It would be doubtful whether such an approach would allow us to achieve agreement on the factors sought and the method of identifying them. Even then, it provides little scope for training and development.

The best we can do is identify the individual strengths of people that have a common accord, and seek to maximise these. For example, the leader who is seen to be fit and energetic may well be more suited to a particular type of job or organisation. In this way, we can at least acknowledge the strengths in each individual without assessing all potential leaders under one set of quality criteria and thereby establishing a 'have got' or 'have not got' leadership ability. One result of this is the assessment category of 'not yet a born leader'.

Situational

Two main schools emerge from this approach to leadership. The first is based on having the leader most suited to the immediate situation. This can happen through either the natural leader arising from the group according to the activity, or the group appointing that leader through consensus. In either event, we do not have a practical solution to managing at work, where the leader is appointed by those above. Yet many organisations unwittingly tread this path, by the way they promote the best secretary to be the office supervisor; the outstanding sales person to be the sales manager; or the reliable accountant to be the accounts manager. Little wonder that, without training in leadership skill, the department flounders.

Leaders must have the technical competence to recognise the standards and quality in their organisation necessary to meet customer requirements, but there is more to it. Leaders must have the necessary understanding and skill for their position of having to get work done through and with other people.

The second 'situational' school is based on leaders adapting their style to meet the situation in which they find themselves. This can apply to both the organisational activities (e.g. fast growth, retrenchment, start up, diversification) and the individual's capabilities (e.g. experienced, fresh in job, fast-track). Its strength is in the recognition that leaders should be aware of what is going on around them and take such observations into account. The weakness is that it can be difficult to identify sufficiently, and accurately, the style necessary for any particular situation without resulting in a confused workforce.

Functional

This approach concentrates on the actions a leader must take to be successful. From this premise of concentrating on the leadership functions of management, a number of different schools have arisen, each seeking to encapsulate a range of activities within a simple framework or model. One of the most practical and established is that describing the leader as existing to get a job done through the efforts of individual human beings working as a team.

As a result, there would appear to be three inter-related areas in which to work:

- ensuring that the required TASKS are continually achieved
- building and reinforcing the TEAM and fostering TEAM-WORK and TEAM SPIRIT
- developing each INDIVIDUAL member of the team.

Action-centred leadership

Taking this functional approach to leadership, we can focus on the actions required which are relevant to any level of management. This has become an organisational philosophy for companies in search of excellence. This approach is based on the three areas of work, with each influencing the other:

- achieving the TASK

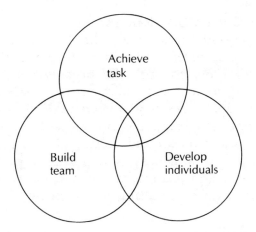

Figure 1.1 *Action-Centred Leadership*

- building the TEAM
- developing INDIVIDUALS

This can be illustrated with the simple model of Action-Centred Leadership (*see* Figure 1.1).

The leader is not a part of the team, but is a member of his or her own peer group and, as such, is engaged in tasks as a team member at that level of management. Invariably, this level will have longer time horizons, larger financial responsibilities, and more significant decisions impacting on employees and customers. From this position, the leader should stand back in order to be able to monitor progress towards desired results through the activities of individuals, and also the extent of teamwork. The effective leader then evaluates what is learnt and acts accordingly, with praise or corrective measures. For example, it may be necessary to become part of the team in providing an extra pair of hands, or additional brain power. The skill is to know when to stand back again before being accused of 'interfering'. Of course, the leader who is seldom visible and rarely supports the team will be accused of 'not caring' – so observation and evaluation are vital in determining the right balance.

Putting it into practice

Considering this in a little more detail, we will first examine the integration of the three circles by an effective leader.

Achieving the task and objectives

The need to accomplish the tasks for which the team, unit, department and, indeed, organisation exists, is the primary and most obvious duty of the manager. A leader who consistently fails to achieve targets and budgets is unlikely to remain a leader for very long! However, we must also accept that never to fail is probably never to take risks – in today's changing world, that is a balance every manager must continually be assessing if they are to be a leader. It is therefore vital to be clear about what our objectives are, how we are going to achieve our tasks, and to what standards.

However, in their zeal to reach the objective for which they are responsible, managers will too often yield to the temptation to 'do it themselves'. The chief engineer will use the tools the engineers should be using; the chief chemist cannot resist finishing the delicate crystallisation on which so many month's experiments depend. They may actually be capable of doing it better, but it is not the job of the leader. Managers that find themselves doing these things more than occasionally should stop and consider why.

Building and maintaining a winning team

Although we are employed by organisations on the basis of individual contracts, it is in teams that the majority of our work is conducted – in the office, the purchasing section, the 'twilight' shift, the 'heavy' gang, or on a project. These teams exist because the task cannot be achieved by one person alone. Neither can it be most effectively achieved by a 'group' of people. In too many organisations there are groups that lack teamwork, particularly where complex organisational structures are used.

It is the leader's responsibility to build teamwork by directing each individual's efforts towards the achievement of the organisation's objectives. The leader must consciously set about gaining the loyalty of members to the team, their pride in belonging, their desire to work together as a team, and the standards they accept.

Teams differ from groups because in teams, each individual understands and values the contribution of the other members. They work to a common goal – some people call it 'group synergy'. The leader should also make effective use of the energy which will arise in the team by listening to the ideas generated. Clear decisions are then taken regarding which ideas are to be used and how and why others are not currently being pursued.

We can therefore see how much the 'team circle' overlaps the 'task circle'.

Developing individuals

We must not forget that all members of the team need to continue to live and express themselves as individuals; to provide for those dependent upon them; to find satisfaction in their work and play. In order to satisfy these needs, people must exert themselves – they must get involved. Fortunately for the manager, there is a high coincidence between these needs and the management obligation to achieve results through the best use of resources – in this case, human.

The leader must ensure that individuals: know what is expected of them; feel they are making a significant and worthwhile contribution to the task; and receive adequate recognition for it.

Ideally, every job should: draw out the best from each human being; use abilities; match responsibilities to capabilities; stretch; challenge and enable people to grow. An individual should be able to look back and think 'a year ago, I would have been really worried about doing this job, and now I'm taking it in my stride'.

Occasionally, the leader may need to help or counsel individuals over some problem which is new, unfamiliar, or even daunting.

If the leader does not develop, or pay sufficient attention to, individuals then they may withdraw from the team. They may be at work, but not working.

Keeping a balance of action

It is the leader's responsibility to take action in all three areas. However, circumstances will not always allow equal attention to be paid to all three areas. There will be occasions when all of your energies will be devoted to achieving the task (e.g. during a period of crisis or when there is a rush job to complete). But whenever that vital period is past, it is important to reassess the impact of that action on individuals and teamwork. This may simply be a case of acknowledging the efforts made during the crisis with a well meant 'thank you'.

The interaction of these areas can also be seen when a department or project is continually failing to achieve targets. Team morale tends to drop and individual reaction can turn to apathy or aggression. Equally, if the team is torn by internal dissension and jealousies, its performance, as well as individual satisfaction, will suffer. This can identify itself in absenteeism, staff turnover, poor timekeeping, and a general fall in standards. It is quite false to address ourselves to these 'problem' people — it is to their manager that we should be looking for corrective action.

Task orientation

Poor leadership can also be seen through over-identification with one area of activity. Consider the manager who is continuously 'task orientated'. This can be represented by Figure 1.2.

Figure 1.2   *Task orientation*

The 'task master' is driven by the figures – always striving to improve performance by whatever financial or technical criterion is considered most appropriate. Little attention is paid to team members as human beings that have considerable responsibilities of their own outside of work. Neither will teamwork play a very large part in this leader's approach. In today's climate of shorter working hours, longer leisure time, and greater amenities, this leader will indeed have little commitment from his or her people. They will do their best to keep out of trouble, looking forward to their income for the ability to pursue life outside of work. Little creativity will be seen here, apart from getting around management rules. Money will become an increasingly prime motivator, with management responding in numerous ingenious incentive schemes – which probably breed greater discontent. Frequently a symptom of the organisation basing its managerial promotion on technical criteria at the expense of leadership potential.

Team orientation

Then there is the leader who wants to be seen as one of the team and be 'popular'. So we see distortion as represented by Figure 1.3.

Leaders have to take difficult decisions, many of which may be unpopular. Indeed, it would be most worrying if all management decisions were popular. By identifying so closely with the team, the leader is unlikely to take timely corrective action if, for instance, standards of customer service are failing

Figure 1.3   *Team orientation*

or discipline dropping. The longer these things are left unchecked, the more difficult it will be to face up to them. On the one hand, the leader is trying to work hard at team spirit. On the other hand, through misguided action, the leader is failing to maintain individual standards, is not achieving the task, and morale is flagging. A really severe case of 'over identification with the team'. This can be a particular problem when the leader has been selected from within the team and not been given sufficient leadership training to cope with the changing position.

Concentrating on individuals

Finally, there is the manager who concentrates on a few individuals in the team. This is represented by Figure 1.4.

Figure 1.4 *Concentrating on individuals*

At one extreme are those individuals receiving the majority of the leader's attention, possibly because they are 'high fliers'. They benefit from particularly demanding or challenging assignments so that others seldom have the opportunity to equally demonstrate their abilities. At the other extreme are those gaining the leader's attention through lack of skills or ability, resulting in undue support by the leader, or even excessive monitoring and disciplining.

As equal opportunities become a more established part of company culture, there will be a need to make even greater efforts to balance individual development with team building and task accomplishment. Excessive attention to someone in the team of different sex, colour, religion, age, or disability, could well result in dissension or jealousy which will affect overall performance.

Leadership processes

We now need to identify the processes that will help us towards leading that winning team. To win, we can determine five key stages in the process.

1 *Defining the objectives*. Being clear what is required in quantitative and qualitative terms.
2 *Planning*. To meet these objectives. This will almost certainly involve two phases.
   - Gathering of information, ideas and suggestions. This is the phase that will probably demand management activity in collecting relevant data, and a leadership approach to the involvement of others through gaining ideas and suggestions. There are many aspects to these activities, broadly grouped under 'consultative' processes (e.g. quality circles, task forces, advisory committees, staff councils).
   - Taking the decision. This must have clarity of timing so that everyone understands that the consultative phase is complete and that minds are not focused on actually getting the work done.
3 *Briefing*. It is vital that everyone understands the plan so that teamwork is part of the process from the beginning. The leader briefs the team, checks for understanding and gains commitment to the work ahead.
4 *Monitor and support*. In achieving results through people, the leader has now created the environment for individuals to work willingly and well at what needs to be done. Standing back is a vital part of the leadership function. Yet we also find that if you stand back too far and are seldom seen, then the team is likely to consider that you do not support, or are not particularly interested in, their work. Visible leadership, 'management by walking about', or, as The Industrial Society prefers to call it, 'Walking the Job', so that you observe, listen, and learn, is extremely important.

5 *Evaluate.* Walking the job is not a fitness exercise. It is learning by listening and seeing, so that we can decide what follow-up action needs to take place. It is quite possible that we may wish to modify our aims; alternatively, perhaps we haven't achieved what we set out to achieve. In such cases, if we are to meet original specifications, it is almost certain that we will want to return to the planning process.

These five key stages could be viewed as an action cycle as shown by Figure 1.5.

This cycle represents both small, or relatively easy tasks, and the more major tasks or overall objectives. In developing the leadership process for a major task or project, constraints may be identified at an early stage without ever reaching the briefing stage. Similarly, having planned, we might be briefing the team when, as a result of questioning, it becomes clear that some aspect of the plan is seriously flawed. It could be argued that this

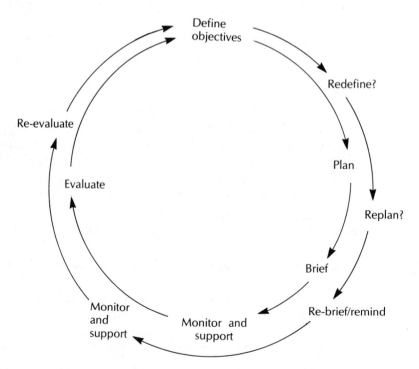

Figure 1.5 *Five stages of leadership action cycle*

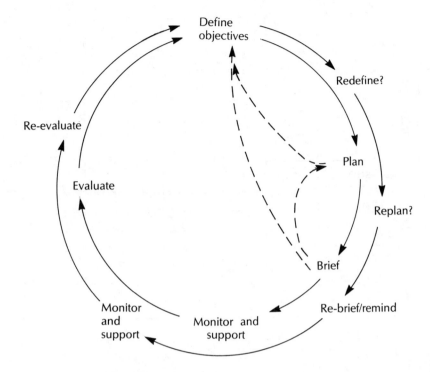

Figure 1.6   *Modified action cycle*

should have been identified during the gathering of information and consultative processes. But it would be a foolish leader who ignores such a flaw and carries on with the original plan. As visible leadership strikes a balance between 'spying' and 'not caring', the desire to admit that you are not always right has to be balanced with being indecisive. If a plan needs modification at first briefing, then it is because it is *not going to work*, rather than because it could be *slightly better*. So we can modify our action cycle, as in Figure 1.6.

It is by following these leadership actions of defining the objectives, consulting, deciding, briefing, followed by supporting, monitoring, and evaluating against objectives, that identifies the manager as a leader.

Table 1.1 *Framework for leadership*

KEY ACTIONS		TASK	TEAM	INDIVIDUAL
Define objectives		Identify tasks & constraints	Hold team meetings Share commitment	Clarify objectives Gain acceptance
Plan	Gather information	Consider Options Check resources	Consult Develop suggestions	Encourage ideas Assess skills
	Decide	Priorities Time scales Standards	Structure	Allocate jobs Delegate Set Targets
Brief		Clarify objectives Describe plan	Explain decisions Answer questions Check understanding	Listen Enthuse
Monitor Support		Assess progress Maintain standards	Coordinate Reconcile conflict	Advise Assist/reassure Counsel discipline
			Recognise effort	
Evaluate		Summarise Review objectives Replan if necessary	Recognise & gain from success Learn from mistakes	Appraise performance
			Guide & train	Give praise

Framework for leadership

We can now bring the action cycle together with the three-circle model in order to identify our framework for leadership.

The framework shown in Table 1.1 on page 14 relates the three job areas to the key processes so that actions can be identified. These actions are so inter-related that their position in one part of the framework does not mean that they do not have relevance in another. However, for practical purposes they have been grouped under the area to which they *mainly* relate.

Checklist: achieve the task

- be quite clear about what the task is, put it over with enthusiasm, and remind people of it often
- understand how the task fits into the overall short- and long-term objectives of the organisation
- plan how to accomplish it
- define and provide the resources needed, including the time and the authority required
- do everything possible to ensure the organisational structure allows the task to be done efficiently
- pace progress towards achievement of the task
- evaluate results and compare them with the original plans and the objectives of the organisation.

Checklist: build the team

- set and maintain the team's objectives and standards
- involve the team as a whole in the achievement of objectives
- maintain the unity of the team by seeing that dissident activity is minimised
- communicate regularly with the team face-to-face, at least once a month, on matters of people, policy, progress, and points for action
- consult with the team, whenever time permits, before taking decisions which affect them

- explain the organisation's results and achievements
- communicate any changes taking place in the organisation and how they will affect the team.

Checklist: develop individuals

Every leader must:

1 Provide a challenge and scope for development by:
   - setting targets, after consulting, and reviewing them at regular intervals
   - providing relevant training – where appropriate by using people to train others, in the specialist skills they may have
   - arranging any necessary internal and external contact
   - restructuring or grouping tasks to use people's skills to the fullest
   - rotating jobs to broaden experience
   - providing scope for individuals to take greater responsibility
   - training thoroughly at least one deputy.

2 Make people feel valued by:
   - knowing their name, their place of work, and interests outside of work
   - regularly monitoring and appreciating individual effort
   - sharing an interest in whatever they hold important
   - creating a good working environment by being approachable
   - ensuring everyone understands the importance of their contribution to the team's objectives
   - ensuring everyone understands the function of the organisation.

3 Recognise achievements by:
   - praising and communicating individual successes
   - holding regular meetings with each individual to

monitor and counsel
- providing guidance for a personal development programme
- operating a fair and open policy of linking salary to
performance.

Providing the right climate and opportunities for these
needs to be met for each individual in the team, is possibly
the most difficult, and certainly the most challenging and
rewarding part of the leader's responsibilities.

In summary, the job of a leader at any level is to:

- get the required results (ACHIEVE TASK)
- build an effective and cohesive team (BUILD TEAM)
- 'grow' and develop each individual, and provide the
satisfaction of having a valued member of an effective team
(DEVELOP INDIVIDUALS)

These are the actions of a leader. This is the 'work' a manager
has to perform to be a successful leader. They are not inborn
traits. They are skills which can be recognised, practised and
developed.

The entire emphasis is on the actions leaders take, upon what
they DO rather than the sort of people they are. It has been
shown time and time again that by DOING, one BECOMES a
more effective leader.

2 THE MANAGER'S RESPONSIBILITY FOR COMMUNICATION

Why does communication matter?

The success of managers depends, primarily, on their ability to communicate to all the people for whom they are responsible, what they need to do, and the importance of doing it. Failures in communication are costly.

Example

In a production job where a new manager was appointed, but all other variables were the same, a saving of 5 per cent was achieved, amounting to £80,000 per annum, because the new manager laid down an effective system of communication. The main difference, as far as the employees were concerned, was that under the new manager they knew what the problem was, what they were trying to achieve, how he wanted the problem tackled and what part they had to play in order to get improvements. They knew, too, the extent to which they succeeded in reaching the individual targets set.

Example

Out of 35 stoppages in a large organisation, eighteen were due to failures of communication. The cost of these stoppages could not be measured in the hours lost alone; the stoppages upset the whole rhythm of production and lessened co-operation between employees and their managers.

Where there is change, the full benefits can only be achieved where there is an adequate communication system for explaining face-to-face, directly to employees, what is required, and why.

Example

A large company negotiated centrally a productivity deal with the unions, to achieve greater flexibility in the use of manpower. In practice, the only sections of the company that succeeded in getting the flexibility were those with a direct and systematic method of communication, through managers and supervisors, to their own employees.

Adequate communication results in greater productivity through more effective work and greater co-operation.

Example

An organisation in the City gets a measurable increase in staff productivity following each monthly briefing by management to the staff. Progress against local targets, and the priorities for the coming month, are explained.

Executives with good potential will leave the staff if they are unaware of their prospects within the company. Finding and training a successor is costly; it will have repercussions in the section and it lowers morale among colleagues. Failures in communication are not limited to factories or to shop-floor level.

There is no monopoly of wisdom at the top of organisations. We cannot afford to waste the ideas and inventiveness of employees at any level.

> *Example*
>
> A company set up a formal consultative system to tap these ideas at shop-floor level. One employee with 30 years' service suggested using a domestic oven cleaner to prepare some of the surfaces used in production. It solved a long standing problem. When asked why he had not suggested it before, he answered that management had given no indication that they wanted employees' views.

We need to bear in mind that the new generation of employees is much more used to being involved – at school, college or university – and they therefore expect that involvement to continue at work.

People will only give of their best if they fully understand the decisions that affect them and the reasons behind those decisions. People need to understand:

- what they have to do and why
- how they are performing against budgets and set targets
- what their conditions of employment are.

They can then be involved in what they are doing, resulting in greater efficiency, higher morale, and greater co-operation.

The need for a properly organised system of communication applies as much in offices, research laboratories, drawing offices and hospitals as it does on the shop floor. If effective communication is to be achieved, it cannot be left to casual methods.

What to communicate

The first things to decide are our priorities, because the conclusions will affect the communication method to be used. Clearly, you cannot tell everybody everything – or consult everyone on everything, otherwise no other work would be done.

The normal approach has been to try to tell people what their managers think will be of *interest* to them, omitting those things they must understand whether they are interested in them or not. Such a yardstick is misleading; it results in much of secondary importance being explained.

Example

The end use of a product from another works may be of some interest to employees. On the other hand, in times of industrial peace, the dispute procedure may be of no interest at all. To communicate the first point is of no great importance. To communicate the second is vital, for once a dispute is on, it is too late to try to explain the need to keep to procedures.

If employees are not interested it will be more difficult – but no less vital – for management to get them to understand.

This understanding is also the first step in achieving successful consultation with employees. Too often, managers seek ideas and opinions in formal consultation structures without having first given employees that understanding of the work from which realistic ideas and opinions can come.

First principles

The priority, then, is for managers to communicate *understanding* of those matters that significantly affect a person's will to give the best of their work. People do not have to agree in order to co-operate with a decision, but they must understand how and why it has been made.

What are these matters which must be understood?

Things that affect a person's job

- What is the job?
- Who is my boss?
- What contribution does my work make to the total job?
- Where does the work come from and go to? What is it? What is the end product? What is it for?

- What are my work targets? To what extent are they being achieved? What are the standards?
- To what extent can I influence costs?
- What are the safety standards?
- What changes are being made and why?
- What are the priorities in my work over the next month?

Things that affect a person's employment

- What is the rate of pay? How are salaries or wages calculated? What is the basis for the bonus? What are the arrangements for overtime pay?
- What are the holiday arrangements?
- What is the sick pay?
- How do I get promoted? How do supervisors get selected?
- What is the length of notice? Are there any redundancy arrangements?
- What are the negotiating procedures? How do I make a suggestion or a complaint? Where can I get help with personal problems?
- What is the company's attitude to my membership of a trade union?
- What changes are being made and why?

Some argue that many such matters cannot be communicated because there are no understandable reasons for the policy decisions taken. In the vast majority of cases this is untrue and is merely a further example of communication failure by senior management. If only the person who took the decisions and decided the policy can be discovered, it will normally be found that they took them for reasons that are understandable.

Which method to choose

All methods of communication in industry and commerce can be grouped under three headings.

- *Managers and supervisors.* Face-to-face communication by the manager or supervisor.

- *Representatives*. Communication through the representative, who may be a member of the staff committee, a shop steward, a staff representative on the employee council, the production committee, the safety committee, or a fellow worker.
- *Mass methods*. People being informed through reading the noticeboard, company newspaper and magazine, manager's newsletters, booklets, circulars, attending mass meetings (when more than 40 people are involved), receiving a popular version of the company's annual report, hearing loud-speakers, using phone-in programmes, seeing films and closed circuit television.

Managers must decide which method of communication is to be used and be clear about what each can do and its limitations. Much of what goes wrong in communication is caused by managers not having thought out clearly what each method can achieve.

Managers and supervisors

Strengths

- The manager or supervisor, as the representative of management to the work group in the office or on the shop floor, is the appropriate person to explain the most important matters, that is, the first principles referred to on pp. 21–22, because these things result from managerial decisions or, in the case of negotiated matters, from joint management/union decisions.
- Part of the job of being a leader is to be the person to whom people look for explanations about things that matter. By becoming the communicator the manager or supervisor will become a more effective leader.
- Supervisors can tailor their explanations to suit the particular group and, following the explanation, questions can be asked. What needs to be explained to one group will be different for another. The opportunity to ask questions is vital for understanding.
- Much of what must be communicated is already common knowledge to the manager. For example, the reasons for a change in production plans which affect a person's job.

- Face-to-face communication with the group saves time, ensures common understanding, and is the most powerful method of 'selling' ideas and building group commitment.

Weaknesses

- With a line of leadership of more than two levels between the top manager and the person on the shop floor or in the office, communication by this method does not happen adequately unless organised.
- Unless planned, it can be expensive in terms of management time.
- The line of leadership cannot, alone, adequately handle upward communication. The top of an organisation is seldom aware of the vividness of attitudes at the bottom if what is reported to them has been passed through a number of levels of the hierarchy.

Representatives

Strengths

- They provide an opportunity for management to explain a policy directly to a few of the employees affected, saving much repetition at different levels.
- They are a necessity for adequate upward communication and invaluable in bringing home to senior management the vividness of feeling in the office or factory.
- The formal contact in representative meetings can and does bring an increase in informal contact.

Weaknesses

- Although management's explanations get over to the representatives, they normally fail to pass on the explanations satisfactorily to their constituents, particularly when the decisions are unpleasant. This is because the representatives of the employees find themselves trying to act as the representatives of management in explaining management policies. This is not the representative's job and puts them, as well as the supervisor, in an impossible position.
- If shop stewards are the main communicators they, not the

supervisors, will become the leaders and bosses of the work group.

Mass methods

Strengths

- They offer the cheapest way of giving particular information to large numbers of people.
- They are quick, e.g. loudspeaker, notice at the exit.
- It is possible to ensure that the information transmitted is accurate.
- They are a necessary aid in support of communication through management.

Weaknesses

- Mass methods are not good for transmitting understanding because you cannot ask a noticeboard or a letter a question. In theory, you can ask a question at a mass meeting; in practice the majority of British people will not do so in meetings of more than 20.
- Although the information transmitted is accurate, it does not necessarily follow that it is accurately received.
- The most important matters to be understood are those that affect the individual or working group. These need separate explanations for each group and the mass method can only cover the general aspect.

Using the grapevine

No mention has been made of communication by rumour – the grapevine. It exists, but managers use it at their peril. The grapevine will pass facts accurately – sometimes, as in the case of an appointment, before the decision has been made. But it very often puts forward an *uncharitable reason* for the decision. The grapevine *can* pass the 'why' in terms that are bad for co-operation: 'X has got the job and you know *why* that is'.

A grapevine withers in those organisations where people know that there is a systematic way of learning about the things that matter from the supervisors or managers.

The importance of questions

In considering the strengths and weaknesses of the various means of communication, stress has been laid on the importance of providing the opportunity for people to ask questions if understanding is to be achieved.

Today, many people think that if you write something clearly enough, people will understand. There is all the difference between providing the information and getting people to understand. Experience of everyday life shows that face-to-face communication must take place and the opportunity to ask questions must be given before understanding will be obtained. Explanation to a small group affected will be more effective than to individuals. In the group, each person will benefit from the answers to another's questions.

Example

An engineer who wants her draughtsmen to understand what she would like them to design will not rely on putting instructions on paper. She will go and see the draughtsmen and tell them face-to-face. After questions, some of which will merely involve repetition of what she has already said, the draughtsmen will understand. The engineer can then confirm the instructions in writing.

When choosing a method of communication, recognise that any systematic method is better than none at all. The mass method is the easiest to work. The hardest is through managers and supervisors. But communication up and down will not be satisfactory in a large organisation without some use of all three methods, and the most important task will be making it work through managers and supervisors.

Effective communication through managers and supervisors

All members of management – including, of course, supervisors and foremen – must be made to appreciate the importance and benefits of adequate communication. The busier their working lives, the more necessary a systematic drill becomes. They cannot afford to leave communication to casual or *ad hoc* methods.

Example

In an organisation, the decision of the works manager to change the production rate was passed down to the deputies and section leaders at their weekly meetings. Thereafter, it was left to casual explanations down the line of command and the reasons for the change were lost in the conglomeration of plant managers, superintendents, foremen and supervisors. This resulted in the changes being made because: 'They had decided,' or it was a 'management decision'. When this happens in an organisation it can discourage hard work.

That 'they' gave it is reason for obeying an order, but not necessarily for co-operating with it. *The difference between co-operation and obedience is often the difference between profit and loss.*

If communication down through line management is to be effective, it must be systematic. The object is to ensure that employees have the decisions that affect their job or conditions of employment explained to them face-to-face by their immediate boss. Two steps are needed. First, establish a drill for team briefing that ensures communication right down the line to the work group, through supervisors. Second, ensure that the necessary information is known by managers.

Team briefing

Team briefing is simply a systematic drill to ensure communication takes place. Each department or section will organise its system of team briefing differently, depending on the number of people involved, the different levels, and the work arrangements, i.e. shifts. The drill for each group must be written down and made known to everyone in the group.

The crucial element is that the information briefed to the group should be relevant to that group. The drill that ensures this happens is that all briefers prepare the local items that need to be briefed, before receiving a briefing from their immediate manager. So at each level, the brief from above is being added to an existing local brief.

Example

The individual foremen in a large engineering company write their own briefs on the first Tuesday in each month, the items being such things as work in progress on that line, the need to complete job cards each day, and the proposed finishing date for the new canteen. They then give their briefs to their departmental managers who read them and suggest additions as necessary. On the Thursday, all department managers brief their supervisors with the brief from above. The supervisors then add this to their local brief, and brief their teams on Thursday afternoon.

Briefing structure

A typical structure for briefing would be for a director, having been briefed by the board, to brief the works manager, who would in turn call the deputies and section heads together and brief them. The section heads then brief the foremen who go on to brief the shop floor. At this level, at least two thirds of the information being briefed by the foremen should be 'local', to do with the job that the group is doing. Local information could include: items collected since the last briefing; procedures that people need to be reminded of; and, very important, a local breakdown of company performance, i.e. the group's output against target, quality record, safety record and absenteeism record. Here, local relevant yardsticks should be used.

In this way, five levels of management can be covered in three steps. In some organisations it might be possible to get the whole management team together at one meeting, but the groups should be no larger than fifteen. Understanding of policies and decisions is only achieved if the group is small enough to allow questions and discussion: fifteen is normally the maximum.

It is important that where information has to go through more than three levels of management, a written brief is prepared and a briefing folder is kept. For three levels or less, note-taking may be sufficient. *Briefers must be made to make notes. This is vital.*

Briefing routine

It is also important that the drill becomes an accepted part of a manager's and supervisor's job, and it is remembered that team briefing is communication with the work group by a management spokesman, not just to a selected few. It is management's job to communicate management's message, and it is vital, particularly at the lower levels, that this is done by the team leader (boss). Communication targets can be written into job descriptions and specifications.

When?
Management must decide when briefing sessions should be held. In the case of day workers, this is often done following the lunch hour. Shift workers may be brought in early or held late and paid overtime. A more economic method is to hold over or bring in the shift supervisor. This often prevents communication failures between shift supervisors. Office and shop workers are briefed either first thing in the morning or just before closing time. Where none of these is possible, some companies find it necessary to bring people in on a Saturday morning. It has been found that where such arrangements have been made, the people concerned have appreciated the fact that they have had things properly explained to them. Perhaps the best situation, in the case of a widely scattered sales force, is to post the brief, then follow it up by a telephone call.

Frequency
For briefing to be credible, it must be regular, with dates set aside in the diary. This also ensures that communication does

not only happen in times of crisis. Many companies have found that monthly is the best frequency: most relevant figures are produced monthly and, at many levels, monthly meetings take place already and briefing can be incorporated into these. Another benefit is that the work group knows when the next briefing will be and will often wait to hear management's view of things before reaching conclusions. Also, once briefing is firmly established, should there be a vital message to pass on quickly, the system can be used at a moment's notice.

Subjects
The subjects covered by the manager will be the decisions and policies which affect people's will to work. The four main headings are: *progress* (how the section is doing); *people*; *policy*; *points for action and the priorities in the coming month*. Local subjects and matters must be predominant at all levels, as well as examples of how major decisions affect a particular work group. This ensures that the majority of the information is relevant to the work group. The relevance of information at each level of briefing is vital. Appendix 4 on page 343 shows the type of subjects covered in team briefings.

How long?
Team briefing sessions should normally last not more than half an hour. A useful guide is for the supervisor to spend two-thirds of the time explaining management decisions and policies that affect those present, leaving one-third of the time for questions on the matters that have been briefed.

Who takes the briefing session?
Normally the foreman, or section head in the office. If people have difficulties in doing this (and this happens less often than managers think), they should be given some practice in:

- the skills of briefing
- writing a local brief
- delivering the brief
- handling questions and feedback.

Deputies able to 'act in absence', etc. should also be appointed to cover sickness, absence, holidays, and so on.

Monitoring

Systems only work when checked. A co-ordinator should be appointed who is accountable for the smooth running of the system. However, the success of the system depends on the commitment shown by managers at all levels to making the system work.

All those running team briefing groups should note in their special folders the time of starting and ending, who was absent, and a one word description of what was discussed, e.g. progress, time-keeping, quality, reorganisation. There are no minutes and no agendas, but the more senior managers should 'walk the job' and ask people what they know about a point briefed. Indeed, they should also sit in on at least one first-line brief each year.

Getting started

First, senior management must be committed to the system of briefing. Second, all briefers at each level must understand the system, and its benefits. A two day training course is the best way to gain their commitment and give them some basic instruction in briefing. Third, the first few briefs should not contain controversial subjects.

Where there has been no tradition of the supervisor or manager talking to the working group, some planning will be needed to get it started. It can start as a training session on doing the job better. A lead-in may be achieved as a result of something not being properly explained, followed by a subsequent request for correct information. The introduction of safety talks is another starting point. As confidence is achieved, the subjects will extend to cover the job, promotion policies, and finally, after consultation and with the shop stewards playing their part, joint management/trade union matters.

The main argument against taking such systematic steps as these is that we cannot afford the time. Where time studies have been made of a supervisor's duties, a very high proportion, 80 per cent, is accounted for by communication. The time involved at shop floor level is less than 0.05 per cent of working time each month.

The systematic method as set out will shorten this time, not lengthen it. Most important of all, where supervisors have shouldered this leadership function of explaining to their working group the matters that affect them, they have been found to become more effective managers.

Getting information to line managers

Certain information, about personnel policies in particular, must be fed into the line of leadership accurately and speedily. Most of the other information is there already. A management bulletin will be required, which can be distributed at a few hours' notice on a pre-arranged distribution list to each manager and supervisor, whenever some decision affecting large numbers of employees has been taken.

The management bulletin should state briefly what has been decided and the main reasons for the decision; as, for example, with details of trade union settlements, changes in a staff job, the introduction of a new way of working.

Each manager and supervisor should receive an individual copy of the management bulletin and not just be placed on a circulation list, since this may result in their hearing important information many days later. It is false economy to restrict the number of copies circulated.

Only urgent matters should be included in the bulletin, otherwise there will be a tendency for it to be put at the bottom of a reading pile.

The bulletin must also state whether the information is to be communicated further and if so – how?

Example

The intermediate results of a round of wage negotiations are circulated in the management bulletin to all managers and supervisors within 24 hours of the negotiation meeting ending. In this way, first line managers are as quickly and well informed as the trade union representatives and the employees.

Making better use of employees' knowledge

Effective communication of ideas and opinions upward from employees to management is essential for all organisations who seek full efficiency. At one end of the scale is the system of representatives and consultative committees; at the other is the local level problem solving team. Both types of consultation improve efficiency and increase the employers' sense of involvement.

Making better use of representatives and consultative committees

Direct discussions between employees and senior management are essential if managers are to be aware of the attitudes and feelings of those who will be affected by management decisions. Without such discussions, wrong decisions can, and do, result. Except in very small companies, some systematic committee meeting with elected representatives is necessary. To look on the committee as a sop to the workers, or as a waste of management time, is to miss an opportunity to increase efficiency and to take a proven step forward in any participation policies.

Purpose and function of a consultative committee

It is not the purpose of a consultative committee to put over management policy; that is the job of managers and supervisors in team briefing. Its purpose is:

- to give employees a chance to improve decisions by contributing comments *before* decisions are made
- to make the fullest possible use of their experience and ideas in the efficient running of the enterprise
- to give management and employees the opportunity to understand each other's views and objectives at first hand.

The main function of the committee is to discuss, before

decisions are taken, any matter affecting the efficiency of the enterprise and the interests of employees to which representatives can contribute.

Subjects for discussion

There should be no limitation on the subjects discussed except for:

- matters which can genuinely be called trade secrets
- matters which should be settled directly between employees and their immediate supervisor
- matters covered in union agreements if the committee is non-union.

The last limitation is a serious one because it prevents the committee from dealing with a whole range of subjects which are of immediate importance to employees. It is therefore a great advantage if the employee members of a committee are union representatives, so that there is no such restriction on topics for discussion. This does not mean that the committee becomes a negotiating body. Even in cases where the same committee is responsible for negotiation and consultation, the two processes are best kept separate, and the chairman should make sure that the committee understands what it is doing at any one time.

The following are examples of subjects which can be the concern of consultative committees:

- output and productivity, e.g. improvements in work methods, office planning, central services, design of machines, transport, office equipment
- manpower policies and procedures, e.g. principles of promotion
- education and training, e.g. induction of new employees, the training of young people
- safety, e.g. investigation of the causes of accidents
- selection and training of supervisors
- effectiveness of communication.

In addition, a committee which is union-based will be in a position to discuss, before negotiations take place:

- wage systems
- job evaluation
- hours of work
- holidays and holiday pay.

Agenda

This should be circulated in advance, with supporting information. More than half the agenda should be initiated by management. It is helpful to have one major subject at each meeting; this is best introduced at the previous meeting so that representatives have time to go away and think about the issues involved and discuss them with colleagues. Major items should also be introduced at the briefing meeting so that everyone knows that the subject is coming up for discussion.

All agendas should include an item which allows the chairman to talk about the progress of the works, or office, or department. This is not with a view to it being passed on, but to remind representatives of the organisational background against which they are talking.

Representatives

There is no need to have an equal number of representatives from each side. A membership of not more than sixteen will produce a good committee; with such a number it should consist of about eleven elected representatives and five appointed representatives. It may be better to re-elect half the elected representatives each year. There should be a minimum service requirement for standing as a candidate; perhaps one year.

If the firm recognises trade unions, then the elected representatives should emerge through the union machinery in the organisation. It is best to include the shop stewards as representatives wherever possible.

The appointed representatives should consist of: the chairman, who should be the manager of the unit; there should always be a supervisor sitting as one of the management-appointed representatives; there should be someone who is a senior manager; and someone who is representative of the younger managers. The latter should be selected for ability and potential; this person will undoubtedly embarrass management by their contributions, from time to time, but their presence on the committee will do more good than harm.

If an additional appointed representative is desirable, a person might well be chosen from a group which is not represented as a result of the elections.

Constituencies

Constituencies for the elected representatives should be drawn in such a way as to produce the maximum community of interest in the group concerned. In case of doubt, it is better to draw them on the basis of the job being done, rather than on the status of the group, e.g. it will be better to have a representative for the whole of the degreasing plant or pension department, rather than to have one representative for the clerical workers employed throughout the organisation.

Meetings

Committees should meet at least every two months if they are to make a useful contribution. Provision should be made to allow for special additional meetings to be held when required.

Reporting back

Representatives may need assistance to communicate the outcome of consultative meetings. Minutes on the noticeboard alone are not satisfactory. More can be achieved by supplying some or all of the following.

- A committee news-sheet immediately following the meeting. The committee news-sheets are not minutes and briefly cover only the most important items discussed. Within 24 hours, copies should be placed on pick-up racks at clocking stations, office entrances and canteens. People can then take a copy for themselves. If a newsletter exists, it may be possible to use this instead of the committee news-sheet. Publication dates must then be tied up satisfactorily with the consultative committee or committees.
- An occasional statement of what has been said for representatives to distribute among their own constituents. This is not as satisfactory as the news-sheet, although it may be easier to accomplish.

- Coaching in speaking for representatives. Four hours' practice with an effective speaker can make a real difference.
- An allotted time for reporting back.
- Management briefing of the decisions taken after consultation, stating that consultation has taken place.

Local level problem solving

Consultative committees, by their very structure, are limited to discussing overall company topics. Specific problems to do with the actual task in individual departments are best dealt with locally.

First line managers should regularly meet with their teams (or volunteers from their teams) to identify and solve their own local work-related problems. This will:

- reinforce the role of the first line manager
- encourage employees to use knowledge and ingenuity to make their areas more efficient
- 'crunch' local problems earlier rather than clogging up the consultative committee.

Many companies have made this step beyond consultative committees, using small, local, problem-solving meetings either on the local manager's own initiative or by installing quality circles.

Example

A team of problem solvers on a battery line looked at a newly installed conveyor belt. They presented suggestions to the management. These ranged from filing down the corners of the safety barriers so as to prevent the operators' hands being cut, to filling up the areas between the bench and the belt and so reducing the scrap level.

Mass methods

Of all mass methods of communication, the most effective are: noticeboards; company magazines and newspapers – including the annual report to employees; the manager's newsletter; employee handbooks; loudspeaker systems; phone-in arrangements; and mass meetings.

Noticeboards

Location is important. They should be where people not only pass, but can also stop to read, e.g. by entrances to plants, offices, canteens.

There should be either two noticeboards, or one board divided into two. One section can then be clearly labelled and used only for urgent and new notices. Once a notice has been on this section for 48 hours, if it is of interest for more than a few days, it should be moved to the other section where notices can be left for reference.

A particular person should be made responsible for each noticeboard. It is best if this person can be the departmental supervisor.

Notices should be signed by an individual, rather than by some legal entity such as the XXYZ Company, which makes people feel they are part of an impersonal web.

When drafting a notice, managers should bear in mind how they would tell its contents to a person face-to-face on the shop floor or in the office.

Company magazines and newspapers

The purpose of company magazines and company newspapers should be:

- to provide a mass means of explaining the company's activities and policies to its employees
- to help employees feel that they are involved in the company
- to create an atmosphere in which change is accepted.

When budgeting and planning company publications, the emphasis should be on frequency and flexibility. It goes without saying that small, casual, inexpensive (e.g. stencilled) newsletters are more topical and urgent than glossy magazines. Ideally, publication should be weekly or fortnightly. Too often, the strict scheduling necessary for the production of glossy magazines inhibits topicality.

The prestige magazine can be sent to an employee's home and is sometimes charged for at a nominal rate. The newsletter should be free: the content should be such that employees need it and will read it, in which case it is in the management's interest to make it as available as possible.

The pick-up racks already mentioned for distributing the committee news sheet, can be used for ordinary issues of the newspaper or newsletter.

Space in company newspapers should be divided into thirds: one-third for the product and other news that affects a person's job; one-third for developments or changes in conditions of employment; and one-third for social events. The third devoted to news that affects jobs will already have been communicated to those directly concerned by their managers and supervisors. Repetition here serves to keep informed those less directly concerned.

Sometimes the magazine is also used as a public relations contact with customers, but it is better to have a completely separate publication for this.

The manager's newsletter

In large organisations where the newspaper covers a wide group of activities, there may be a need for some arrangement whereby the head of department, or works manager, can communicate, in writing, to all employees in their part of the organisation. Invaluable assets are the works manager's or department head's newsletter which goes to all employees, (including members of management) on the site or in the department.

Once more, it is essential that this newsletter appears frequently: at least monthly. Items should not be saved up; when there is something to be said, the newsletter should be sent out. It is a false economy not to run off enough copies for each person or merely to put the newsletter on a noticeboard.

Other advantages of a manager's newsletter between the senior manager and employees are:

- at times of stress and misunderstanding, there is a recognised method of confirming facts in writing
- there is no need to send letters about company matters to people's homes, or to use the pay packet to tell people about things that have little to do with pay; both means of communication are resented.

Accountability charts

People must know who is their boss and who is their boss's boss. There should be available, for each person, a copy of the accountability chart of their department or section, showing the boss's name and who is directly accountable to them. Unlike an organisation chart, it does not attempt to show the complexities of inter-relationships.

Employee handbooks

Each employee should receive an employee handbook setting out the main rules and arrangements that apply to them. The book should be as brief as possible, but it can be supplemented by booklets dealing with specific subjects, such as job evaluation schemes, the disputes procedure with the union, the sick pay scheme and pension fund.

   These booklets should preferably be written in the form of questions and answers which explain specific aspects of conditions of employment. It may be obligatory, for instance, to provide employees with the rules of the pension fund in a legal form, but since this will be virtually unintelligible to anyone who is not an actuary or a lawyer, it will also be necessary to provide employees with an explanatory booklet in everyday language. In the case of works rule-books, a useful form is to set the rule out on one page and on the facing page give the reasons for the rule.

Loudspeaker systems

The great danger of these is that they tend to be used too much. They are not satisfactory for putting over a policy as the listener cannot even see the person speaking, let alone ask any questions. Loudspeaker systems cannot take account of the mood or the particular occupation of the listener.

Phone-in

Some large organisations adopt a phone-in system whereby any member of staff can phone an internal number and hear a recorded tape about current activities, sales position, or the reasons behind other news. Some adopt a system whereby a person can ask a question which is recorded and an answer provided.

Mass meetings

Mass meetings are valuable as the only practical way for people to hear the most senior managers directly. They are not good for achieving understanding, principally because people will not ask questions; they are no substitute for the team briefing sessions.

Example

A mass meeting is held once a year by a director or works manager, to explain to employees the results of the year's working and to talk about plans for the following year. Steps are taken to make it as easy as possible for shift to attend. It is held in the canteen at the end of the normal working day. Such meetings may draw about 40 per cent of the operatives and 70 per cent of the office staff.

In one organisation, the chief executive will speak each year at the time of the annual results, to five hundred senior managers. It is then possible to require each of these managers to speak to similar numbers. This two-tier method of mass communication can be a valuable means of explaining the accounts. It can be supported by a video recording of the first meeting, but the video tape must be accompanied by a manager to deal with the questions that arise.

Annual report for employees

The publication of the annual report of the company gives a major opportunity to help people to understand the vital importance of their work. More and more companies issue a special report setting out the main facts which provides the opportunity to explain that, during the year, people in the organisation have together created five different things:

- they have produced a certain volume of goods and services for other people
- they have generated the incomes of those employed, thus giving people freedom of expenditure
- they have provided tax revenue, both on those incomes and directly, which pays for social needs such as schools, hospitals and pensions
- they have generated saving in reserve for future development
- they have generated a return on people's saving in distributed profits.

Employee reports can also include information about employees, such as length of service, safety, and absenteeism statistics, and time lost through industrial disputes. These are particularly relevant if figures are compared from region to region, or department to department. Other helpful details to include concern:

- customers – who and where they are
- products – what brand names they appear under; what goods will they be part of; which sites make/deal with the various products/services the company offers.

It is important that, when employee reports give figures, they include comparisons and comments. Bald figures tend to produce the reaction: 'So what?' unless it is clear whether or not management is pleased with the results and why the results are better or worse than expected.

The effectiveness of the employee report depends on how it is distributed. Experience suggests it is best distributed in a briefing or before a mass meeting, like the one described in the example earlier. This ensures that everyone receives the report and has a chance to ask questions. Many organisations post reports to employees' home addresses: this is the next best thing as everyone at least receives the report – but it does not encourage them to ask questions or discuss the report with colleagues.

Other mass methods

Other mass visual aids are posters, filmstrips, films, videos, and closed circuit television. All are most effective when they are used as an aid to face-to-face communication.

Example

A company makes an annual video showing company financial results. This is shown to the shop floor in small groups by their supervisor in one of the monthly team briefing sessions. In this way, there is ample opportunity for questions, and the local implication of company performance can be explained.

Written communications and other mass methods can never become the main vehicle for communication. This must be done face-to-face using team briefing or consultative committees. The written word is therefore a useful back-up or a support document, and not the main or only vehicle.

Is communication working?

As in all aspects of management, it is necessary to check that communication is working.

Ways of checking

Walking the job

The simplest method is to ask questions, when walking round offices or factories, about why someone is doing a particular job or why a change has been made. If the explanation is inaccurate, or if the person does not know, the manager should take the matter up with the person's manager or supervisor.

Using consultative committees

After a major change has been made, discuss amongst the

consultative committee whether the communication aspect has been adequately carried out and how it can be improved.

Using courses

Take the opportunity provided by training courses for managers and supervisors (the nearest thing to privileged occasions) for checking the adequacies of communication.

Instituting an investigation

Give a young person, such as a management trainee, the job of examining communication. This is best done by the investigator asking senior management for two or three examples of recent decisions which affect employees and tracking these decisions and the reasons behind them through all levels. Who did the managers talk to? When? How? How did the next level hear? When? How? It is important to note not only if the decision gets lost, but at what point the reasons have changed or become unknown.

Commissioning a written survey

There are two ways of doing this. A group of people may be asked in a questionnaire how they were informed of a particular recent decision: through the supervisor, company newspaper, manager's newsletter, noticeboard, representative, or by rumour? This usually reveals clearly how many people heard by rumour.

The second method is the attitude survey, where employees are asked, with great regard to anonymity, carefully designed questions about what they know of various policies and what their attitude is to their conditions, supervisors, managers and jobs. Many companies have found that this type of survey can be carried out most successfully by an outside body, as the employees are often reluctant to talk in detail to other employees about their problems, etc.

In both cases, the written surveys can produce some surprisingly quantitative illustrations of communication failures.

There is one common and vital factor in all the situations we face at work: the ability of every leader, be they manager or supervisor, to obtain the commitment of people to their work.

We know that a key factor in the leadership of our own bosses in this participative age is the extent to which they pay serious attention to communication both upward and downward. People achieve more, working for a leader who bothers with communication. This is true of each one of us who, as a leader of one or many, has responsibility for achieving people's co-operation.

If we take action to make communication happen, then, like others before us, we shall find efficiency increases because people are enabled to put more into their work. We shall also be rewarded by finding that the working lives of those for whom we are responsible have become rather more worthwhile.

3 SELECTION INTERVIEWING

What is the selection interview?

Selection, as the word indicates, is the act of 'choosing'; in business terms, selection means choosing a person who will give both a department and the organisation as a whole the results that it needs from a particular job. Since selection is a two way process, it is equally important that in today's world, where expectations of work are higher than ever, the organisation is equally able to meet the aspirations of the individual. Any selection which does not give the organisation the results it needs is costing unnecessary money.

An equally important cost, though one more difficult to measure, is the effect that the wrong person in a job can have on other people. If an employee works as part of a team, then any inadequacies will affect the team, producing failures in their performance. Even if the employee works alone, these inadequacies will have an effect on the people with whom he or she comes into contact. The employee who is performing inadequately because he or she has been wrongly selected will also probably suffer loss of morale (and unnecessary stress as a result of this) along with the immediate manager who is trying to put right a situation that would, for all concerned, have been better avoided in the first place.

'Inadequacies,' of course, cannot be measured simply in terms of job performance. An employee might be highly skilled and capable at the job but if their attitude towards colleagues is destructive or un-cooperative it will upset the harmony that is essential to achieve the best results from people.

It is clear then that a manager must look closely at a person's experience, skills and characteristics before taking the major step of choosing that person for a job in the organisation.

Legislation and discrimination

More and more organisations are describing themselves as 'equal opportunities employers'. What does this mean? There is clearly a difference between good intentions and a realised policy which is not just about compliance with the law but improving and broadening the 'talent base' of an organisation and improving motivation, performance and results.

Although this chapter is about the selection interview (and equal opportunities clearly have much wider implications for working practices) there is no doubt that much of what the codes of practice recommend can be implemented through the selection process. Employers will obviously wish to avoid both direct and indirect discrimination in selection where it is illegal and this booklet aims to highlight the 'danger zones' where appropriate. However, the potential benefits of a pro-active policy with the commitment of senior management behind it are far greater than merely avoiding the tribunal courts.

There are many examples of equal opportunity policies, in both the public and private sectors, where management and employee relations have improved and where the problems of finding the right people for the right jobs have been tackled better. In this respect, equal opportunities are no longer a luxury and employers should consider how best they can implement a policy for their organisation. The Equal Opportunities Commission issues guidelines which can be used flexibly according to the size and needs of an organisation. Some employers will require less formal structures than others, while all employers will have to consider a time-scale against which they aim to achieve their objectives.

In this chapter, we will consider the implications of legislation and equal opportunities at each stage of the selection process.

In most organisations, employees, particularly at a senior level, are not appointed without at least a second interview; a second or third opinion is helpful. The role of the 'second interviewer' does need to be clear though – what are they looking for (as distinct from the first interviewer)? Do they have the right of veto? Is it their responsibility to make the final decision?

ACTION Clarify the interview procedure and aim to give the immediate line manager the responsibility for the final decision, even though other personnel specialists, senior management, etc. may be involved in the procedure.

Who selects people?

Most organisations today have a personnel department which specialises in a number of areas, one of which is selecting people for jobs. In some cases, this responsibility has passed completely from the line manager into the personnel specialist's hands. The results of this have been rather varied: at best the new employee's prospective manager sits in at some stage of the interview, or carries out an independent second interview which can be very satisfactory, or, at worst, the earliest the manager meets the new recruit is when he or she turns up for work on the first morning. As a result, the new employee may sometimes prove unable to do the job to the manager's satisfaction or be totally unsuitable as a person for the manager and the existing team. These problems could be avoided if the line manager and supervisor, where appropriate, were actively involved in the selection process, and encouraged to take responsibility for the decisions about the people working in the teams for which they are accountable.

Of course, the specialist skills of the personnel department are essential in establishing the recruitment process which is right for the organisation; attracting the right sort of candidates and sometimes picking out certain characteristics of a candidate that a non-specialist might miss. However, before a final decision is made, the manager in question should have the right to recommend the acceptance or rejection of a candidate, to be fair to the organisation and potential employee.

It is also true to say that many organisations, particularly in the public sector, select by panel or committee. These have both obvious advantages and disadvantages. Where senior public appointments are made for example, the board or committee are present to ensure fair play and a quality decision. However, this may not always be so if the panel are not properly briefed, or prepared, or its key members trained, in the selection process. Panels can be made up of a large number of interviewers and for a prospective junior employee to be faced with a panel of a dozen, or more, is obviously an intimidating experience which may not bring out the best in an interviewee.

How are people selected?

What is the normal chain of events that surrounds the selection of a new employee?

- a vacancy arises
- what is the vacancy?
- who should fill the vacancy?
- where will we find the right person?
- how do we choose which person?
- the interview
- assessment
- placement
- follow-up.

In the sections that follow we will look more closely at each of these.

A vacancy arises

People resign from jobs for a reason. Sometimes that reason is unavoidable – retirement or ill-health, for example. Often the reasons are understandable and leave the organisation little choice in the short-term – a better salary with another company is the obvious example here. At times, however, the reasons are such as to point to a failure in the organisation somewhere. Examples of these are dissatisfaction with the job, prospects, or conditions; conflict with colleagues or boss; or a sense of injustice towards the organisation.

If an employee is leaving because of the latter type of reason, then the organisation has a problem which must be looked into as soon as possible. For if one person is affected in such a way the manager can be sure that others will be – and dissatisfied or disgruntled employees are costly, whether they leave the organisation or stay with it.

What can be done about this? The answer is to find out as

quickly, and as accurately as possible, the reasons for people leaving by giving them a termination interview.

The timing of this interview is important. If it is held immediately the resignation is received, it may be possible to persuade the employee to stay (if that is what is wanted). Otherwise it is better to wait until the final day when they are more likely to tell the manager, or anyone else, what is really wrong.

Sometimes leavers prefer to deal with someone who is seen as neutral, so this termination interview is often done by the personnel officer. If this is the case, the manager must be sure to talk to the personnel officer afterwards to find out what points were made. Where possible, however, it makes sense for the personnel manager to do this interview.

For the termination interview to be of any real value leavers must be made to feel free to say whatever they think – without any defence or counter-arguments – and it must be guaranteed that everything said will be in confidence, certainly as far as colleagues and other employees are concerned. Finally, it is important that all employees see that action is taken to put right any faults of the organisation identified by this type of interview. But be warned – if the interview is as frank as it should be, personnel managers may sometimes hear things they don't like.

Sometimes the interview may reveal some problem with the organisation, or structure, which is making the leaver's job either too difficult, or too easy, or the person is too busy, or not busy enough. If this is the case it may well be that the manager should think seriously about the job, and whether it should exist at all or exist, at least, in a different form.

ACTION Ensure that all employees are interviewed and that the necessary steps are taken to put right the problems which the interview highlights.

What is the vacancy?

When a vacancy arises, it is an opportunity to reconsider overall functions and structure within a department. Does a job need to change, for example, to meet the changing needs and objectives of the organisation? Does the vacancy need to be filled at all, or is there a need to create a new function which did not exist previously?

There is always a danger that where managers have been very satisfied with a previous job-holder they will try to find an 'identikit' person to replace that job-holder. It is essential that managers think more broadly and the best way to do this is to begin by focusing on the job itself.

Therefore before managers can decide whether a job needs to be filled they have to know what the job actually is. This will require a job description.

The important questions that need to be answered in order to produce a job description are:

- What is the job title? (One that reflects the content of the job, and does not imply the sex of the job-holder.)
- Where is the job situated?
- Who will the job-holder be responsible to?
- What is the overall purpose of the job?
- What responsibilities does the job-holder have for staff, materials, money? What are the consequences of any decisions in these areas?
- What are the key result areas of the job and the standards expected?
- With whom does the job-holder work?
- What are the terms and conditions of the job – hours, overtime-shifts, pay?
- What are the future career prospects, if any, for the holder of this job?

It is a good idea to get the answers to these questions from the present job-holder, if that person is available, as well as for the line manager to supply them. The two sets of answers will almost certainly be different, with the real facts lying somewhere between the two. (If the answers produced by the job-holder and the boss are really different, this should be looked into in some depth – it probably means that in several areas of activity each of the two thinks that the other one is responsible for looking after it.) If the job-holder has actually left the company, attention should be paid to the comments made at that person's termination interview.

ACTION Establish the major aspects of the job. Look closely at the job–does it really need to be filled?

Who should fill the vacancy?

Having decided what the job is, the manager must then decide on the skills, attributes and experience required to carry out that job: i.e. a person specification. Care should be taken at this stage not to discriminate.

If the person specification is objectively based on the job description, rather than a prejudicial view of the sort of person 'one would like to see filling the job', discrimination is far less likely.

Person specifications are usually laid down under standardised headings. There does not have to be a set format, although it may be helpful for an organisation to standardise its approach in order to ensure that the selection process is properly applied.

Again looking at the job itself, and considering the 'core' skills required to do that job, will point to the necessary categories for the person specification.

The following headings may be useful. These are examples of the skills and attributes in specific areas that managers may consider:

Physical requirements

What standards of health and fitness are appropriate? Are there any points concerning vision, hearing, dexterity, etc? Ability to work under particular job conditions which are important?

Remember there is no point in putting restrictions on the type of candidate sought unless they are derived from the requirements of the job.

Consider if there are any physical aids or adaptations that could be used to employ a disabled person.

Education and training

General Education. How relevant are specific academic requirements? Consider the job: does it require certain levels of literacy and numeracy rather than specific GCSE passes in Maths and English. The GCSEs may be helpful indicators but candidates may have achieved the required standards by some other means.

Specific Training. For example vocational certificates, professional qualifications, apprenticeship certificates, etc.

Experience

Should this be directly relevant or could similar experience in a different environment be considered?

Should length and breadth of experience be considered, level and range of responsibility, etc?

Special skills and knowledge

Specialist knowledge without which the job cannot be done, for example computer systems. How far does the job require particular aptitudes in understanding mechanical principles, dealing with figures, drawing skills, etc? How will these be assessed at interview?

Personality and disposition

This is a difficult area, often vaguely defined, difficult to assess and most prone to bias at the interview. It is therefore more helpful to define personality traits as closely related to the job as possible. For example:

- *flexible*: (in terms of the job) someone who can easily adapt his or her previous arrangements to carry out a job in another part of the country with just half a day's notice.
- *outgoing*: (in terms of the job) someone who can listen to clients' needs and establish rapport with clients.
- *easy to get on with*: (in terms of the job) someone who can demonstrate that he or she has worked successfully as part of a team. Someone who is prepared to put his or her own work aside in order to help another member of the team with something urgent. Someone who is prepared to listen to and consider the views of others, etc.

For each job it would be necessary to list the key 'disposition traits' and then to define each one if possible. It may be useful and objective to ask a range of current job-holders what they think those 'traits' might be before standardising the person specification.

Special circumstances

This should only form part of the specification where it is relevant to the job – for example travelling, staying away from home, etc.

This can be a 'danger zone' for managers where questions are often asked in the form of 'Do you have any dependants?', 'Do you have children?' and so on. These questions are directly discriminating if they are about the person and not the job. The question should be 'Are you able to travel and stay away from home?'

When compiling the specification, it may also be useful to state whether certain aspects are 'essential' or 'desirable'. The candidate who possesses all the desirable requirements as well as the essential ones will probably do the job particularly well, but sometimes these 'stars' are not available and a company may retain people longer if they are on an extended learning curve and necessary training can be provided. So, whilst we would insist that potential employees must meet the essential requirements, the desirable qualities are extras which may be helpful in assessing one candidate against another, but not a pre-requisite for the job.

When writing person specifications, it is also tempting to describe the ideal and possibly unobtainable candidate. This may mean that potentially good candidates are eliminated and that recruits have higher aspirations than can be met in the job.

Fitting a person to a realistic person specification will help to ensure that the job will be done well.

ACTION Produce a person specification based on realistic requirements. Avoid discrimination. Be logical, specific and honest with yourself.

Where will we find the right person?

Employers need to think broadly about where to recruit if they are to attract a balanced group of applicants. When the job market is buoyant, it is also necessary for managers to make recruitment a priority and to take advantage of opportunities to promote their organisation and form links with the local community. It may be necessary to consider adjusting working practices, for example flexible working hours, etc, in order to attract a wider range of candidates.

Advertising in the national press is very expensive but there are alternative sources which can be considered, for example:

- internal advertisements
- external advertisements in
  - local press
  - specialist press
  - ethnic minority press
- employment agencies
- education and training establishments
- open evenings
- local community groups
- unsolicited sources
  - word of mouth
  - unsolicited letters
  - casual callers
  - recommendations from other employers or employees.

Internal recruitment

As a matter of policy, most companies today notify their employees of vacancies. Some also use a vacancy as a training experience to develop staff. A few have an effective management development system linked to a realistic appraisal system which can produce the replacements virtually automatically. You can be fairly sure, however, that whatever method (or none) operates, there will be people within your organisation who at least deserve to be in the running for a vacancy. Not to make use of these people, if they do have the ability, is a major waste of resources and a sure way of demotivating staff. It is also a sure way of losing them – if they cannot obtain promotion within your organisation they are likely to go to one where they can.

Advertising

If you chose to advertise and have selected the appropriate publication on grounds of specialism, circulation within the community, level of vacancy, locality, etc, it is worth considering the content of the advertisement.

A good agency will advise on the layout and presentation. Again remember that the advertisement promotes an image of the organisation. You need to consider the content and the following points may be helpful:

- the company: name, logo, what it does, size, etc
- the job: title, duties, location
- the person required: summarise the points from your person specification
- benefits package: salary – phrases like 'salary negotiable' may be interpreted as meaning low salary.

ACTION Check that your advertisement is not breaking the sex or race discrimination acts. Job advertisements should not state or imply that the job is only for applicants of one sex or race. Make sure the information is accurate, as the advertisement may form part of the contract between you and your new employee. Also consider including an equal opportunities statement to encourage a wider variety of applicants.

How do we choose which person?

Whatever method of attracting candidates you have chosen, you will now have a number of applicants. You are now going to work through the stages to the final acceptance of a candidate.

Application forms

Forms can present a professional image and are on the whole easier to pre-select from. A common format means that you are asking candidates for more easily comparable information. However, CVs are often used and do tend to speed up the recruitment process. There may also be certain cases where requiring applicants to complete application forms is an inhibiting factor and puts potentially good candidates off. Such potential employees should be encouraged to come direct to the company.

The legal status of forms
Although case law has not provided definite guidance, it can be assumed that forms are part of what, in the Sex Discrimination

Act are described as 'arrangements made for deciding who should be offered employment' (Section 6(i) (a)).

This means that some questions could be unlawful. Examples of such questions deal with family, ages of children, marital status, etc. Some of the unfair beliefs which frequently influence judgement about the suitability of women for a job are, for example:

- women with children are unreliable
- women are more likely to have time off work owing to illness (particularly 'women's problems')
- women of marriageable age are interested in only short-term employment.

However, each case must be considered in terms of its own particular facts. These cannot be elicited by questions on paper. There is no point, therefore, in asking questions which suggest 'stereotyping' and arouse suspicions of prejudice and discrimination.

Information for monitoring purposes
Where a monitoring procedure is carried out as part of an equal opportunities policy, the information which includes points about racial origin, marital status, and so on, is usually provided on a separate sheet, or tear-off slip, which is not made available to those making decisions at any stage of the selection process.

Pre-selection
Unless candidates are attending an 'open day' or coming directly to the organisation, this is usually done by comparing the application form to the person specification. There are drawbacks to this because often information is incomplete and preselection may be carried out by someone fairly inexperienced in selection. It may be worthwhile involving line management and at least a second opinion at this stage. CVs can present problems because you are pre-selecting on the information candidates have chosen to give you rather than information common to all candidates that you need to have.

It is worth bearing in mind that even if candidates fail to meet the essential requirements for a particular job they may still be worth considering for another post in the organisation. On the other hand, it may mean that the type of candidate required is not available, the person specification over ambitious, or the advertising was not specific enough or was incorrectly placed. The decision must then be whether to re-advertise, or to retrain, or to take the 'best of those available' – often a vacancy is better left unfilled and temporary measures taken rather than to appoint the 'wrong' person out of desperation.

ACTION Use application forms where possible, unless it is a job which does not require one.

Acknowledgements

It is obviously important to acknowledge all applications immediately and let candidates know as soon as possible whether their application is to be progressed further or rejected.

ACTION Tell the candidate as soon as possible what is happening.

Preparing the candidate for interview
It is worth deciding what information about the job and the organisation should be sent out before the interview. You may even do this prior to pre-selection when initial applications are made, not just to those short-listed for interview.

You will then present both a more professional image of the organisation and cut down on the amount of time spent giving information during the interview. You also help the candidate to make selection decisions about your job and your organisation: remember the interview is a two-way process.

Short-listing
It is difficult to prescribe how many candidates to interview; it may be that those pre-selected on the basis of person specification criteria constitute a large number. Much will depend on how many apply in the first place. Where there are large numbers, it is best to try and limit yourself on the basis of pre-selection but also to work through your list of 'less likely' candidates where necessary. It is probably better to see more candidates than less, although time is obviously a crucial factor. Consider the time well invested if you select the right person – you must also allow enough time for each candidate that you see; too many in-depth interviews in one day may not help the interviewer or candidate.

Where the urgency to appoint and not to risk losing candidates through delay is a factor, it may be necessary to consider interviewing outside normal working hours.

The interview

Preparation before

Brief reception, and anyone else involved, and give the name of those expected for interview. If appropriate, arrange for a tour of the place of work. Sometimes informal discussions with other members of a department already doing the same or similar job may help candidates to form a more realistic picture of the job and organisation. It is also useful for candidates to meet those people they may be working with. There is little mileage to be gained in raising expectations too high: candidates need to understand as far as is possible the true nature of a job.

This means sometimes stressing the less attractive and more mundane aspects of a job, for example, being an air-steward is not about glamorous international travel.

The interview room

If a true picture of candidates is to be gained they must be made to feel as relaxed as possible. Provide a comfortable, private room for the interview with few, if any, distractions in or around if. Often an interviewer sits behind a desk, but this can very easily act as a psychological barrier between the interviewer and the candidate, and is certainly not likely to help the candidate relax. Sometimes it is better to have two fairly comfortable chairs with perhaps a small table next to them on which to rest notes and so on. However, some people find the lack of formality off-putting – judge each situation on its own merits.

The interviewer should try to ensure privacy by arranging for there to be no unnecessary interruptions and for telephone calls to be transferred elsewhere.

Planning the interview

Interviewers should look over the candidate's application form before the interview to familiarise themselves with the candidate's history, and, by comparing it with the person specification, to pick out the points that need to be investigated further.

With this and the person specification available, interviewers should then prepare a plan of how they want the interviews to go in terms of areas to be explored. Of course, the actual interview will have to be flexible, according to the candidate, but a plan helps to guide the interview systemataically through all the relevant areas missing out nothing of importance.

It is probably a good idea for interviewers to think of the sort of question they will begin with. The candidate is probably a little tense at the beginning so a neutral question tends to open the interview up without putting the candidate under any real pressure. A good topic, for example, would be to find out how the person travelled to the interview.

Structure
A useful structure may follow the categories selected for the person specification. Questions which are related to these categories should be prepared beforehand; these key questions, which are therefore relevant to the job, should be asked of each candidate. In this way, employers can demonstrate that they have treated candidates fairly, and assessing one candidate against another is more easily validated.

Obviously, the pursuit of these key questions will depend on probing, and following up, leads to individual answers given, as well as individual issues which arise from application forms.

It is also useful to plan information supplied, and to reserve this for the latter part of the interview, so that valuable time is not wasted talking about the job instead of finding out about the candidate.

Finally, interviewers should make sure they have all the relevant papers, including information on terms and conditions, renumeration, etc, that they are likely to need.

Objectives of the interview

It is important that interviewers are quite clear what their objectives are in an interview:

● to find out whether the candidate is suitable for the job and the organisation

- to find out whether the job and the organisation are suitable for the candidate
- to ensure that the candidates have a fair deal, thus developing a positive public image.

The importance of the first two cannot be over-emphasised: but while the importance of the candidate's suitability is fairly obvious, the question of the organisation's suitability for the candidate is often overlooked. Yet the commitment of candidates to an organisation and a job that suits them is crucial to its profitability and effectiveness.

Opening the interview

Having greeted the candidate, and checked the name (interviewers have been known to interview the wrong person), interviewers should introduce themselves, and offer the candidate a chair.

At this stage interviewers should then use their prepared opening question to break the ice. After that it is well worth telling the candidate that this is really a two-way situation. It is amazing how often candidates are surprised at being told that they are expected to gain information from the interviews as well as give it. It is a good idea to stress to candidates that they must feel free to ask questions whenever they are not sure of something.

Explain the structure and order of questions so that the candidate knows what to expect.

Interviewers should ask if the candidate objects to them taking notes – purely as reminders of the more important facts in the interview. The notes themselves should be short phrases, often trigger-words, to remind the interviewers to return to a point later, or to help summarise at the end. A useful tip is for the interviewer not to make a note immediately after candidates say something which could be a point against themselves, but to wait until the conversation has moved on to another topic.

ACTION Put the candidate at ease. Tell the person what the interview is trying to achieve. Get agreement to the taking of notes.

What to do in the interview

Using the prepared plan and the person specification, interviewers should make sure they work steadily through all the relevant areas, collecting facts and opinions (of the candidates) as they go along. It is up to interviewers to make sure they have got all the facts they need, and that they are complete and correct. It will be too late after the interview has finished!

Certainly it is important that the interviewer probes the apparent facts. For example, it is not enough to note that a candidate was a supervisor in his or her previous job. How many people were supervised? In what jobs? What were the actual responsibilities of the supervisor? In other words, what do the facts really mean?

ACTION Get all the correct facts required. Probe these facts to obtain the details behind them. Supply necessary information about the job and ensure the candidate has the opportunity at the end to ask questions or supply relevant additional information.

The interviewer's skills

If interviewers are to form a realistic picture of a candidate they must get the candidate to talk. A sure way of failing to do that is by asking 'yes-no' questions. Instead the interviewer ought to ask open-ended questions that force the candidate to give wider and more complex replies. For example, the question 'Did you enjoy your last job?' gets the answer 'Yes' or 'No' – and that won't really tell the interviewer much. On the other hand, the question 'What did you think of your last job?' requires candidates to express their own opinions in their own way, which is far more valuable to the interviewer. Open-ended questions usually start with 'How', 'What', 'Why', 'When', or 'Where' – try to use these whenever possible. Such questions will lead to other – probably more specific – questions.

Often the best way to assess a person's future performance is to gather evidence about their past performance. In addition to open questions which get candidates talking, the so-called behavioural question is a way of exploring what people have actually done in areas relevant to the job. They may be questions which start off 'closed' to establish a specific fact and then a follow-up 'open' question is asked to explore the facts.

They may begin with phrases like:

'Give me an example of a time when you have had to do . . .'
'In what circumstances did you have to make a quick decision . . .?'
'What did you do in your last job to contribute towards teamwork? Be specific . . .'
'Give me an instance when in your last job, you had to let others
know how you thought or felt . . .'

Hypothetical questions – the 'what would you do if . . .?' –
variety are often used but can be unrealistic and discriminatory if
the hypothetical situation is totally outside the candidate's
experience. Use this type with care. Information supplied
through behavioural questioning is probably a more objective
frame of reference on which to base decisions.

It is also important to give candidates time to think of their
answers and to summarise throughout, both to clarify misunderstandings and to keep the interview on course.

Often the candidate, for a number of reasons, will leave out
facts or bend them to suit the situation. If interviewers are
concentrating on listening to and observing the candidate, they
will pick up clues to these situations and can then explore them
in more depth. It is enormously important that the interviewer
listens closely to what is being said and actively observes the
manner in which it is being said. Nervousness when answering
particular questions may possibly be a sign of extra tension
caused by telling a half-truth or even a lie.

The other advantage of the interviewer concentrating on the
candidate is that it impresses on the person his or her importance
to the interviewer and to the company. A candidate in that
position is far more likely really to open up, with obvious
benefits to the interviewer.

ACTION Ask open-ended questions and behavioural questions. Listen to
what the candidate says. Watch what candidates do and how
they react to questions. Summarise throughout.

Pressures during the interview

There are pressures on the candidate throughout the interview.
It is the interviewer's job to minimise these in order to achieve

the frame of mind in the candidate that will allow the person to talk freely and objectively.

There are all sorts of stories about 'stress' interviews – bright lights or direct sunshine, tall chairs, aggressive questions. For the selection interview, the interviewer should concentrate on reducing stress, not producing it.

Objectivity has already been mentioned in relation to the candidate. It is impossible for candidates to be completely objective about themselves and in the same way good interviewers should recognise that they, too, are unable to be totally objective, unless a really big effort is made to recognise and accept these failings and compensate for them when interviewing. The interviewer should particularly watch out for positive and negative bias toward a candidate. An example of positive bias would be the subconscious assumption that the candidate was a 'good person' because he or she came from the same town, or went to the same school, or played the same sport as the interviewer.

Equally, something that irritates the interviewer – colour of hair or skin, sex, background, accent – could produce a subconscious dislike of the candidate, a feeling that the person could not really do the job properly. Either feeling is dangerous to interviewers. Their job is to obtain the facts about a person and to compare them objectively with the requirements in the specification.

Only after that has been done should judgement take place. And even then it should be an honest judgement uninfluenced by the interviewer's own personal likes and dislikes. Interviewers who say they can tell straight away 'just by looking at them' whether people will be right for a job or not, are doing themselves, their company, and the candidate a grave disservice.

One way to test one's subconscious prejudices is to seek alternative evidence. If you have very positive feelings about an issue or aspect of a candidate, test or try out the negative or opposite aspects of the same issue and *vice versa* – in other words, seek contrary evidence, whether positive or negative.

Gut feelings cannot and probably should not be ignored. However, they should be 'pushed aside' during the interview and not permit a premature decision to be made ten minutes after the interview has begun. If you have doubts and suspicions, it pays to be honest and open with candidates so that they have every opportunity to allay your fears. Your honesty may even help them to realise that they may be making a wrong decision about the job which is also in your interests.

You may reflect upon your feelings after the interview when you have the facts before you and perhaps the benefit of a second interview and another opinion.

ACTION Remove as much stress from the interview as is possible.

Finishing the interview

When interviewers have got all they need from the interview, they should check that the candidate has no further questions and then signify the end of the interview. They should:

- check that the candidate's expenses were covered if this is the policy
- tell the candidate what will happen next, i.e. offering the job, rejecting the applicant (explaining why), or telling the person when to expect a decision, or second interview
- thank the candidate for coming and see the person out.

ACTION End the interview firmly. Tell the candidate what to expect next.

Assessment after the interview

The decision

Now interviewers come to the often difficult process of matching what they know of the candidate against what they want (the person specification). This is a difficult task, and it must be done carefully and honestly; mistakes are expensive and a company of any repute realises that it has a moral responsibility to the candidate, as well as to itself, to make as correct a decision as possible.

One of the best ways of reaching a decision is for the interviewer to work steadily through the person specification giving the candidate a rating against each part using the following type of scale:

A = much above average – 150 per cent
B = above average – 125 per cent
C = average – 100 per cent
D = below average – 75 per cent
E = much below average – 50 per cent

The ideal candidate for the job (bearing in mind that the person specification prescribes the person who will do the job satisfactorily) will have all Cs. Anyone with As or Es is probably too good, or bad, for the particular job. Someone with Bs is probably acceptable if there is a foreseeable move for them in twelve months' time or so. Someone with Ds will require some training.

Weighting

Very often one of the factors (e.g. training) will be of particular importance. Decide this when the person specification is being drawn up to avoid bias after the interview. The effect of this extra importance is to weight the decision. For example, if training is important and the candidate is rated C on that point, one other C plus three Ds should be enough to lift the overall rating to a C, thus making the candidate acceptable.

Another useful technique that the interviewer can employ to help with the decision is to visualise the candidate in typical situations that the job will provide and to consider how the person might get on, for example, how would the candidate cope with Bert Jones when Bert's machine goes down for the third time that day?

Many companies use a standard interview assessment form. This requires interviewers to put down their own comments, assessments and decisions under various headings. The value of this is that it allows one candidate to be compared against another fairly objectively. This is particularly valuable if one candidate was seen at 9.30 on Tuesday and the next at 3.15 on Thursday.

When the decision has been made, particularly if it is to reject the candidate, the interviewer should make sure that the record of the outline of the interview includes why the candidate was rejected. If a rejected candidate alleges discrimination because of race, union activities, sex, or against rehabilitating certain offenders, it is up to the company concerned to prove its innocence. Records of the decision and the reasons behind it are highly valuable in this situation.

ACTION Assess the facts. Keep a record of the interview.

The offer of employment

If the decision is made to offer the job to the candidate, it is normally made subject to a satisfactory medical examination and references. The contract issued should contain all the aspects required by the Employment Protection (Consolidation) Act 1978.

References are always a problem. Testimonials brought by the candidate to the interview should be viewed with great suspicion unless the interviewer can verify them with the company concerned.

The normal type of written reference from a company is a wordy statement about a candidate's moral integrity and so on; not very helpful at all. The interviewer can improve on this considerably by writing to the referee asking specific questions, such as:

'What are the dates between which Mr/Ms . . . worked for you?'
'What was the job title?'
'What did it involve?'
'What was the rate of pay?'
'How many day's sickness did the person have in the last two years?'

and the crucial question

'Would you re-employ the person?'

Some companies will refuse to answer some or all of these. Of those who do, a favourable reference should not carry a great deal of weight with the interviewer, whereas, on the other hand, an unfavourable one obviously deserves further investigation.

ACTION Make it clear that the offer is subject to satisfactory medical examination and references. Look particularly at poor references.

Placement

Once the candidate has accepted the offer of employment, and the medical examination and references are satisfactory, the line manager should take steps to make sure that the new employee will be properly received on the first day, and given induction training and whatever job training is necessary to make the person an effective member of the organisation as soon as possible.

Remember induction begins once a future employee has been made a job offer.

ACTION Plan the induction and the training of the new employee.

Follow-up

When the employee has been fully inducted and has properly settled in, the manager should stand back and take a long hard look at the months passed since that person was appointed to see if the employee is really what the interviewer thought he or she would be at the interview. If the person is not, what aspects were missed or wrongly interpreted at the interview, and what can the interviewer do to try to avoid making the same mistake again? In the short term this will show up in appraisal interviews, but eventually the termination interview will have very good feedback also on the validity of the choice.

ACTION Was it the right decision?

4 INDUCTION

Recruitment and training are a major cost to any organisation. Employers therefore need to maximise staff retention to ensure that this investment is not wasted. The employees' initial impression of an organisation usually stays with them, and it is therefore important to make this experience a positive one. Induction is a greatly neglected area of management policy which aims to achieve just this.

New members of staff need to have basic information about their terms and conditions of employment, trade union membership and their immediate working environment. However, this is not enough. People, whatever their industry or profession, want to know how they fit into the organisation as a whole and how their work relates to that of other people and other departments. Naturally they also want to meet their colleagues and line managers.

All these things should be covered in an induction scheme. However, all too often there is no formalised system for ensuring that this takes place.

Recruits are left to 'pick things up as they go along' or taken on the traditional handshake tour. This is simply asking the new employee to adopt an indifferent attitude towards the organisation, thereby reducing the chances of that employee staying long enough to contribute his or her full potential. Labour turnover costs money too. In addition it reveals an unacceptable wastage of an organisation's human resources – the most valuable assets it has. Induction programmes assist in reducing labour turnover by integrating new employees effectively into the organisation.

The process of induction

Induction is the process by which new employees are integrated into an organisation so that they become productive as soon as possible.

69

In order to ensure that this happens quickly and effectively, the process needs to be planned, managed, and adopted into the organisation's overall training plans.

In order to arrive at an induction action plan there are three main points to be considered.

1 what they should be told
2 who should tell them
3 when they should be told.

What they should be told

There are five main categories of information that should be given to new employees:

- organisational information
- procedural information
- job information
- personal information
- team information.

Organisational information

This should include information about the organisation including size, history, and if appropriate details of who the parent company is and/or its subsidiaries. It is important that employees know exactly who it is that they are working for.

Procedural information

This comprises information concerning organisational procedures which affect all members of staff. The information provided should include:

- terms and conditions of employment
- disciplinary and grievance procedures
- fire and bomb procedures
- standards or codes of dress
- rules on entering and leaving the premises.

Job information

This relates to what is necessary for a new employee to know in order to do the job effectively. The information provided should include:

- a job description detailing the major tasks and accountabilities of the job
- details of any training which is involved
- procedures for obtaining equipment, stationery, or tools
- a copy of relevant sections of an organisation chart as it is important to inform recruits not only of what they have to do but also why it is important and how it fits into the department and organisation.

Personal information

This is the area which affects a new employee's private life and personal needs, for example, how salaries are paid, where to eat, and the location of the toilet facilities. Everybody has anxieties on starting a new job and to have to ask about these fundamentals only adds additional stress.

Team information

Team information will provide knowledge of all those things which will encourage employees to integrate into the working group. This category needs to cover the informal as well as formal aspects of working life, e.g. the fact that 'we all go for a pint at lunch time on Fridays' can be more important to this process than knowing who the shop steward is.

Who should tell them

The golden rule governing the passing on of information is that when in doubt, the informant should be the new employee's immediate line manager or supervisor. However, there are a number of people who could be involved.

The personnel department

The main role of the personnel department in induction is in devising and maintaining an effective system. Initial induction may be done in group sessions or individually, depending on the organisation. In either case personnel should be responsible for providing information on specialist areas such as contracts of employment, pension and sickness schemes, share option schemes, etc. They can also be responsible for passing on organisational and procedural information.

The immediate boss

This is the person who has the greatest vested interest in an effective induction procedure and who is responsible for ensuring that the employee gets the right balance between job, personal, and group factors.

Induction also represents an ideal opportunity for boss and subordinate to get to know one another and to start developing their working relationship.

Responsibility for the induction of a new recruit should never be delegated. Other people in the department may become involved, but the immediate line manager should introduce them to new employees and follow up to ensure that their work has been satisfactorily carried out.

On-job trainer

It can be of great benefit to give delegate responsibility for induction to one of the new employee's fellow workers. It can give the new recruit an opportunity to make a 'friend' which will be particularly helpful in the passing on of personal and group information. Every working group develops its own unwritten customs and habits and for someone to unwittingly contravene these customs can be both embarrassing and humiliating.

The shop steward/staff representative

New employees should be introduced to their shop steward or staff representative. As well as being able to provide information, these people are important in making sure that the new employee is aware of the channels of communication within an organisation.

A director or senior manager

A short interview with one of the new recruit's senior line managers will allow the recruit to recognise senior management and can give a wider appreciation of the role of the department. It also gives the manager an opportunity to meet every new recruit and to monitor the effectiveness of the induction programme.

When they should be told

Induction is a continuous process and may well spread over several days or weeks after the recruit starts work. New employees are only able to take in a limited amount of information at any one time, and the aim of a systematic induction programme should be to cover all the ground in the shortest effective time.

Pre-employment

The induction process begins during recruitment and selection. Before joining an organisation, the new employee should be aware of the important terms and conditions of employment, and these should have been provided in writing. However, the recruit also needs to be given specific instructions for the starting day. These should include:

- where and when to report
- who to ask for
- what to bring
- where to park.

   Employers should also prepare for the recruit's arrival by providing:

- all equipment, clothing, safety wear, etc.
- a timetable for people who are involved in inducting the new employee.

Day one

Whatever the size of the organisation, what happens on the first day at work makes a big impression. Recruits should therefore be made to feel welcome by everyone they meet. It is usual for new employees to report to the personnel department who will cover the essential paperwork with an employee either as part of a group induction or individually before taking them along to their department.

Once all the necessary paperwork has been completed – bank details, pension forms, etc – organisational and procedural information should be given. This should include disciplinary and grievance procedures.

New employees should be introduced to the people whom they are going to work with so that there are some familiar faces in the department the next day. This should include the on-job trainer allocated to the recruit.

It is important to remember to restrict the information given on day one in order to maximise what is retained by the employee.

In the department

The aim of departmental induction is to ensure that new employees settle down into their work and that their levels of performance reach a set standard as soon as possible. The complexity and length of the departmental induction programme will vary according to the job.

Individuals should have their induction programmes detailed to them by their immediate line manager or supervisor. This means that they will understand what has been planned for them and will also allow them the opportunity to prepare questions in advance, minimising the tendency to think only of important things after the event.

The areas covered at this stage are job information and personal information. These can be given by the immediate line manager or supervisor and the on-job trainer. The extent of the role of the on-job trainer will be dependent on his or her skills and experience.

Follow-up induction

After 8–12 weeks, the new employee should be settled into the organisation. Some will find this easier than others and some may develop problems which are potential reasons for leaving. All starters should therefore be followed-up individually and problems and concerns dealt with before they result in a possible resignation.

A formal follow-up induction also gives the opportunity to impart further information, e.g. education and training facilities or transfer policies, which it was not appropriate to cover in the initial induction period.

All new employees will have questions after this length of time and will probably want to know more about the organisation. It may therefore be appropriate to arrange a tour of another part of the company, e.g. Head Office or a staff visit to the factory.

Special cases

While the principles outlined so far are the guidelines to good induction, there are some special cases. These require additional considerations over and above the normal induction process.

School leavers

Most school leavers will be nervous and excited about starting work and therefore need to be put at ease as soon as possible. They need to develop a positive attitude towards work and an effective induction programme provides an opportunity to ensure that any initial interest and enthusiasm which exists is developed and encouraged.

The induction programme for school leavers needs to place particular emphasis on ensuring that they appreciate their importance to the organisation and understand where their job fits into the greater whole.

In order to build commitment, there is a need to place considerable emphasis on why something should be done or done in a certain way, rather than just giving instructions. Opportunities for training and development should also be clearly outlined.

The use of an on-job trainer or 'mentor' can be of particular benefit to this category of new employee. A school leaver's confidence can easily be destroyed and such assistance will help ensure that they do not break any of the 'unwritten laws' of the workplace, as well as aiding the formal induction process.

Graduates

In graduate induction, emphasis needs to be placed on giving an appreciation of how departments are inter-dependent. Technical graduates tend to see their own objectives simply in terms of their own subject and need to develop an appreciation of the constraints in which they will work. Management trainees need to understand the 'business'.

For this process to be fully effective, it is essential that a graduate's induction programme involves undertaking specific jobs or tasks at all stages. This will ensure that induction is perceived by the graduates as relevant. This helps to maintain their motivation and interest.

Women returning to work after a career break

Women returning to work have special anxieties. One of these may manifest itself as lack of confidence – feeling that they will not be able to cope because of the changes in working practices and technology.

An effective induction programme should recognise this and place particular emphasis on skills training. This will build confidence and enable the employee to feel that they can make a worthwhile and valued contribution to the organisation.

Minority groups

Induction programmes should take account of any special needs of minority groups. If language is a problem, training should be arranged in order to help the new employee integrate into the organisation.

How induction is carried out

Whatever the size or resources of an organisation, induction should be:

- part of a systematic plan
- written down
- recorded at each stage as completed
- constantly monitored.

The best method of achieving this is to draw up a checklist of the items to be covered as shown in Table 2.1.

The basic principles of induction should always be the same. However, the specific way that a programme operates is dependent upon the individual organisation and the resources that it has available.

Table 2.1 *Induction checklist*

Name of employee......................... Date of starting ....

SUBJECT	RESPONSIBILITY	SIGNATURE (of employee)	DATE
1 ORGANISATIONAL INFORMATION			
Group Information			
Name	e.g. Personnel		
History	Manager		
Products/services			
Locations			
Company Information			
Name			
Organisation			
Product/service			
Customers			
Managers' names			
Welfare and Benefits			
Canteen			
Lockers			
Medical			
Sports			
Social			
Share option			
2 PROCEDURAL INFORMATION			
Contract of employment			
Hours of work			
Notice periods			
Wages/salary where/when/how			
Bonus schemes			

Pension scheme			
Sickness			
notification			
certification			
pay			
Holidays			
Pay slip			
Rules and			
Procedures			
Company rules			
misconduct			
codes of dress			
Disciplinary			
Grievance			
Appeals			
Safety			
fire and bomb			
exits			
extinguishers			
first aid			
accidents			
safety reps			
Communications			
Procedures			
T.U. recognition			
Staff council			
Company newspaper			
Briefing groups			
Manpower			
Development			
Policies			
Day release			
Fees assistance			
Performance			
appraisal			
Promotion			
Transfer			
3 DEPARTMENT			
INFORMATION			
Organisation			
Names			
Rules			
Meal breaks			
Clocking in			
Clocking out			
Job description			
Equipment			
Standards of			
performance			
Hours			

Large organisations

In large organisations with a personnel and training department, group inductions can be arranged. These can cover the organisational and procedural information categories. It is useful to use visual aids such as films and slides whenever possible, as what is seen makes more impact than what is heard.

Specialists should be used wherever possible to talk about their own subjects. These should include:

- the Personnel Officer (terms and conditions of employment)
- the Security Officer (security policies and procedures)
- the Health and Safety Officer (accident reporting and standards of health and safety).

A number of different speakers will break up the day, making it more interesting and therefore aid the retention of facts.

It is important to ensure that new employees are introduced to their line manager or supervisor at the end of the group induction day and are given clear instructions as to where to report the following day. They will then be ready for their departmental induction, which is when they will start to receive job information.

Small organisations

In smaller organisations with no personnel and training department, it is not possible to arrange group inductions. Induction programmes therefore need to be specifically tailored to each individual's needs from day one. The induction will be wholly the responsibility of the new employee's immediate line manager or supervisor. The same checklist for large organisations can be used, but the line manager or supervisor will have to decide who is best qualified within the organisation to cover the various items. This will then mean arranging meetings with specialist members of staff including:

- the person responsible for wages and salaries
- the union/staff representative
- managers/supervisors from other departments.

It is essential that everybody involved is fully aware of the programme and the role that they are expected to play in it.

Group induction timetable

9.00 a.m.	Welcome and Introduction	Personnel Manager
9.30 a.m.	Paperwork Collection of P45s Bank details	Wages Supervisor
10.00 a.m.	Video History of the Organisation	Training Manager
10.30 a.m.	Coffee	
10.45 a.m.	Conditions of Employment	Personnel Manager
11.30 a.m.	Company Rules and Procedures	Personnel Manager
12.15 p.m.	Welcome from Managing Director	Managing Director
12.30 p.m.	Lunch	
1.30 p.m.	Welfare and Benefits	Personnel Manager
2.00 p.m.	Education and Training	Training Officer
2.30 p.m.	Safety Procedures	Safety Officer
3.00 p.m.	Security Procedures	Security Officer
3.15 p.m.	Tea	
3.30 p.m.	Issue Uniforms	Training Officer
4.15 p.m.	Meet Department Heads	
5.00 p.m.	END	

5 APPRAISAL AND APPRAISAL INTERVIEWING

Staff appraisal is gaining increasing importance as a contributor to the success of organisations in industry, commerce and the public sector in Britain. Increased competition, rapid changes, reduced resources and employee expectations, have all combined in such a way that organisations are being expected to achieve more with less. Appraisal offers a method of developing the most important and valuable resource – people.

Consequently, many organisations are revising their existing appraisal schemes and introducing appraisal for all employees, not just 'staff' grades. In addition, the education sector, health and local authorities and many other employers are recognising the importance of appraisal. The method of appraising is also now tending towards openness, dialogue, and performance, rather than personality. Planned future actions are taking on more importance in comparison to past actions.

Key elements and basic requirements of appraisal

Appraisal is one of the mechanisms to help gain people's commitment towards achieving the stated aims of the organisation. Therefore the objective of appraisal is *to help improve individual performance, realise potential and achieve better results for the organisation.*

Key elements

Any appraisal scheme should be concerned with these three essential areas:

- a review of past performance, from which lessons can be learned

- an identification of the future needs of the individual, the department and the organisation
- an action plan specifying what has to be done, by whom and by when.

Different organisations may have different objectives for their schemes and will need to identify these objectives, for example, development, control, training, financial reward. What is called the appraisal scheme can be a reflection of these objectives. For example:

- staff assessment or annual report implies a situation in which job holders are told about their past performance by their boss
- staff development or performance coaching suggests that the future should be considered and that this is done by discussion

The title and objectives should be compatible with the culture and aims of the organisation.

Basic requirements

Experience suggests that in the most successful systems:

- top management is committed and involved
- appraisals are carried out by the immediate boss
- all line managers receive training and the drill is monitored through the line
- in large organisations a senior person is accountable for monitoring the mechanics, consistency, and results of the scheme
- the method of looking at performance is objective and regular
- the job holders' views are taken into account
- the appraisal looks to the future as well as reviewing the past
- the objectives and workings of the scheme are explained to the appraisees.

Benefits to be gained from an appraisal system

There are three main areas where benefits may be drawn from a successful scheme.

Benefits to the job holder

An appraisal system includes a drill which gives the job holder the opportunity to discuss all aspects of the job, with the boss, in-depth and away from the pressures of the daily work-load. It clarifies for the job holders how they can contribute best to the objectives of the department and the aims of the organisation. This forum helps identify strengths and weaknesses, building on the former and addressing the latter. It also gives clear direction on what is expected in the job, and involves the individuals in planning their work and their future. The input of other people and the support of their boss will also be discussed at this meeting. Finally, the recording of the interview and action plan means that a commitment has been made to make these things happen. It also means an individual should not have to start all over again if a new boss arrives.

Benefits to the boss

An important benefit of an appraisal system is that it creates the opportunity for managers to think seriously about what they expect of their people and, in particular, what their plans are for the period ahead. It provides a forum for recognition of new ideas and helps to tackle problem areas. It also clarifies and improves the relationship between the two parties and strengthens the position of the manager as leader. Appraisal is as much about developing managers as about developing staff.

Benefits to the organisation

Appraisal is a visible commitment by an organisation to recognising the importance of its people and this can be reflected in the morale of staff and be transmitted to potential employees. An organisation should aim for greater individual effectiveness and commitment in areas such as: corporate aims; succession planning; identification of training needs; feedback from employees; recurring problems; obtaining objective information (on performance) for use in business planning, promotion or salary decisions.

Checklist

- Clarification of jobs and expectations.
- Shift from reacting to events, to controlling.
- Greater involvement and commitment from staff.
- An objective record of achievement and future action plans.
- Better use of human resources, training and succession planning.
- Improved results.

Methods of assessing performance

Grading

Many systems rely to some extent on trait grading, that is, ticking a series of boxes which give grades for a number of qualities, for example:

Qualities	Unacceptable	Below average	Average	Above average	Excellent
Honesty					
Communication					
Initiative					
Co-operation					
Integrity					

The problem with this approach is that it concentrates on looking 'backwards', forces the job holder to react, is very subjective in interpretation, and tends towards middling. If there is a direct link to salary, it is likely that managers will be over-generous in their assessment: the so-called halo effect. As it is straightforward it creates the opportunity for lazy managers to give insufficient thought to the process. Often gradings reflect boss/job holder relationships rather than achievement.

Organisations defend it on the grounds that: it forces a decision to be made about performance; it provides a guideline for salary reviews; it makes a statement about the manager. If it is to be used, ratings should be substantiated by written comments, guidelines on rating definition should be fully explained, and it should relate to performance not personality. Managers should be prepared to take into account job holders' comments and alter ratings if these are justified. Finally, it should be only part of a larger process which allows for development action to be discussed.

Written assessment

Written assessment requires consideration before committing pen to paper. The narrative of the appraiser needs to be specific and substantiative. However, it depends upon the questions asked or the discretion of the manager as to exactly what is recorded. The narrative often states more about the writing skills of the manager and the relationship between the manager and the job holder than it does about actual performance.

It will be more effective if it results from a discussion and if the job holder has given some thought to key questions before the interview, rather than the job holder simply reacting to the boss.

Management by objective

In order to overcome the problems associated with personal qualities and subjective judgements, an objective method of appraising is required. The technique of management by objective (MBO) or an interpretation of it, when based upon measurable or recognisable job results, does provide a concrete way of assessing performance. It may be developed by ranking results against standards of performance to take into account the importance or difficulty of the tasks concerned.

The danger of MBO in practice is that some systems have

become complicated. They can restrict discussion to a few objectives and miss other important areas. Rapid changes may not be reacted to or anticipated quickly enough.

Target setting

Increasingly, organisations are using target setting as the best means of measuring the performance of individuals. Such a system relies upon two key elements.

- Identifying key result areas for the job and setting standards of performance which are measurable, recognisable and achievable. These are ongoing and relate to the job.
- Setting targets which are priorities over and above the routine work. They are about change and development and relate to the individual job holder.

Target setting provides objectivity but is also dynamic, as it relies on a series of regular discussions between the two parties throughout the year, i.e. every one or two months, or quarterly. Records of targets, and success or failure, are for use at the main appraisal interview. Consequently, the annual interview does not reflect merely the last couple of months' work. Shortfalls can be identified and rectified at an early stage rather than being placed on the record at the end of the year as a failure to meet a target.

Providing that this system includes regular meetings and consultation and is not an imposition, it is the best method of meeting the need to have an objective appraisal scheme which is based upon a dialogue.

Checklist

- Methods of appraising people should be based upon performance, not personal qualities.
- The standards of performance expected must be made clear to the job holder.
- Systems must encourage forward-looking dialogue as well as looking at previous work.
- The job holder should be able to consider and inject

information into the review of performance.
- Systems must include regular reviews in order to update the information base and to maintain impetus.

Introducing an appraisal scheme

If an appraisal scheme is to be successful it is important that line managers can identify with the scheme and that they perceive it as a useful tool. Therefore, it is essential to involve them in the evolution of such a scheme in order to increase their commitment. This can involve consultation during the early stages or trying out a draft scheme with representative departments and including their ideas for improving the scheme. This will help to sell the idea to the rest of the organisation.

Deciding on the scheme

There are a great many areas which need to be looked at when considering how a scheme will operate. The key steps to take before and during introduction are as follows.

1 Decide why a scheme is needed, what its objectives are and how it will help achieve the aims of the organisation.
2 Decide on the structure of the scheme
   - paperwork
   - frequency and timing
   - who is involved
   - what support information will be produced
   - how information will be used (e.g. salary, training, career progress, etc.)
   - how it will be monitored.
3 Ensure that there is commitment at the most senior level.
4 Produce the required documentation.
5 Train the appraisers.
6 Communicate the objective and method of the scheme to all concerned.
7 Monitor the early stages closely and review its success at a pre-determined date.

Other factors to consider

Title. The name of the scheme can be important in introducing its purpose and in the effect it has on people's expectations. For example, 'annual report' suggests a purely backward-looking assessment with no dialogue. 'Performance coaching' suggests support and a forward-looking attitude, and emphasises performance, not personality.

Objectives. The organisation must make clear why it has installed or is installing a scheme. It is important to be realistic about results. Appraisal is normally about fine-tuning individual performance in the present job. Naturally, other objectives like planning, succession planning, and salary review can be introduced. It is vital that people see it as positive and not directly concerned with discipline, grievance or redundancy.

Mechanics. Is the scheme to be seasonal or rolling? This may depend on the link with money or corporate objective setting. Rolling schemes are easier for busy managers in theory; in practice an extended season, for example two months, gives a clear and realistic time span for managers to complete appraisals.

The scheme

1 Appraisals should be conducted at least annually, but this must be supplemented by more frequent and regular reviews throughout the year.
2 The immediate boss should do the appraising as he or she is closest to the job holder's work. No-one should have to appraise more than fifteen people. Using higher levels or personnel people weakens the boss–job holder relationship. The boss's boss should be involved to monitor action, check consistency of comments and gain upward information, they should also be the first line of appeal. This is important to ensure fairness and gain credibility. Project management produces problems which can be mitigated by appointing a 'mentor' boss responsible for the individual's development. They will closely consult with others during the year. As appraisal is principally about looking forward, it should be the current boss who undertakes it even if new to the position.

Clearly they will need to consult closely with others.

3 Personnel departments should prompt the system and can have a useful administration and collating role. They can also assess corporate and individual training requirements and succession planning.

4 Participants should be able to see what is being recorded and have an input into this. Action plans should be a working document.

5 Everyone should be appraised, and this should be done regularly throughout the year by means of review meetings. This will make the system dynamic and a part of the normal management function, and reduces the chance of surprises at the annual interview. The forms used may be different for managers, blue collar workers, and administration staff. In the case of junior staff, large developmental targets may not be as appropriate as they are to management or professionally qualified people.

6 Plans must be made for training all participants, supplying back-up paperwork, inducting new staff and training newly promoted managers. Decisions need to be made on how the success of the scheme will be monitored and reviewed and the resulting involvement of line and personal staff.

Checklist

- Decide on the consultative process.
- Set dates for key stages of implementation.
- Design the mechanics of the scheme.
- Ensure commitment of top personnel.
- Produce support literature and paperwork.
- Train the appraisers.
- Communicate the objectives and methodology to all those concerned.
- Review the practical results of the scheme.

Linking salary and performance

Some organisations do link salary increases to individual performance in order to encourage and develop, and to reflect the job holder's contribution to results.

Clearly, by this system there will then be a link between salary review and performance review. If people see this as an automatic link or if salary is discussed at the appraisal interview, then this can direct attention away from the main purpose of the system and reduce the honesty of the two parties. Managers may raise their judgements in order to avoid conflict; job holders may try to bargain down their targets in order to inflate achievement next time around.

Salary is a recognition of past performance. Appraisal is principally a discussion about future performance. Therefore, it is wise to have a different drill for each with two interviews being separated by time.

If recommendation on salary follows the interview, it is good practice to base this on performance and achievement against clearly understood objectives and to allow the job holder an input in the discussion of these results. However, other factors may affect any discretionary part of salary awards, e.g. length of service, position in scale, corporate or departmental results, and the amount of money available.

Checklist

- Have a separate drill for salary review and performance review.
- Relate salary only to those parts of performance which can be substantiated.
- Ensure staff and managers are clear about factors which affect salary.

Paperwork

Appraisal depends upon dialogue and action, not paperwork. However, the paperwork is important because it imposes a drill to ensure that the meeting occurs and that a record is kept of what happens. It is also useful in that it ensures certain aspects of a person's performance are addressed and provides helpful feedback, and a means for senior managers to monitor the effectiveness of junior line managers and their appraisals.

With proper training and management experience, a blank sheet of paper may be more useful than an oversophisticated system which takes little account of the pressures on busy line managers. Any form should include: a review of past performance against key result areas and specific targets; overall comments by the job holder, the boss and the boss's boss; a clear plan for development and action.

Support guidance notes to both appraiser and job holder should address the objectives of the scheme, the mechanics and structure of appraising, guidance on areas of performance to consider, and how to make the best use of the interview.

Paperwork should be as simple as possible. It will be more likely to succeed if it is geared towards line managers rather than management development specialists.

Checklist

- The paperwork is a vehicle, not an end in itself.
- It should be kept simple.
- Apart from forms, it should include guidance notes for appraisers and appraisees. Appendices 9 and 10 on pages 357 and 358 may be of use here.

Measurements of performance

A *standard of performance* relating to the job is a continuing yardstick for judging whether performance is at an acceptable level. *Targets* are priorities over and above the normal work. They are about change and development and relate to the individual. The following chapter is devoted to explaining target setting.

Standards of performance

When key result areas have been identified, standards of performance need to be drawn up. Whereas targets are specific to an individual and tend to be short-term, performance standards relate to the job or position and are longer-term. They act as yardsticks for judging acceptable performance and help job holders to understand what is expected of them. Standards must be objective. Thus, they will either be measurable or recognisable (by adherence to a previously agreed system, for instance).

If no standards are set, it is difficult for job holders to know how they are doing. It is important that both job holder and manager have the same understanding of what standards are expected.

Standards should cover quality as well as quantity, and should emphasise what result the job holder should achieve rather than what function has to be performed.

There are some jobs which lend themselves easily to measured standards: a salesperson can be judged by the service given or the goods sold. But for others, such as research scientists, teachers, or solicitors, it is far harder to commit to paper an acceptable level of performance. However, it is always possible for the manager to outline acceptable and unacceptable methods or results. Setting standards ensures that this is clearly explained and understood.

People need to be able to monitor their own performance against such standards as well as expecting their own boss to check results throughout the year.

There are six areas in which standards may be set:

- *numeric*: sales or production figures, defect levels, paper flow, visiting rates
- *deadlines*: completion of projects to time, turnaround of correspondence, statutory time limits, regularly meeting dates, answering 'phones, accounting deadlines
- *financial*: working to budgets on income and expenditure, meeting profit forecasts, stock levels, reduction in costs
- *procedural*: stages in writing a computer program, organisation liaison systems, timing on replies to customer complaints, giving information

- *negative*: number of complaints, feedback from colleagues, cancellations of work
- *recognisable*: corporate approach to customers, standards of dress, presentations to meetings, typing errors, house style.

Examples of standards of performance

A standard of performance is a continuing yardstick for judging when performance is at an acceptable level.

- Sales representative – call rate averages eight per day at an average of eighteen miles per call.
- Social worker – in category 'A' cases, visiting takes place at least every four weeks and is followed by a full report to the supervisor.
- Plant manager – no more than two export orders per year fail to meet the shipping date.
- Office manager – all job applicants are acknowledged within two days and updated at intervals of not more than three weeks.
- Scientist – at least two research papers are produced each year.
- Teacher – meetings to consult and liaise with parents are set and attended.

Assessing potential

There has recently been a general move away from judging career potential at the same interview as current performance is discussed. This has been because of the problems caused by managers not distinguishing between performance in present tasks and the potential different set of needs in a new job, often simply due to insufficient knowledge. Lack of opportunities, fear of the self-fulfilling prophecy of those not perceived to have potential, or disappointed expectations, are also factors. The spotting of potential also presupposes the identification of lack of potential and may restrict the beneficiaries to those who may fill a few high-level jobs to the detriment of developing potential on a broader range of skills.

If potential is to be discussed, it is important that promises are not made which cannot be kept. More often the discussion highlights areas to concentrate on and provides guidance to make people more 'marketable' should suitable vacancies arise. The best indicators are where people have shown consistent improvement in a job, particularly over a wide spread of disciplines and environments, or where they have coped with increased responsibilities. People's support for the work of colleagues or other departments and a non-parochial approach may also be usefully considered as indicators of potential.

Checklist

- Managers must check with senior management or personnel before making recommendations which may fall through.
- Promises should not be made unless they can be kept.
- Performance in similar job aspects or cultural environments may give an indication of potential.

Appraisal interviewing skills

The lynchpin for any system is the main appraisal interview which is normally done on an annual basis.

Preparation for the interview

Prior to the interview it is important to collate the information which should have been collected throughout the year, refer to previous records and speak with other people who are affected by the work of the job holder. Bosses should give plenty of thought to what they want to say, have ideas for the future, have done their homework regarding the possibility of secondments, training, etc., and try to anticipate the comments, problems, and aspirations which the appraisee may raise.

A brief meeting with the appraisee should be held to give notice of the interview, stress the objectives, outline areas for discussion and to hand over any relevant paperwork (*see* Appendix 9 on page 357). Up to two hours should normally be allowed for an interview, although some interviews may not take this long. Back-to-back appointments should be avoided and managers should also avoid doing more than two per day. All ideas, key points and the structure of the interview should be recorded on paper to assist in conducting the interviews.

Conducting the interview

In order to promote discussion the room should be laid out informally, the appraisee welcomed and put at ease. It is imperative to start with a reminder of the purpose and structure of the interview. Although managers must give their view, it is useful to get the appraisee talking by using open questions, probing their answers, not interrupting and giving recognition where due. Problem areas must also be addressed, but as a sharing of a problem on performance, not a character assassination. There should be no surprises at the interview and managers must always be able to justify any comments they make. The use of summaries is to be recommended: to note key points, check acceptance, and move on to new areas. Even if it has not been a good year, an interview should always finish positively with a plan of action.

Follow-up

It is wise to write up interview notes immediately after the meeting and pass these on for further comments if required. Always set deadlines for this process so that completed forms are placed with the parties concerned as quickly as possible. Targets may have been set for the appraiser as well as the job holder (for example, to check availability of particular courses). Always ensure these are met in order to maintain the credibility of the system. Managers should then review progress with their people regularly throughout the year.

Checklist

- Allow time to prepare and give notification to the appraisee.
- Consider the previous period and prepare an overview.

- Consider departmental and individual needs for the future.
- Establish the purpose of the interview.
- Establish a dialogue and obtain the job holder's views.
- Use summaries throughout.
- Always finish on a positive note.
- Set deadlines to complete the process.
- Meet regularly to review progress throughout the year.

Implementation and maintenance

Having decided upon the scheme and its mechanics, a suitable timetable for implementation would include training all appraisers in:

- the objectives and benefits of the scheme, mechanics and paperwork
- setting standards and targets
- conducting an interview
- formulating an action plan
- ensuring it becomes part of the management function by holding regular reviews.

This is not the time to make changes in the paperwork otherwise the whole system may lose credibility.

Appraisees should also receive a face-to-face appreciation session on why and how the system is to run and what they can do to ensure they find it successful. Support literature should be supplied at these sessions.

After completing an initial round of appraisals it is a good idea to review the initial response and effectiveness and make improvements as necessary.

Maintenance

A great danger point for a successfully launched scheme is at two to three years, when people may become stale or run out of things to address. It is desirable to have refresher sessions and ensure newly appointed managers receive proper induction into their responsibilities as appraisers.

Senior management, in conjunction with personnel, should review the success of the scheme periodically, consult with those affected and make the changes required, particularly during the early stages.

Checklist

- Train all appraisers.
- Hold appreciation sessions for all other affected people.
- Ensure support literature is available.
- Address appraisal at induction sessions for new managers and appraisees.
- Hold refresher sessions every two to three years.
- Review the scheme periodically and communicate any changes.

Key points to consider in order to install and maintain an effective appraisal scheme are:

- gain involvement and commitment from the top
- let the scheme be owned by line managers
- appraise people on identifiable performance
- concentrate on the future
- review performance regularly
- train all appraisers and appraisees
- ensure people are clear about the scheme's objectives.

Examples of complete appraisal systems are available free of charge from:

The Information Department
Robert Hyde House
48 Bryanston Square
London W1H 7LN
Telephone: 071–262–2401

6 TARGET SETTING

Targets are priorities or special tasks which need to be achieved in addition to the routine work. They relate specifically to an individual and are about changes and development. They may be intended to improve performance, to redress a drop in performance, or to develop a trainee to the required level.

Targets are about short-term shifts in performance, whereas standards are continuing yardsticks. This can be shown as in Figure 6.1.

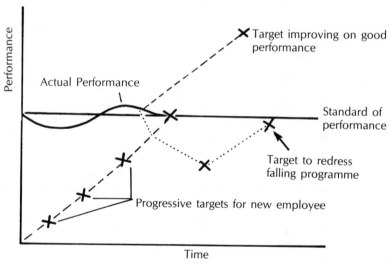

Figure 6.1 *Relationship of performance to targets over a period of time*

Why set targets?

Targets are set to:

- get results

- improve people's performance
- develop skills, ability and knowledge
- provide a challenge and sense of achievement.

If people are to contribute effectively to the organisation they need to know the answers to certain questions.

- Who is my boss?
- What is my job?
- What is the standard expected of me?
- How am I doing?
- Where do I go from here and how do I get there?

Target setting helps to answer the question 'How am I doing?' and provides a means to address 'Where do I go from here?' and 'How do I get there?'

In order to be effective, target setting requires a drill by which both individual and manager regularly review performance and set new targets. Moreover, clarity of structure within the organisation is helpful as ambiguous structures can produce contradictory targets from two or more bosses. An overall understanding of acceptable standards of performance will also help to provide the baseline for target setting.

Establishing job responsibilities

The next step is for the employee and line manager to establish what contribution the employee is expected to make and how they will measure success.

Traditionally, this has been done by means of a job description, but recently job descriptions have fallen into disrepute for being too complicated and inflexible, and for failing to reflect the actual work done. For a job description to be effective, therefore, it must be updated regularly with the emphasis on what is to be achieved rather than the duties that have to be performed.

People need to know the overall aims of the organisation and department, and, more specifically, the areas to which they will contribute. These are often called key result areas and cover fairly broad headings such as stock, sales, supervision, internal communication, external communication, administration, training and development. They are not a comprehensive list of duties, and it is unlikely that there will be more than six to eight of them. Key result areas will, effectively, state the objectives of the job. Standards of performance will need to be added or incorporated in order for the objectives to express expectations clearly.

Targets are set throughout the year. Key result areas should be set separately by the job holder and the line manager before the two discuss them. This will immediately highlight any discrepancies between their expectations of the job.

Setting targets

Having established the requirements of the job, the next stage is to consider how targets can be used throughout the year as a normal part of the management process to enable staff to give their best performance.

Areas for target setting

Targets not only relate to sales or production figures, but also to results which cannot be as easily quantified. Therefore, providing both the boss and the job holder understand the tangible results which are expected, improving relations with another department can be as valid a target as reducing expenditure by 4 per cent.

Targets may therefore be set to:

- set a standard of performance
- raise a standard of performance
- re-establish slipping targets or standards
- progressively train job holder up to standard
- achieve a project often put aside
- innovate
- broaden individual skills
- develop the individual
- cash-in on unforeseen circumstances
- implement a new policy

- develop a new area of work
- change priorities due to altered circumstances
- direct the high achiever.

How are targets set?

The manager has now discussed with the job holder what is expected from the job and what standards of performance must be maintained. Before setting targets, the manager should also look at available examples of what has been done – this will help in deciding what can be done.

Targets are set by the manager after consultation with the job holder. To avoid future argument about whether or not they have been achieved, targets should always be kept clear and simple, set at a face-to-face meeting, and recorded. People need to know what is required, when it is required and what priority it has in relation to other targets or routine work. The manager should not tell the job holder how to achieve the target but should allow scope for the job holder to exercise initiative.

Examples of targets

A target is a special task which needs to be achieved over and above the routine work.

- Sales representative – to gain three new accounts of at least £200 per calender month in 'x' month.
- Social worker – to establish regular liaison meetings with the local community policeman commencing . . .
- Office manager – to install a house style manual for departmental letters and forms by . . .
- Scientist – investigate availability of new instrumentation for 'x' and present the investment proposal to the Research Committee Meeting in . . . .
- Teacher – to take 'x' month on secondment with local industry and to produce a report for the Curriculum Committee on how the school can improve links with local businesses.

Clearly, every effort should be made to get the job holder to agree to the targets as this will make their commitment greater.

In cases where this proves impossible, the manager must have the final say. Providing the job holder has been consulted and the reasons for setting the targets are clearly explained, it should be possible to get the job holder's acceptance. Appendix 11 on page 360 gives a sample questionnaire which is intended to help this process.

How many?

If more than half-a-dozen targets are attempted in any one period, success in all of them is unlikely. People will not be able to concentrate on too many unless they are routine, in which case they lose their challenge. The number will reflect the difficulty and time span but it is not necessary to spread targets clinically over each result area. They should rather attack those areas where the need is greatest. Remember that targets are *special tasks over and above the routine areas* and, as performance standards have already been drawn up, other key result areas will not be neglected.

How precise?

Targets should be precise enough to avoid argument as to whether or not they have been achieved, but not so precise that they state the method by which the target is to be attempted as well as the goal itself. People need to know what is required, the deadline and what is the priority in relation to other targets or routine work, but the manager should allow scope for the job holder to exercise initiative in carrying out the relevant target.

For what period?

There is no ideal time limit for a target but if more than one or two targets have been set, it is wise to stagger the deadlines. Human nature determines that most people only complete a target close to deadline; if several all fall at once there will not be enough time for the job holder to concentrate on each and the quality of the results will suffer.

The time span for carrying out a target could be anything from a day to a year. However, if a job holder's enthusiasm is to be maintained, shorter time limits (one to six months) are better.

How difficult?

If targets are to improve performance and motivate people, there is no point in making them too easy. They should be challenging and stretching to develop a person and give them a real sense of achievement. They must also be realistic: what may be an easy target for an established employee may be too difficult for a new employee working through an induction period. Moreover, if the job holder does not think a target is realistic, commitment at the beginning is unlikely. This re-emphasises the need for the manager to get the job holder's views before setting a target. However, it could be that the manager will have to tone down an employee's enthusiasm and set an easier, more realistic target. Remember that whereas standards of performance relate to a job, targets relate to an individual and therefore should be more flexible.

How subject to change?

Flexibility is important as there is always a danger when setting targets that other factors may change their priority, rendering them irrelevant, too difficult, or too easy. Frequent monitoring will assist greatly. It is important also that targets are not dropped at the first sign of trouble as this rapidly discredits the whole concept and allows people to make excuses. The job of a manager when faced with a problem is to identify what other actions need to be taken to overcome it, rather than move the goal posts. Difficulties encountered in achieving targets should be viewed in this light.

How to monitor?

The likelihood of change and its effect on targets set means that the process must be monitored and, indeed, there is little point in setting a target unless there is some means for checking progress. The method for monitoring should be established when targets are set so that job holders are not taken by surprise or feel spied upon by a manager who has no faith in them.

Walking the job

Apart from regular systems for exchanging information such as monthly figures, reports and so on, a more informal method of checking on progress is 'walking the job': that is, simply going around the team and asking how they are getting on. This can also be a useful occasion to recognise progress and proffer informal advice if needed.

One-to-one meetings

However, it is important that meetings for reviewing due targets, considering progress on others and setting new ones are arranged regularly. This will ensure that target setting becomes part of the management process and that targets and progress are considered throughout the year and adapted to the needs of the organisation, department and job holder. It will also give job holders a regular opportunity to discuss their work away from the hurly-burly of daily pressures, and shift the balance of work away from 'fire-fighting' to looking ahead.

Ideally, review meetings should take place monthly and certainly no less than quarterly. They should be short with only a brief confirmation of progress and action, and should include the following points:

- have the targets been achieved and if so what can be learned from them?
- if any targets have not been achieved is this due to:
  - failure on the job holder's part such as leaving it too late
  - the manager's failure such as providing insufficient resources or authority
  - unforeseen circumstances, for example absence through sickness or extra workload?
- if the target has not been met, should the deadline be extended, alternative methods adopted or has the target been rendered irrelevant?
- how is the individual doing in relation to the routine areas of their job?

It is important for the manager to be constructive at these reviews. Successes and failures should be identified and new targets and positive action set. It should not be seen as a chance for the manager or job holder to apportion blame. The emphasis should be on assessing people on what they have achieved rather than on abstract personal qualities.

Records

Target setting is about dialogue and commitment to action rather than paperwork. However, it is important to keep a record if only by means of a memo confirming progress and new targets. A more structured approach will assist, particularly where people are not used to the concept and there is a need to provide information upwards to the boss's boss or to identify training needs. A full scale appraisal should be carried out at least once per year. Appendices 12 and 13 on pages 361 and 362 provide examples of an appraisal policy, a counselling questionnaire, and a review form, respectively.

7 TRAINING YOUR STAFF

Why train?

Training is a means of equipping employees to perform competently in their present or future jobs so as to increase the efficiency of the organisation and their own job satisfaction. It is the *planned* provision of the means of learning on the job or in a training centre. The benefits training can give include the following:

- *Reduction of learning time and cost.* People learn the job quickly, to required standards, safely, and with minimum waste of materials or damage to equipment.
- *Improved job performance.* Increased output, improved quality, work done on time.
- *Less supervision* through reduction of problems such as absenteeism, lateness, accidents.
- *Better recruitment and selection.* Training opportunities help attract right type of employees.
- *Reduced labour turnover* by developing employees' potential and their job satisfaction.
- *Reduced costs* resulting from above benefits.
- *Increased customer satisfaction* through improved goods and services.

Training is a line management responsibility from the top executive to the first line supervisor. Those responsible for the successful accomplishment of the work are also responsible for maintaining the effectiveness of the employees undertaking that work.

This booklet aims to acquaint managers with the main methods involved in training and give them some guidance as to when and how they can be used.

Who is to be trained?

New entrants

All new employees require induction training in order to familiarise them with the organisation, its products/services, its personnel policies, and practices. Some part of this training may be carried out by the personnel department. But it is the responsibility of the manager to introduce newcomers to the department, to train them from the start in the way the department is run and the standards of performance and behaviour expected from them.

The importance of induction cannot be over-emphasised, especially where young employees are concerned. They are at an impressionable stage in their development, when attitudes to work can be influenced to an extent which may last a lifetime. Failure by the manager to give the necessary time and attention to this aspect of training can result in high staff turnover during the first few months; poor time-keeping and absenteeism; and a general lack of interest in the work and commitment to the organisation.

New employees seldom bring to the job the full range of knowledge and skills required. In addition to induction, they must therefore be trained in the necessary job knowledge and skills. The selection procedure, whereby the applicant is matched against the requirements of the job, should have shown the gaps which training needs to fill.

Special attention is given at the end of this chapter to young people and development training.

Existing employees

Those who require improvement in present job

If performance standards are to be maintained, it is essential that employees are *appraised* regularly so that any weaknesses, whether owing to deficiencies in the employees themselves, or to changes in the job, can be made good. Identification of such training needs is the duty of the manager: no one else is so well placed to do this.

Those preparing for promotion

To be successful, every organisation needs to exploit its resources: the most valuable of these is the human resource. Time and money must be invested in training and developing employees to meet future, as well as present, operational needs. Individual employees also require opportunities to develop their latent talents and abilities. 'Talent spotting' is also the manager's responsibility.

Those needing retraining

An important factor in achieving success, whether as an individual or an organisation, is the ability to recognise and respond to change. Changes in products, technology, markets, legislation and so on, can affect the way jobs are done and may mean that some, if not all, employees must acquire new knowledge and skills. Responsibility for meeting operational changes is a major part of every manager's job: retraining is vital to achieve this.

Those nearing retirement

In the interests of both the organisation and the employees, it is necessary to decide how to maintain their performance at an adequate standard, how best to utilise the knowledge and experience they have, while at the same time enabling them to 'run down' in preparation for retirement. Some may learn new skills, e.g. as job instructors; or apply their experience to special projects which are necessary, but difficult to fit into the normal routine; some may have to be trained to accept lower-level jobs for a period prior to retirement.

Supervisory training

Supervisors are in a key position and have a responsibility both to those whom they supervise and to management, who expect them to achieve their given targets. The role they play varies considerably from organisation to organisation, as does the extent of authority delegated, and the duties should therefore be examined in detail to see what special subjects should be included. Most will look for a wider knowledge of such things as computer applications, accounting procedures, work scheduling, than was previously expected. All should be given adequate help with people–management skills, which call for an appreciation of the following:

- leadership: combining the needs of the individual, group, and the job, and ways of motivating those in the team
- personal counselling
- industrial relations and general negotiations, including the handling of grievances and disciplinary matters
- the basics of employment law and a full understanding of company procedures
- training skills
- the art of effective communication
- safety policies, procedures, precautions and preventive measures
- general employment conditions and career prospects.

Management development

The impetus to an organisation comes in the first place from its managers. It is therefore essential that those in senior positions should be equipped to give a positive lead and that there is a planned succession for key appointments. Management training will cover the specialised aspects of each appointment and may often call for outside help. In addition, a more in-depth understanding of all the people/management issues discussed above will be required of those to whom the first-line supervisors look for support, and this too must be built into the programme.

The management role also includes responsibility for planning, co-ordinating, and budgeting and here, general principles must be taught as well as their application in the local situation. There is no easy way of developing creative thinking, intelligent anticipation and other similar attributes but thought should be given to methods by which they can be stimulated.

Managers will normally be aware of most of their own weaknesses and they should be encouraged to discuss these in a sympathetic atmosphere without any fear of the consequences of exposing their shortcomings to those in a position to influence their future. Their future development will depend partly on the organisation's requirements and partly on their own preferences; continued training should try to take account of both of these.

Shop stewards

Officials of recognised independent trade unions have a statutory right to time off with pay for training in aspects of industrial relations which are relevant to their duties, provided the training is approved by the Trades Union Congress or by the trade union to which they belong. The number of courses organised by the trade unions has increased very considerably in recent years, replacing to a marked extent those previously run in-company, a trend which has been encouraged by government financial support and by the unions' anxiety to see that their particular point of view on a variety of matters is fully represented. Nevertheless, some courses are still run by employing companies, possibly with the participation of an independent third party and/or a union official. Some see special value in holding joint shop steward/management courses which enable each to have a better understanding of the other's view.

Safety representatives

Safety representatives appointed by recognised independent trade unions also have a statutory right to training on full pay and employers recognise the wisdom of extending such a facility to others who are not covered by the legislation. Once again, company courses have been supplemented and substantially replaced by those sponsored by the unions who wish to put across their own view point and approach. There may well be justification for more local arrangements so that attention can be drawn to the particular hazards of the company's work and to the precautions to be taken. These may be made in addition to, or as a substitute for, the union based programme, and where unions are involved it is advisable to discuss the contents with the officials beforehand and if practicable to include a union speaker in the programme.

What training is to be done?

In order to train effectively, it is first necessary to decide in some detail what specific knowledge and skills the jobs involve, what the individuals already possess, and what gaps in such knowledge and skills training can fill.

A systematic approach to the identification of training requirements is described briefly below. To undertake such an approach, the manager will probably need to enlist the aid of a specialist, e.g. a training officer, or consultant.

Identification of requirements

Examine the job

Make a preliminary examination of the job to find out what is involved in its satisfactory performance. Managers may well think they already know all the jobs in their departments. But it is worthwhile observing the whole job, and questioning the job holder about the nature of the activities involved in it. This will be of particular importance when training new entrants, since the previous holder of the job may have modified the way the job is done to suit his or her own strengths and weaknesses – such variations may not suit either the new entrant or the manager's requirements.

Describe the job

Prepare a *job description*, i.e. a document stating the job title, where located, job relationships, purpose, activities – or overall objective, main objectives, and performance standards.

Analyse the training requirements

Examine the main activities given in the job description so as to identify the tasks involved and the knowledge/skills required for their efficient performance. The extent and depth of this examination depends upon the complexity of the job. There are a variety of analytical techniques, of which the job instruction breakdown is the simplest and can be applied to a variety of jobs.

The work study or method study breakdown and the skills

analysis breakdown are more sophisticated techniques usually reserved for more complex operations, and require specialist training and skill on the part of the analyst.

The result of analysis will provide a *job specification*, i.e. a summary of the specific knowledge and skills required, but not necessarily in the order they should be taught.

Assess individual performance

The process so far has taken no account of the individual who is to do the job. The new entrant's degree of competence to perform the job should have been assessed when he or she was selected. Existing job holders need regular appraisal to determine how they are measuring up to required performance standards, and what training they need to make good their deficiencies or develop their potential. This assessment will give a detailed statement of what the trainee needs to learn, i.e. a *training specification*. In the case of a new entrant with no knowledge of the job, the job specification and the training specification are the same.

Corporate training needs

Identification of training requirements is not related solely to individuals' performance. Managers need to be alert to the training implications, both for their own departments and the organisations as a whole, of such matters as technical developments, new systems and procedures, market forecasts, changes in employment policies and practices, financial results, etc. Such changes may call for a 'one-off' programme to meet a temporary situation or emergency. But if the organisation is to achieve its objectives, there must be a continuous review of manpower resources to ensure their effective use throughout the organisation.

How to train

Not only are managers responsible for training their staff but, in many respects, they are the best people to do the training. They know the jobs, they know their staff, and have a direct interest in their successful performance. But the way training is carried out will depend upon the numbers to be trained, the complexity of the work to be done, the difficulty of the training process, and the facilities at the manager's disposal. Training can be done:

- on-the-job (on-site, desk training), e.g. assignments/projects, coaching, job instruction, job rotation
- off-the-job (in the organisation), e.g. internal courses, programmed instruction, packaged programmes
- off-the-job (outside the organisation), e.g. external courses, special duties, correspondence courses, guided reading, TV and radio programmes.

The training programme

A training programme may employ any one or more of these means, e.g. an on-the-job instruction programme for a new packer; an internal course for a group of supervisors with common training needs; a combination of external courses, coaching and counselling by a manager for a former sales representative newly promoted to supervision. Appendices 14 and 15 on pages 365 and 366 show examples of individual training and course training programmes.

Planning the programme

This should contain all the items in the *training specification* and give details of the order in which they should be taught, the methods to be used, instructional staff, location, timetable. In planning the programme it is helpful to ask – and answer – the following questions:

- Who is to be trained – number and type of employee?
- Why are they to be trained – training objectives?
- What should be taught – knowledge and skills?
- How should training be done – methods?
- Who should do the training – instructors?
- When can it be done – length and frequency?
- Where will it be done – location?
- How will it be assessed – evaluation?

Designing the programme

In designing the programme, consideration should be given to the following points:

- *Sequence*: chronological; order of priority; common/related items.
- *Load and pace*: how much information trainees can absorb and how quickly they can learn.
- *Variety*: subject matter, methods.
- *Feedback*: to test learning, e.g. by setting targets, exercises.

Follow-up

If training is to improve job performance, it is essential that the manager gives trainees an early opportunity to practise their newly acquired knowledge and skills in the job. This may be done by a period of practice under supervision, by coaching and counselling, by assignments or projects, by temporary second-ment or job rotation.

Whatever means are employed, the manager must continue to check to see how well the information is retained and used, until he or she is satisfied that the trainees can perform their jobs competently on their own.

Methods

The following sections describe the main methods, the purposes for which they can be used, brief guidance on how to use them, and some indication of their advantages and disadvantages.

Assignment/projects

This is a form of exercise which requires trainees to complete a definite task, generally within a time limit. Such tasks should be based on actual problems facing the trainees' department or organisation, e.g. a high accident rate, customer complaints, high staff turnover.

These exercises are used to give trainees practical experience in applying the knowledge and skills learned previously through formal education or training.

Trainees should be given briefs written in clear, specific

terms, e.g. 'list the causes of all lost–time accidents which have occurred in the machine shop during the last two years and suggest how these could be prevented in future'. The brief should also include reference to the type and sources of information required.

The amount of guidance given will depend upon the level of competence of trainees and the complexity of the problem, but as much as possible should be left to the trainees to do for themselves. Trainees should produce specific, practical answers which take account of the policies, practices and general constraints of the situation. The results of their efforts should be presented to and be assessed by their boss, and anyone else who may be concerned with the problem – safety officer, maintenance engineer, etc.

The advantages of this method are that: training activities are directly related to the practicalities of the job; it is a simple means of monitoring trainees' progress and evaluating the effectiveness of the training itself; recommendations produced by trainees may be adopted and the 'pay-off' measured in financial terms. However, this method can be demanding in terms of the time of a number of senior people. Suitable for individual or group training.

Business exercises (in-tray)

Some problems have to be solved and decisions made by individuals working on their own. One exercise which deals with this is the in-tray. It simulates the working situation by presenting trainees with a number of items such as letters, memos, reports, similar to those which arrive on their own desks. They must deal with these by writing down whatever actions they think appropriate in the circumstances described in the exercise. The results of their efforts are analysed and discussed on the basis of the decisions made.

This exercise can be used to develop skill in: problem–solving; planning use of time; establishing work priorities; written communications, etc.

It can be run in a variety of ways and the time required will vary accordingly. If it is run as a problem-solving exercise it can take several hours, but if it deals with only one aspect it can be done in about an hour.

Like all business games and exercises, it can provide realistic experience of the techniques and skills of the job. However, the benefit is realised only if the exercise material selected is relevant to the needs of trainees. Suitable for group training; adaptable for individuals.

Business games

Groups of trainees, each representing an imaginary organisation (or some aspect of it) operate in a defined situation.

There is a wide variety of business games. A common type involves the planning of a plant, staffing it, scheduling a product, assessing the potential market, planning the sales campaign, and running a viable business for a set period of time. During the exercise, decisions made by trainees are evaluated by 'umpires' (or computers). The results of one set of decisions made by trainees influence their next set of decisions, and decisions made by one group affect the results of competing groups.

Business games enable trainees to appreciate which key factors they must observe in order to understand the state of a business. They can also learn such techniques and skills as planning, budgeting, marketing, problem-solving and decision-making. They can also learn to appreciate the interdependence of various functions in an organisation and the importance of teamwork.

Business games require time (anything from one or two hours to several days) and the resources to run them effectively.

They can provide realistic experience of the techniques and skills needed to run an organisation, and trainees generally become very interested and involved. However, 'playing games' may overshadow the learning experience and too much reduction of the time-span in the situation results in superficial learning. Suitable for group training.

The case study method

A case study is a record of a real situation, including the surrounding facts, opinions and prejudices, given to trainees to analyse and discuss. It may deal with one event (e.g. the launching of a new sales campaign), or with a situation involving a number of events (e.g. a strike arising from proposed redundancies following a merger). It may be presented in writing, orally, on film, filmstrip, or slides.

It can be used to teach such subjects as administration, sales, industrial relations, human relations. It is especially useful in supervisory/management training for dealing with such concepts as authority and responsibility. It can also help trainees to develop analytical ability, problem-solving and decision-making skills.

The case study is given to trainees for analysis, discussion and decision as to the type of action which might be taken. In some case studies, however, the action taken is included in the case history: consideration should then be given as to why such action was taken or what alternatives the situation offered. A short, simple case study can be dealt with in 20–30 minutes. Longer, or more complex cases need several hours. If the group is small (five–fifteen) the cases can be discussed by the total group; if larger, trainees may be divided into syndicates, each discussing the whole case simultaneously, or each dealing with a different aspect, and reconvening for a summary session.

In conducting a case discussion, the leader should encourage trainees to 'project' themselves into the situation described so that they deal with it in a responsible way. This is especially important with human relations cases which can develop into a 'witch hunt'.

One advantage of this method is that trainees can draw upon experience and exercise skills which are used in their work without incurring real risk. However, unless the cases used are relevant to the needs and interests of trainees they may be regarded as unworthy of serious attention. In some types of case study, the lack of detailed information about the situation and of a conclusive answer can create a feeling of dissatisfaction on the part of trainees. Suitable for group training.

Coaching

This is a way in which managers can systematically increase the ability and experience of their staff by giving them carefully planned tasks coupled with continuous appraisal and counselling.

Managers should consider the following points:

● *Opportunities* (for coaching) may arise through assessment of an individual's needs for improvement, or through changes in departmental or work procedures.

- *Planning* – agree a coaching plan and timetable with the trainee. Consider: what changes have to be achieved; when have they to be achieved; how will achievement be measured; how will progress be monitored?
- *Assignments* or tasks should be relevant: seek and use suitable work problems. Set high but attainable targets.
- *Monitor progress* – correct if necessary; offer advice, guidance and encouragement.
- *Evaluation* – at the end of the coaching period, review and evaluate the trainee's performance and consider further development plans.

Coaching is a low cost means of improving individual performance and departmental efficiency. However, it is only effective if trainees can see its relevance and value to themselves as well as to their work, and the coaching is carried out in a systematic and purposeful manner. Suitable for individual training.

External courses

These are training courses which are organised and directed by an authority other than the trainees' employer. A wide variety of such courses suitable for all types of employees are provided by technical, educational, professional and specialist organisations.

External courses provide opportunities to acquire technical and professional qualifications, training in subjects of which there is no knowledge or experience within the trainees' organisation, and opportunities for broadening individual experience. They are useful for meeting specific individual needs, when numbers are too small for an internal course, or when employees cannot all be released at the same time.

It is important to select the right courses for trainees. Consideration should be given therefore to the following factors:

- type and reputation of the organisation providing the course
- timing – frequency and duration
- location – does it involve travelling time and expense?
- cost – direct/indirect; grant available if any
- the programme – objectives – explicit, realistic

- content – well-balanced, appropriate to trainees' needs
- methods of training – appropriate to content and type of training
- staffing – qualified
- status of course members – comparable level
- facilities and amenities
- administration.

If in doubt on any of these points, the course organisers should be contacted for further information – they generally welcome such enquiries.

A number of bodies maintain advisory services on external courses and will give enquirers assessments of particular courses. Managers or training specialists can also build up their own dossiers on courses which have been found suitable for their employees.

In some circumstances it is possible to liaise with a local technical or commercial college, or other training agency, and get them to organise the particular type of course required.

If trainees are to benefit from external courses, they must be briefed beforehand as to why they are attending and what they are expected to get out of it, and after the course they should discuss the application of their newly acquired knowledge and skills with their boss so that further training or experience may be given. One way of ensuring that what has been learned is put into practical effect is by giving trainees project work. This can also be used as a means of evaluating the effectiveness of the training courses.

Among the advantages of external courses are that they are ready-made, quick and easy to arrange, offer a wider choice of training facilities than can be provided internally, and give trainees the benefit of meeting people outside their own organisation with different ideas and experience. However, the disadvantage is that courses catering for a wide variety of trainees tend to be generalised, and the right course may not be available at the right time. Suitable for individuals or groups.

Group discussion

This is an interchange of ideas and experience among the participants, who are guided to achieve the training objectives.

Group discussion can be used to give trainees an opportunity to learn from the knowledge and experience of others, or to promote changes in opinions, attitudes, behaviour. It is a technique which can only be used where relevant knowledge and experience exist within the group, e.g. through prior experience, or can be supplied in a lecture, film or demonstration. The size of the group must be limited: five–fifteen should enable all to take an active part.

To ensure that all trainees benefit from the time spent in discussion, discussion leaders must prepare a plan. They should:

- analyse the subject and decide which aspects should or can be covered in the time available, e.g. 20–60 minutes
- break down the subject matter into manageable steps
- prepare an introductory statement which: defines the subject; explains the discussion plan; and includes an opening question to get discussion started.

In conducting the discussion, the leader needs to keep the objectives clearly in mind and periodically focus the group's attention on them. Control of the discussion depends mainly upon the guidance exercised by the leader.

The leader's functions are:

- to listen
- ask questions
- clarify misunderstandings
- correct errors
- reject irrelevances
- co-ordinate ideas
- evaluate members' contributions
- give information if necessary
- give interim summaries
- summarise final conclusions.

The advantages of the discussion method are that it gets trainees involved and committed; provides for cross-fertilisation of ideas and experience; gives trainees an opportunity to examine and test their own ideas, attitudes or behaviour and to change them. However, unless it is well prepared and conducted it can produce confused thinking and frustration. Suitable for group training.

The incident method

A variation of the case study method, the case consists of a short statement of an incident which has actually taken place. For example: 'The chargehand found two operators fighting. One operator fell against a nearby machine and injured his hand. The chargehand reported the incident to the foreman.' Trainees have to search for the rest of the information by questioning the discussion leader before proceeding to discuss the problem and deciding what action should be taken.

This method aims especially to inculcate in trainees the habit of asking questions and getting relevant information before determining the issues to be resolved and making decisions.

In this type of case discussion, the leader only supplies the information asked for and should allow trainees to come to a decision with insufficient information if they so choose. Their mistakes will become self-evident when they have to justify their proposed actions. As these 'incidents' have actually happened, the action taken by the people concerned is known and can be compared with the action proposed by the trainees. ('Incidents' from the discussion leader's or trainees' own experience are a useful source of material for this exercise.)

Among the advantages of this method are that it: gives trainees practice in obtaining and assessing information; provides an answer to the problem posed and thus overcomes the dissatisfaction which can arise from some case studies. When trainees are organised in syndicates the competitive element can increase involvement. However, unless the discussion is carefully handled, there is a risk that trainees attach more importance to getting the 'right answer' than to learning the requisite skills, and also that the group is divided into 'winners' and 'losers'. Suitable for group training.

Internal courses

These are courses for which the organisation and direction of the sessions is the responsibility of the employer of the trainee.

Such courses may be organised and conducted by managers for groups of employees in their own departments, by the organisation's training specialist, or with the assistance of an outside agency such as a technical or commercial college, consultant, etc. However, the involvement of members of management is essential to the success of such courses. Not only are they able to pass on some of their knowledge and experience to the trainees, but the courses give them an opportunity to get to know what the trainees are doing and thinking about their own jobs. The feedback can provide some useful information regarding methods, equipment, products, policies, and may also indicate further training needs.

Internal courses serve to meet training requirements where a group of trainees have common needs e.g. a number of new entrants needing induction or basic job instruction; or when some operational change, such as the introduction of computers, means that a section of employees require retraining, or when there is an overall need, e.g. for a general improvement in supervisory performance.

The advantages of internal courses are that: they are 'tailor made' to meet specific needs, so that issues are dealt with in terms of the organisation's own policies and practices; a body of knowledge and skills is developed which is generally recognised and applied, i.e. a common language and way of doing things; where trainees are drawn from different units, they can get to know and understand one another and acquire a sense of identity; courses can be arranged when required and at a convenient place.

However, unless care is taken to include some sessions which inject new ideas there is a danger of 'in-breeding'. Suitable for group training.

Job instruction

A systematic four-step plan of instruction. Mainly used for training in manual tasks, it can also be adapted for training in procedures and systems.

Prior to instructing, it is necessary to: break down the job into stages; list the operations or instructions which have to be carried out to perform each stage; note the key points (e.g. safety factors, special points of difficulty, variations from normal procedure) which must be emphasised; and prepare the instruction plan, materials and aids.

Instruction plan:

1 *Prepare the trainee* – put at ease; create interest in learning; check existing knowledge

2 *Present* – tell (explain), show (demonstrate) as appropriate, one step at a time; stress 'key points'; instruct clearly and completely, and at a pace trainees can absorb
3 *Practice and test* – get the trainee to do the job or explain the subject; correct errors; check understanding; continue until he or she reaches required standard
4 *Follow up* – put to work; check as necessary.

The advantages of this approach are that it is a simple, economical, and efficient method of job training. However, it is less effective where the knowledge/skill requirements are complex. Suitable for individual training; adaptable to small groups.

Job rotation

A form of accelerated experience in the normal working situation aimed at developing existing knowledge and skills or acquiring new experiences.

Trainees are moved for short periods to new jobs. They must be briefed as to what they are expected to learn, and their progress checked to ensure that they benefit from the experience. The amount of responsibility trainees can be given initially must be judged by the extent and relevance of their previous experience. It is also important that the jobs involved are selected for the training and development opportunities they provide and not as a convenient means of filling temporary vacancies. Certain jobs can be reserved as training positions.

This method enables trainees to acquire the specific practical experience they need quickly, instead of having to wait for opportunities to occur through promotions and transfers. However, it can be difficult to ensure that the right jobs are available at the right time, and this practice of using or reserving specific jobs for training purposes can sometimes block normal promotion prospects for others. Suitable for individual training.

The lecture

A straight talk without group participation other than through questions at the end. Lectures can be used to give new information, introduce or summarise another piece of instruction, present a case for discussion. Good lecturers are 'masters of their subject and servants of their audience'. Lecturers should:

- define clearly and keep in mind who the listeners are, and what they should know by the end of the session
- check what knowledge they already possess; consider how the subject touches their interests
- decide priorities – what they must know, should know, would like to know
- consider how much time is available, e.g. 15–45 minutes
- plan:
    - *introduction:* tells the listeners the ground to be covered and defines terms which might confuse
    - *main points:* arranged in an orderly sequence which help listeners to follow and understand
    - *conclusion:* summarises the main points, or highlights an important aspect of the subject, or raises a controversial point to stimulate discussion
- decide whether any visual aids or handouts might help listeners to understand the message more easily.

When presenting a lecture you should:

- get the attention of your listeners, e.g. by making a provocative statement, asking a challenging question, using a visual aid
- speak clearly, in a conversational manner, looking at your listeners and speaking directly to them
- show enthusiasm for your subject and a genuine interest in your listeners.

The advantage of the lecture is that it can give information quickly to a number of people at the same time. However, misunderstandings can arise, as the speaker cannot be sure the information is being assimilated. This disadvantage can be overcome if speakers invite questions or ask questions during the lecture, so that they can adapt their material or approach if necessary. (When a lecture is structured to ensure audience participation it becomes a *lesson*.) Suitable for group training.

Packaged programmes ('training packages')

These are available on a wide variety of subjects: leadership, appraisal, employment legislation, job instruction, problem-solving, staff selection. They generally include a training manual, exercises, audio-visual aids, and assume that the purchaser has (or can hire) the necessary equipment – slide, filmstrip or film projectors, overhead projectors, tape recorders, etc.

Most of them require tuition before they can be used effectively. For example, The Industrial Society's Action Centred Leadership programme requires managers to first attend an external course, and then work under the guidance of a Society instructor on two in-company courses, before they are recognised as competent to run the programmes by themselves (*see chapter 1, The manager as a leader*).

These programmes can be very useful to the manager, especially in an organisation without a training specialist, as all the hard work in collecting the material, designing the programme and producing instructional aids has been done.

However, they need careful selection, as attempts at adaptation can result in reducing the effectiveness of the programmes in some cases. The initial cost can be high, but is economically viable where the programme can be used for groups of trainees and the material can be retained and used repeatedly. Suitable mainly for group training.

Programmed instruction

The material to be presented appears in small, carefully sequenced segments (called frames). Each frame elicits a response from the learners who immediately find out whether their response was correct.

Two approaches are generally recognised.

1 Linear programming, in which one frame is so carefully constructed and validated that the learner will almost invariably give the correct response.
2 Intrinsic or Branching Programming, which presents several responses from which the learners select the one they think is correct. If they are correct they are told so, and given data for the next frame. If they are wrong they are given further

explanation, then directed back to the previous frame to make another choice.

Programmes can be presented in machine or book form. There is a wide variety of published programmes dealing with subjects suitable for industrial and commercial training.

This method can be used where a number of trainees cannot be spared from their duties simultaneously, or where there are wide differences in knowledge of the subject, or learning ability. But trainees should be brought together periodically to ensure a common understanding of what they have learned and its application to their everyday duties.

Programmed instruction is especially useful as a means of learning factual subjects. However, where training is concerned with promoting changes in opinions and behaviour, or the development of personal skills, it is generally less effective. Suitable for individual training.

Role-playing

A form of 'learning by doing' but in a simulated situation. Trainees are presented with a situation which they have to resolve by acting out the roles of the people involved.

This method helps trainees to recognise their own strengths and weaknesses, increase their appreciation of the differing attitudes and reactions of other people, improve their skill in dealing with people, and learn new techniques. It can be used to train in interviewing, staff selection, staff appraisal, chairmanship, negotiating, instructing, public speaking, selling, etc.

It requires the setting up of a typical work situation (e.g. a sales assistant serving a customer) which trainees handle as they think appropriate, or behave as they think people who normally find themselves in such situations would behave. Their performance is observed and discussed by the trainer and the rest of the group. Role-playing can be combined with other methods, such as, for example, a lecture on the principles of selling followed by role-play exercises in which trainees apply these principles in dealing with customers; or a case study discussion concerning a disciplinary problem which may be resolved by the trainees 'acting out' the roles of boss and subordinate.

Role-playing is a method which should be approached with

care; success depending to a large extent upon the trainer's ability to create a friendly, permissive atmosphere in which trainees feel able to act out their roles and to take and give criticism. It is best done with smaller groups (six–eight) so the trainer can control the whole exercise; larger groups can be divided into syndicates composed of role-players and observers. Time must be allowed for briefing trainees, doing the role-play and discussing it – a minimum of 30 minutes, generally longer.

An advantage of this method is that trainees can practise skills and experiment in behaviour while protected from the real consequences of their mistakes. However, it can expose the sensitive trainee to destructive criticism, or create difficulties in personal relationships. Suitable for group training.

Special duties

These are specific tasks assigned to trainees which will enable them to acquire experience outside their normal job duties.

Such activities might include representing the organisation on external bodies, membership of a professional/technical body, technical teaching, youth club leadership, secondment to agents or subsidiaries, attendance to trade exhibitions, and so on.

These tasks should be carefully selected and assigned at relevant stages in the training programme. They can provide useful experience – especially for employees in line for supervisory or management jobs. However, they may involve absence from normal job duties, and must be planned accordingly. Suitable for individual training.

Miscellaneous methods

Correspondence courses, guided reading, TV and radio programmes, can all provide a means of acquiring knowledge and skills applicable to a variety of jobs. Like all methods they must be selected carefully. Some guidance must be given to the trainees as to how they should deal with the material; specific arrangements made for the reading, viewing etc. to be followed by individual or group discussion; and some tests (oral, written, or practical) devised to assess what has been learned. Suitable for individual or group training.

Evaluation

Time and money spent on training is only justified if the training contributes to the efficiency of the organisation and improves the performance and prospects of employees. Evaluation – the assessment of the total value of any training activity – is therefore essential.

Managers are well placed to do this. Through the methods described in Chapter 3, managers can identify the lack of the knowledge and skill which is needed to do a job to required standards, or those operational problems which training can solve. They can then carry out the training needed. After the training they should reassess the individual's performance or re-examine the problem area, to test what the training has achieved. The manager should ask the following questions:

- Did results meet the training objectives? (e.g. what evidence of improved performance?)
- What benefits accrued to the organisation?
- Were there any spin-offs not directly related to the training objectives?
- What was the cost?
- How will decisions about future training be affected?

In addition to making their own assessments, managers should ask the trainees how they felt they benefited from the training, and get the views of other people who may have been involved, e.g. other managers, supervisors, instructional staff.

Evaluation is comparatively simple in cases like that of new entrants with no previous experience of operating a machine, who after training can demonstrate that they can operate the machine in a safe, efficient manner and produce the required quantity and quality of work. It becomes more difficult with more complex jobs, e.g. supervisory jobs, and in such skills as decision making, where the results of decisions may only be measurable in the long term, and other influences may affect results.

However, although in some cases it may be necessary to accept inconclusive evidence rather than proof, it is still worthwhile evaluating training. Provided the objectives are identified in specific, measurable terms (e.g. to take shorthand dictation at 80 wpm and transcribe it accurately; to reduce errors in invoices, customer complaints; to increase output/sales by so much), it is possible to demonstrate 'cause and effect'.

Training records

Simple records can assist the manager in deciding who needs training and when, and ensure all staff are receiving the required training.

There should be: an *individual* record for each trainee, giving name, department, date of joining, and details of the training – i.e. dates (start and completion), objectives, method, result of training, cost, further action; and a *department* record, giving names of trainees, type of training, dates, results of training, costs, further action.

The training specialist

A competent training specialist can help the manager with:

- analysing jobs
- preparing job descriptions
- preparing appraisal systems
- identifying operational problems that training can solve
- planning the training programme
- giving advice on selection of training methods, techniques, aids
- preparing training materials
- implementing the training programme in specific areas delegated by management (e.g. basic skills training) or areas of particular complexity (e.g. group relations training)
- evaluating training
- preparing training budgets
- keeping records
- training managers, supervisors and others in instructional techniques and skills
- keeping managers informed of developments in the training field.

The function of the training specialist is to advise and assist line management to carry out their responsibilities for training and developing their subordinates. He or she is the specialist in training – they are the specialists in running the organisation.

The training specialist may be employed full-time (large organisations may need a training department), or a senior executive can undertake this function as part of his or her regular job. In either case, the training specialist can only operate effectively with the support and active involvement of line management.

Development training

What is employee development training?

Development training – as opposed to job skill training and technical education – is designed to develop positive behaviour and attitudes and is particularly suitable for young employees. Instead of teaching technical skills, development training aims to inculcate:

- a better understanding of, and involvement in, the working environment
- the ability to assess potential and think realistically about the future
- the importance of being a member of the work group
- the opportunity to develop the basic skills needed to cope in adult life
- an understanding of how society works and the contribution which can be made to it.

Good development training is essential in preparing young people for the responsibilities and ethics of working life. It is achieved when the company has a realistic young employees' development and training policy. It will improve the young employee's overall performance at work. Good development training:

- is supported by top management
- is geared to the practical needs of all young employees
- is on-going and related to the overall training programme

- is seen as an integral part of the young employee's training programme
- enables young employees to learn through experience in a practical way
- allows for the maximum participation by those adults who can influence the young employees in their personal development
- is flexible enough to meet changing needs
- makes best use of outside training facilities and activities.

What should it include?

Development training is not about changing attitudes, but about helping to form them in a positive way. This type of training should occur during the transition from school to work and during induction.

Suitable areas for development training should include:

- vocational skills training
- a residential experience
- areas of special development including leadership and communication skills
- involvement with supervisors who influence young employees
- youth forums and apprentice associations
- further education
- community work.

Determining the need for development training

Answering the following questions about all your young employees, not only those on formal training programmes, will help determine the need for training.

- Are absentee figures high?
- Are they frequently late?
- Do you think they could give more to their department?
- Is labour turnover high?
- Do they lack leadership skills or self-confidence?
- Can they work well in groups and communicate effectively?
- Do they take responsibility and accept challenges?

The development training programme

Development training should be an integral part of new recruits' overall training programme, so planning and timing need particular attention. For young employees with a very heavy college commitment the best time is during holidays, particularly for residential courses.

Some companies use Friday afternoons for running in-company training sessions.

It is important to remember that young employees have recently left school and will not, therefore, appreciate being put back into a classroom environment. The theoretical and academic approach should be avoided. There are numerous methods of training.

Individual tuition

This method is often used by companies employing only a few young employees. It usually involves the person's supervisor providing continuous coaching on the job. A detailed induction programme should be produced which enables the young person to meet various company specialists to discuss what they do. These meetings should be written up in a log which can be monitored and should be spread over the first six months. Visits to other companies and units should be organised initially by the trainee's supervisor, but later by the trainee. Make sure that clear objectives are produced for the visit and that the trainee is briefed on what to look out for and what type of questions to ask. Trainees as they develop should submit the questions for your comments. Wherever possible project work should be devised in order to maintain continuity of the programme. As trainees develop they can assist in devising the next stage of the programme.

Internal training courses

Internal training courses are organised by the company or an external organisation and run on-site. They can be short full-time residential courses or longer part-time courses. Some advantages of the short full-time residential courses are that they:

- take the young employees away from their normal working environment
- make them feel important and thus help to induce a responsive frame of mind
- increase social learning within the company
- allow more concentrated training as the evenings can be used.

Advantages of part-time courses are that they:

- allow information to be presented in small doses which may be absorbed more easily
- permit the course organiser to adapt training to the needs of the group as they become apparent over a period of time
- allow for projects to be carried out between sessions, thus providing an active link between the training and the job.

Internal courses have an additional advantage in that they can be run at times which will produce the least disruption. They also enable managers and union representatives to participate more fully as group advisers and speakers.

External courses

There are a large number of organisations providing development training courses for young employees. They offer a wide selection of courses which vary in content, method, and duration, but they all aim at developing young employees.

The choice, of course, for a particular young employee is important. For instance, make sure that the age group and experience of delegates is correct and that the objectives of the course match the identified training needs.

The young employee, before attending, must be clearly briefed on what the course is designed to provide. A debrief should be carried out on return to work. You can then assess the value of the course. Allow the young employee to identify the knowledge gained and to set the actions needed to improve performance. It is important that the young employee feels confident and knows what has to be achieved. The impact of an external course may be reduced by the young employee's anxiety or even hostility. There may be a feeling of inadequacy, nervousness, or of 'Why have I been sent?' This may prevent the person from responding to the tuition offered. Other sources of anxiety are: what clothes to wear, the question of expenses, i.e. will the company pay for books and photographs bought on the course?

A useful way of giving the young employee confidence is to send more than one person. This is also helpful when they return to work. It provides them with a common experience which can be discussed with other managers and young employees. They may also have some common action points.

The external course is also of value to the company with very few young employees. It provides a breadth of industrial experience, points of view which may not be expressed within their company, and the challenge of mixing with a large group of people.

8 INVOLVEMENT OF YOUNG PEOPLE AT WORK

Few would doubt the growing importance of young people in today's workforce. Demographic changes and the impending skills shortage mean that organisations will increasingly depend upon dynamic recruitment and training programmes for young people in order to sustain a skilled workforce.

Although young people's importance in the recruitment market has increased dramatically over the past ten years, they are, still, a fragile section of any employer's staff. They differ from other groups in that they are unaccustomed to the practices of a business environment. They need more encouragement and attention than older employees as they go through the transition from school to work.

In addition to the actual skills and techniques of the job, they need development training to encourage their understanding of how a job fits into an organisation and of their own importance in playing a responsible part in the adult world.

This book gives practical guidance to managers about how to develop training and induction programmes for recent recruits. It also covers how organisations can forge links with education to aid their recruitment of young people.

Recruitment

Achieving a motivated, young workforce begins with recruitment. It's no good having a well-thought-out system for training and involvement if you fail to attract and select the kind of employees that will benefit from it.

Ask yourself the following key questions when reviewing your recruitment policy for young employees.

- What image do we portray?
- How do young people see us?

- Do we train people in recruitment and selection skills?
- Are we using all available recruitment sources?

Surviving the shortages

The declining number of young people means that good recruitment practice and flexibility are more vital than ever.

Long term strategies

To management recruitment shortages employers will need to consider the following actions.

- Examine your recruitment policy and practices. Is discrimination, whether conscious or not, depriving you of important recruitment sources?
- Examine your recruitment standards. Are they justified by the needs of the job? An increase in post-entry training could compensate for lower initial requirements.
- Adjust recruitment strategies. For example, provide training from scratch yourself, rather than looking for qualified applicants.
- Reconsider the type of person you recruit to trainee positions. Could your training schemes be extended to other groups of people? Could some jobs be converted to part-time or job share?
- Maximise the potential of existin employees through training and retraining. Invest time, effort, and resources to keep employees' skills up-to-date and to develop new capacities at work.

Good recruitment practice

Determine your needs

The first stage in recruitment is to determine your exact requirements. Consider:

The job
What is the vacancy? Does it need to be filled? Does it need to be changed? Using this information, produce a job description. Define the main tasks, responsibilities, training and career

prospects, accountability, and the terms and conditions of employment.

The person

Having defined the job, you then need to decide what skills, characteristics, and experience are required for a person to perform it satisfactorily.

This list of qualities required to fulfil the job description is known as a person specification. When writing one, it is useful to consider the following categories.

- physical requirements
- education and training
- experience
- special skills and knowledge
- personality and disposition.

It is helpful to look at who has done well in the past in your organisation and why.

Plan your campaign

In planning your campaign for recruitment, these central questions should be addressed.

- What do you have to offer the young employee?
- What do your target candidate group know about you?
- How can you best communicate with them?

The best publicity for attracting the right kind of people comes from a positive, lasting image in schools, colleges, the community, and with fellow employers. If they are to give their best as employees, young people must *want* to join your organisation. It is vital to inform influential people about your organisation and to offer young people an employment package that is attractive, worthwhile, and known about.

Increasingly, young people are looking for a comprehensive programme of training, skills development, and involvement at work. Projected labour market changes suggest that no one will be able to rely on an initial burst of training to sustain them through working life. Attracting the right kind of people means demonstrating a long-term dedication to career development opportunities from the start.

- Analyse what aspects of the job, training and organisational culture are most likely to appeal to your target group and make sure that they are clearly represented in recruitment literature. Clear information on training – such as an 'at a glance guide' – will help build your image and aid self-selection by candidates, thereby saving you time later on in the recruitment procedure.
- The most convincing publicity comes 'from the horse's mouth', so involve recently recruited employees and trainees in the recruitment procedure. For example, send them to careers events at schools and colleges or involve them in work experience schemes.
- Capitalise on existing contacts, formal or informal, that employees may have with recruitment sources, such as youth organisations, schools, and colleges. Set up a sustained programme of contact.

The role of the line manager

Young people are greatly influenced in their view of their job, the management, the trade union, and their own future by the attitudes of their immediate managers.

The immediate line manager is responsible for getting their commitment and enthusiasm. They should also seek specialist help and advice, but without the real support of 'the boss' – the direct supervisor – training can be a waste of time.

The manager must be involved in the following areas:

- Induction – making young people feel valued.
- Appraisal – providing scope for development.
- Involvement – recognising achievements and providing a challenge.

Induction

- Introduce the trainee to the working group.
- Place the trainee with a young 'sponsor'.

- Discuss the training programme with the trainee.
- Make sure they know what you expect of them.

Appraisal

- Give trainees a properly planned programme of work and be sure that they are stretched to their full capacity on worthwhile jobs.
- Maintain close contact with the training department through regular progress reports and discussions. Check that the training matches the need.
- Where applicable, discuss further education with the trainees. Help them to see the relevance of their studies for the future.
- Have regular progress reviews at least every three months. Use these sessions to encourage and advise. Tell trainees what is going on in the organisation and encourage them to feel involved.
- Set short- and long-term targets or projects relating to training objectives. Delegate and give responsibility.

Involvement

- Encourage trainees to keep a log book, describing the jobs they do and the progress they have made.
- Invite their suggestions on how they feel the job could be improved.
- Ensure that they are briefed before any courses and that they understand what you expect them to achieve. If it is their first course or their first time away from home give them some idea of what to expect. Debrief afterwards and help identify achievements.
- Encourage participation in youth forums or apprentice associations.
- Seek ways to involve trainees on consultative committees where appropriate.
- If unionised, encourage them to become members, attend meetings, and speak up for what they believe to be the best for people at work.
- Take an interest in trainees' outside activities and encourage them to hold responsible positions in clubs and societies.
- Encourage them to take advantage of any recreational

facilities and development courses the organisation offers, such as Community Service Volunteers, Outward Bound and the Duke of Edinburgh's Award Scheme.

- Encourage them to see their work as a challenge and to 'have a go'.
- Talk to colleagues and other departments to see how they have developed and involved their young people.

Mentoring

Many organisations employ a 'mentoring' system which involves a senior manager not directly 'in the line' taking on responsibility for the informal guidance of a young employee.

Meetings between the two will, more often than not, take place outside working hours and probably off the premises. This is a good way of keeping the senior people in the company in touch with the workforce whilst showing the young employee that the organisation cares for and is committed to its future generation of managers.

Feedback and evaluation

In order to assess the progress of development training and ensure that maximum benefit is obtained, certain conditions must exist on their return to work. Often trainees return full of enthusiasm but find that the attitude of the well-established employee forces them back to their old ways.

Follow-up is, therefore, particularly important in linking the training to the person's job.

The follow-up

- Meet regularly with the trainees to discuss the training and any action to improve performance.
- Trainees should produce a report on the course, which includes what they intend to do to improve their performance at work. Evaluation can take place as to whether course objectives were met.
- Trainees should make a presentation to other young employees and managers about the course.

- Monitor action points and modify where necessary.
- Produce on-going projects based on some of the factors raised on the course.
- Guide the commitment of time on behalf of the trainees (e.g. projects should be done in both company and own time).
- Relate project work to three areas:
  - work
  - individual
  - community.
- The trainee's immediate supervisor must be committed to follow-up work. His or her role is that of catalyst or enabler.
- The supervisor should initiate and encourage action.

Examples of follow-up activities

At work

- Participate in real departmental problems (i.e. in sales, personnel, production) to give insight into all departments and to provide contact with management.
- Have them accompany training officers to schools to talk about their training scheme and to give career guidance. This gives the young employee a sense of belonging to the organisation.
- They could be involved in the initial induction programme of new young employees – enabling closer contact between employees – and could provide guidance on how future programmes could be improved.

For the individual

- Monitoring by supervisors.
- Duke of Edinburgh Award Schemes.
- Local affairs involvement.
- Involvement in a youth forum/apprentice association.

In the community

- Involvement in physically- and mentally-handicapped centres, old people's homes, money-raising projects, sports and outdoor activities in order to create social awareness.

- Involvement in intermediate treatment programmes in conjunction with social services and education.

Youth forums and apprentice associations

This is a widely practised form of self-development, involving many thousands of young people all over the country. A youth forum/apprentice association at work consists of a group of male and female employees under the age of 24 years from all sections of the workforce. It is a vehicle for involving young employees in the management of their own affairs. It aims to:

- establish and advance the identity of the young employees within the company
- provide a structure through which young employees can exchange ideas with each other, the management, and unions
- provide a common meeting ground for social and recreational purposes
- promote a social life for young employees
- further the worthwhile interests and personal qualities of young employees.

The benefits to young employees

- Gain recognition within the organisation and establish an identity.
- Develop skills – such as leadership, administration, and motivation.
- Get to know others from different departments, sections, etc.
- Get their problems aired – the forum/association is able to discuss problems relating to the organisation's young people with the Personnel/Training Department.
- Improve their relationships at work.
- Be involved – feeling part of the organisation leads to job satisfaction.

Structure

There is a main committee which is made up of:

- chairperson (usually a senior trainee or fourth-year apprentice)
- secretary
- treasurer
- representatives (made up from each section of the organisation, i.e. departments, sites, or year groups)
- a member of the management, who is invited to sit on the committee to offer advice and guidance but has no voting rights
- a President – an honorary position, usually the organisation's Chairperson/Chief Executive.

Finance

They are totally self-financing. Money is raised through weekly/monthly subscriptions and by running fund raising events. All funds are kept in the forum/association bank account.

Getting started

Although the initiative for starting a forum can come from management or union representatives, one of the fundamental characteristics of a forum or association is that it is run by the young employees themselves. A line manager may be called upon for advice and support.

In order to establish and maintain a forum or association, young employees should take the following steps.

Call a meeting

Management, trade unions, and young people should discuss plans, objectives, programmes, a method of electing a working party, and the extent of management and trade union involvement.

It is advisable to select a working party for six months in order to draw up a constitution and organise the inaugural meeting at which officers will be elected for the next year. During the time of the working party, a programme of activities should be run in order to maintain interest.

Form a committee

The committee should comprise a:

- chairperson
- meetings/programme secretary
- recruitment officer
- treasurer
- public relations officer.

If there are a large number of young employees, other committee members can be elected to give a fair representation.
The committee should determine:

- the aims (*see* Appendix 1 page 331)
- the constitution (*see* Appendix 2 page 336)
- the frequency, timing, and venue of meetings – not more often than once a month, and ideally half in and half out of working hours, taking into account the working hours of all the members, e.g. shift work
- membership fees, how they should be paid, and whether the organisation should contribute.

Most youth forums are self-supporting but have started with a loan from the organisation for six months. Monthly financial reports should be produced and entered into the minutes.

Plan a programme

It is important to hold a survey of members' views and ideas. This will help achieve a balanced programme that caters for minorities.
The programme could include the following:

- meetings with invited speakers from inside the organisation. Trade union officials, department heads, supervisors, or shop stewards could talk about their jobs, what they are trying to do, and why

- meeting with speakers from outside the organisation, for example from neighbouring organisations, community groups, training and development organisations, Social Service Departments, or the local media
- visits within and outside the organisation, including exchange visits with other youth forums
- conferences for members to discuss topics of common interest, such as personal skills-building, what supervisors look for in the people they promote, market changes and their implications, or industrial relations. Talks by members of the forum and appraisal by other members are very useful in developing ability and confidence
- social activities, including community work and weekend trips.

Publicise the forum

If the forum is to become an effective group within the organisation, it is important to make its voice and presence felt. Publicity can be gained by:

- appointing a publicity/press officer
- making use of notice-boards
- asking for regular space in the house journal or newsletter
- producing a forum newsletter or magazine
- publishing reports of activities, meetings, and plans
- keeping in contact with local media.

Recruit members

Recruitment should be planned and a recruiting team formed that includes someone from each section of the forum. This team should:

- delegate recruitment targets to each team member
- try to get the youth forum incorporated into induction programmes
- invite sceptics to a committee meeting.

Maintain commitment

Apathy is the most common problem with youth forums. It can be prevented by:

- forming a committee from as wide a base as possible
- changing the committee and office holders from time to time
- ensuring a lively and varied programme of activities
- delegating the responsibility for specific areas or projects.

Building links with education

Imaginative collaboration with education is an important way for employers to demonstrate a commitment to young people, their training, and their involvement at work. There are benefits for both sides. For industry it can:

- generate goodwill – many customers will be parents of school children and students, and the pupils themselves are potential customers
- provide opportunities for employee development training
- aid recruitment – collaboration establishes contact with potential employees and careers advisers at an early stage; liaison with industry can help pupils be better equipped for recruitment and the world of work
- improve employee motivation – passing on skills and answering questions about their work helps current employees to develop pride in the job and the organisation
- produce positive publicity
- yield specialist advice.

For schools it can lead to:

- practical resources
- improved vocational preparation
- data for problem solving activities
- specialist advice
- increased pupil motivation
- project collaboration.

To be effective collaboration should be:

- two-way
- task orientated

- sustained
- have specific objectives that are agreed upon by both sides.

Types of collaboration

The opportunities for collaboration are numerous and will improve as the working relationship develops. They may take various forms.

Resources

Industry can offer immediate practical help to schools and colleges by providing:

- funds for specific projects, e.g. staff training courses
- materials for classroom use, e.g. raw materials such as fabric, timber, or metal; proformas and documents for vocational work; and equipment – even those that have exceeded their normal working life can be of use – like typewriters that have been replaced by word processors
- specific prizes, awards, or endowments
- the use of facilities, e.g. printing services, training rooms, sports centres
- sponsorship of City Technology Colleges – employers are asked to provide building and running costs.

Industrial governors

Becoming a governor is a long-term commitment with opportunities for helping staff determine curriculum content. This develops a close working relationship with a school or college.

Visits

Visits can be two-way but should always have clear objectives and be related to curriculum activity.

Students may visit in order to see industrial processes or to get an insight into the ethos and experiences of work.

Employees can visit schools to provide specialist technical knowledge or a personal insight into the experience of work. Apprentices, for example, can talk about the transition from school to employment or help students on projects which draw on the apprentice's experience at work. Such visits can be part of development training.

Senior employees can provide specialist involvement with teachers in demonstrating key industrial processes, such as marketing or production techniques. Trade unionists can also contribute specialist knowledge and skills.

Secondment

Seconding a teacher into your organisation can be a good starting point for establishing collaboration since it allows the teacher to assess liaison possibilities. Secondment gives the teacher:

- an understanding of the challenges facing young people starting work
- knowledge of recruitment needs
- classroom data from 'real life' work situations
- development training.

The objective could be to:

- perform a specific task in one department
- take part in a multi-department project
- carry out specific research
- observe.

All secondments should include:

- a detailed action plan and objectives
- briefing and debriefing
- a written report produced by the teacher
- an action plan for their return to the school or college.

Work experience and work shadowing

These schemes for teachers or students have many of the benefits of secondment. They offer short-term insights and should be project related.

Compacts

Compacts are Training Agency administered collaborations between schools and employers in inner city areas. Employers agree to give preferential recruitment treatment to pupils if they work to agreed goals, such as levels of literacy and numeracy.

The scheme gives pupils the incentive of gaining employment and provides employers with better trained and motivated young people who understand their needs. Contact your area Training Agency office for details of schemes in your area.

Acting as client

Organisations can usefully act as 'real life' clients in vocational exercises in schools and colleges with gains on both sides, e.g. sociology students conducting a survey among employees, or a media class producing a promotional video.

Advice and discussion

Employers can contribute advice in areas such as curriculum planning, for example in the design of a particular course or module.

Participation in school/college based events

This might include careers events, presentations to parents, mini-enterprise schemes, or special conferences such as The Challenge of Industry or The Challenge of Management (*see* Appendix 3 page 340).

Being a patron

An employer can become the 'patron' of a particular school or college collaborating at a range of levels.

Making contact

Schools and colleges can be contacted directly or through the local education authority. Many will have an industry co-ordinator, but the initial formal contact should be made with the head. To make contacts successful:

- ensure you have an education liaison co-ordinator
- set liaison targets
- make use of existing contacts employees will have.

9 MOTIVATION

What is motivation?

Motivation is what makes people do things. In another sense it is what makes them put real effort and energy into what they do. Positive motivation occurs when people 'give' to a request – motivation ceases when people are 'compelled' to surrender to a demand. Obviously it varies in nature and intensity from individual to individual, depending on the particular mixture of influences at any given moment.

In short, a simple definition of motivation is:

'Getting people to do willingly and well those things which have to be done.'

The importance of motivation

Motivation is vital in any job if people are to give their best to it. Assuming that employees are given opportunity for good performance and have the necessary skills, then effectiveness depends on their motivation. People are undoubtedly a most critical resource and however sophisticated our technology, we will still depend on the 'human factor'.

Who is responsible?

It is the job of work-group leaders or team leaders to motivate their teams. It is they who are best placed to create the correct environment in which people will 'grow' and give of their best to their work. It has to be recognised that certain factors are often outside their span of control or influence, e.g. pay, status, terms and conditions of employment. However, practical experience has shown that these people can provide recognition, responsibility, and work which is challenging – all of these having proved to be among the greatest motivating factors.

Behaviour of employees

The attitudes and behaviour of employees very often reflect motivation or the lack of it. Examples of the signs of motivation are:

- high performance and results being consistently achieved
- the energy, enthusiasm, and determination to succeed
- unstinting co-operation in overcoming problems
- the willingness of individuals to accept responsibility
- willingness to accommodate necessary change.

Conversely, employees who are de-motivated or who lack motivation often display:

- apathy and indifference to the job
- a poor record of time-keeping and high absenteeism
- an exaggeration of the effects/difficulties encountered in problems, disputes and grievances
- a lack of co-operation in dealing with problems or difficulties
- unjustified resistance to change.

Managers generally deplore employees' lack of motivation and interest in the company and in their work. Many men and women turn their excess energies and talents to hobbies and merely tolerate their jobs as a way of earning their living so they can afford to meet the challenge of life in leisure-time activities. It is not leisure as a pursuit, but work as a drudgery, that is to be condemned.

So many repetitive, monotonous, and uninteresting jobs could be made more palatable if managers recognised the rights of individuals. Countless people have the elements of challenge and interest in them destroyed by managers' failure to recognise human needs and motivations.

The behavioural scientists

Over the years a growing number of behavioural scientists have carried out their own investigations into what makes people 'tick'. It would be wrong to ignore this accumulated knowledge, but equally wrong to pretend that each viewpoint in itself holds the key to solving our problems of motivating people. The results and findings of some, however, do give an insight of practical significance which can be helpful to the understanding of the line manager.

A. H. Maslow

Maslow's thinking is centred on a hierarchy of the individual's needs (*see* Figure 9.1 on page 154) and is outlined as follows.

The needs hierarchy

1 Based on needs not wants.
2 Operates on an ascending scale. As one need becomes fulfilled the next ascendant need is uncovered.
3 We can 'revert back', i.e. people operating at level 4 or 5 will revert to level 2 if a feeling of insecurity takes over. Once this need is met, however, they will return to their former needs area.
4 Needs not being met are demonstrated in behaviour, and managers must create an 'environment' in which motivation can take place.
5 To avoid apathy, which finally results when needs are unfulfilled, managers must be able to implement the right action at the right time.

Put another way, Maslow is asking the questions:

● Where do you think you really are?
● Where are you going?

D. McGregor

Douglas McGregor (quoting A. H. Maslow) suggests that people's needs can be depicted in a kind of hierarchy. At the

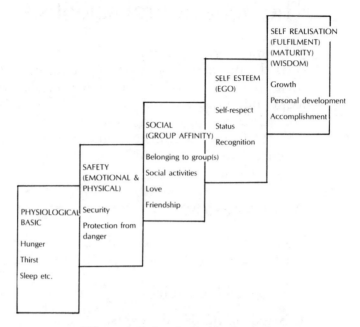

Figure 9.1 *Individual needs*

bottom of the triangle are the needs of our animal nature for self-preservation – for sleep, for food and water, for shelter and warmth. These needs are basic; as someone aptly said: 'Mankind does not live by bread alone, except when there is no bread.' Once satisfied, they cease to be strong motivators to action. Thus, as western societies begin to feel more materially secure, their higher needs for self-expression (including the drive for achievement), for an objective, for self-fulfilment, clamour for satisfaction. It follows, therefore, that in suitable circumstances and with proper management, the majority of people can be self-directed if they become committed to an objective they value. They will not only accept responsibility but often will seek it. Further, to work is as natural as to eat or to sleep. Creativity is widely, not narrowly, scattered among the population. (This is McGregor's 'Theory Y'.)

In short, people can be self-motivated. The task of the manager is to create conditions of work in which, and through which, self-motivation can find its release. In situations where this is difficult to achieve – as in dull, repetitive work – higher pay remains of paramount importance, since workers are forced

For self-fulfilment

for self-expression

to belong

security, shelter, warmth, etc.

psysiological needs, hunger, thirst etc.

Figure 9.2 *A. H. Maslow's hierarchy of needs*

to find satisfaction outside the work situation.

If Theory X is to be our assumption and we treat people accordingly we find out nothing about them and our beliefs will become a self-fulfilling prophesy, i.e. people will need close supervision, firm discipline, incentive schemes, etc.

If, however, we believe that Theory Y is correct and treat people accordingly, we shall find out what they are really like. The answer will be that they are all different and we can then manage them according to their strengths and weaknesses.

The key is in not making assumptions but in giving opportunity for achievement, responsibility, creativity and in utilising talent, abilities, interests, etc. in so far as the task allows (*see* Table 9.1).

F. Herzberg

Frederick Herzberg asked many people in different jobs at different levels, two questions.

- What factors lead you to experience extreme dissatisfaction with your job?
- What factors lead you to experience extreme satisfaction with your job?

He collated the answers and displayed them in the form of a chart which shows the order and frequency in which the factors appeared (*see* Table 9.2 on page 156).

Table 9.1 *Attitudes to work (the X–Y theory)*

Theory X	Theory Y
1 People dislike work and will avoid it if possible	**1** Work is necessary to people's psychological growth
2 People must be forced or bribed to make the right effort	**2** People want to be interested in their work and, under the right conditions, they can enjoy it
3 People would rather be directed than accept responsibilities, which they avoid	**3** People will direct themselves towards an accepted target
	4 People will seek, and accept, responsibility under the right conditions
	5 The discipline people impose on themselves is more effective, and can be more severe, than any imposed on them
4 People are motivated mainly by money	**6** Under the right conditions, people are motivated by the desire to realise their own potential
5 People are motivated by anxiety about their security	**7** Creativity and ingenuity are widely distributed and grossly under-used
6 Most people have little creativity – except when getting round management rules!	

Dissatisfaction

Factors on the left of the chart show a greater potential for dissatisfaction than satisfaction. Improving them or giving people more of them:

1 Does not create a motivational atmosphere.
2 Creates only short-lived satisfaction, because they become accepted as the norm.

Table 9.2 *Herzberg's factors of satisfaction and dissatisfaction*

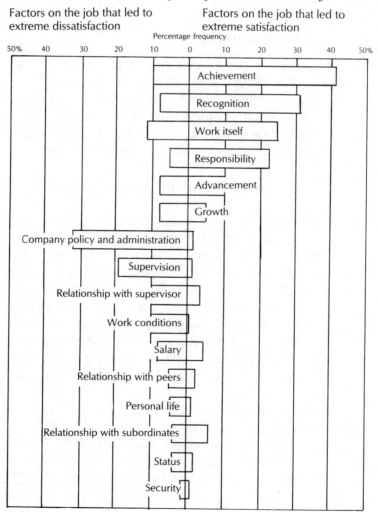

In Herzberg's words: 'You just remove unhappiness, you don't make people happy.'

These factors match levels 1, 2 and 3 of the Maslow hierarchy and are connected with the job context. Herzberg called them the 'hygiene factors'.

Satisfaction

Factors on the right of the chart have little to do with money and status; much to do with achievement and responsibility. They match levels 4 and 5 of the Maslow hierarchy and are connected with the job content. Herzberg called them the 'motivators'.

The work itself

The chart shows that the nature of the work itself has potential for both satisfaction and dissatisfaction. The moral for managers is clear – they should pay particular attention to the kind of tasks they expect people to do. Where these are boring and repetitive they should strive to create a motivational atmosphere by paying special attention to other factors.

The Hawthorne experiments

Management has been unwilling to recognise the impact of motivation on the conduct of employees and hence on the productivity of the enterprise. Although the most significant findings on this subject became known more than 40 years ago and sounded the death knell on the totally mechanistic approach of scientific management, many thousands of practising managers have failed to pay heed to these findings. In its attempt to eliminate variables and predict results, management has tried to depersonalise the organisation. Scientific management, with its accent on efficiency, believes people are motivated only by material considerations and, therefore, their actions can be ordered without regard to personal attitudes and behaviour.

The shortcomings of these beliefs were first brought to light in what later became known as the Hawthorne experiments which were conducted between 1924 and 1927 at the Hawthorne Works of the Western Electric Company in Chicago. The management wished to increase the productivity of its workers and experimented with working conditions.

While productivity went up and later settled at a lower level, which was still higher than the initial level, the conclusions that were drawn were:

- that improvements in working conditions in themselves will provide only a short-term stimulus to higher performance
- that, in the long run, continued improvement is dependent on other factors, for example the extent to which people are allowed to grow within the job.

Table 9.3 *The Hawthorne experiments 1924–1927*

Changes in working conditions	Results
Day work to piece work	Increased output
Five minute rest periods morning and afternoon	Increased output
Rest period increased to 10 minutes	Greater increased output
Six 5-minute rest periods	Output fell: workers explained that their work rhythm was interrupted
Return to two rest periods, the first with a free hot meal	Increased output
Girls permitted to go home at 4.30 p.m. instead of 5.00 p.m.	Increased output
All improvements in working conditions rescinded. Girls returned to 48-hour week, with no rest periods, no piece work, and no free meals	Output increased to highest point recorded during entire period

Practical steps in motivation

There are four kinds of people in the world:

- people who watch things happen
- people to whom things happen
- people who do not know what is happening
- people who make things happen.

If managers are to be the ones who make things happen through other people, they must be aware of how they can get people to work willingly and well, to increase people's satisfaction in their job, and the organisation's efficiency.

Managers must then *make their staff* feel valued by:

- regularly monitoring the employee's work
- sharing an interest in employee's lives and in whatever they hold important
- creating an atmosphere of approval and co-operation
- ensuring every employee understands the importance of his or her contribution to the team's/department's/organisation's objectives
- ensuring every employee understands the function and philosophy of the organisation and why work matters.

They must provide opportunities for development by:

- setting standards and targets for all employees
- providing on and off the job training
- arranging any necessary internal and external contacts
- using employees to train others in the specialist skills they may have
- structuring or grouping tasks to use the employees' skills/ gifts to the fullest.

They must recognise achievements by:

- praising and communicating individual successes
- reporting regularly on the team's progress
- holding regular meetings to monitor and counsel on an

individual's progress towards targets
- explaining the organisation's results and achievements.

And they must provide a challenge by:

- setting and communicating the team's/department's/organisation's objectives
- providing scope for individuals to take greater responsibility
- encouraging ideas and where practical by allowing your staff the responsibility for implementing them.

Motivating change

Change is normal. Change is an inherent part of life. Why then do all people, managers and workers alike, constantly resist it?

Can resistance to change be regarded as abnormal or pathological? One point of view holds that it is more a 'symptom' than a disease.

When resistance does appear it should not be thought of as something to be overcome. Instead it can best be thought of as a useful red flag – a signal that something is wrong.

Undoubtedly one of the most challenging roles which a manager plays is that of *motivating change*.

Implementing change is about starting, changing gear, stopping, accelerating, slowing down and arriving. The theme throughout is about involving others and being co-operative, willing, and flexible. While we may not waver from our final objective, our activities and circumstances may change in the process of reaching that goal.

Motivating and managing change requires:

- the full co-operation of all concerned in the business
- an effective method of communication which is two-way at all stages and levels
- effective feedback to the decision-making centre of progress and obstacles.

Change has very often to be effected while maintaining present procedures and, if this is to be achieved, it requires the

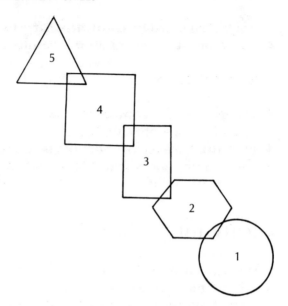

Fig. 4. *Symbolic illustration of stages during a process of change.*

full co-operation of the participants, e.g. subordinates, managers, all employees below first-line supervision, customers, suppliers, and trade unions.

Gaining *willing consent* throughout the course of effecting change is positive motivation.

Introducing changes

Examples of change

1 *Major changes:*
- altering pay or bonus systems
- introducing new equipment or machinery
- making a major change in procedure
- introducing work measurement.

2 *Minor changes:*
- moving a subordinate from one job to another
- making a small alteration in work method
- modifying the time of tea or lunch breaks
- altering canteen prices.

Change is inevitable and is a continuing process. Even minor changes may have major repercussions; for what appears to be a minor change to the manager may seem a major one to the employees affected.

Why do people resist change?

They resist not because of the change itself, but because it means adjusting themselves to a changed situation, and because of fears such as:

- loss of job
- loss of skills
- inability to cope with change
- loss of earnings
- loss of status
- loss of companions (owing to work reorganisation)
- loss of familiar surroundings.

How should managers introduce change?

'Communication and consultation are particularly important in times of change. The achievement of change is a joint concern of management and employees, and should be carried out in a way which pays regard both to the efficiency of the undertaking and to the interests of employees. Major changes in working agreements should not be made by management without prior discussion with employees or their representatives.'

(*Industrial Relations Code of Practice*)

1 *Plan:* taking into account who it will affect and how it will affect them.
2 *Explain:* the need for change – by managers briefing down the line to all those affected.
3 *Consult those affected or their representatives:*
   - it tells them that their views are being considered, resulting in increased willingness to co-operate
   - it tells you of their specific anxieties, allowing you to take these problems into account
   - consultation may bring out important factors previously overlooked.

Analyse

Consider and act on the results of consultation. In particular:

- reconsider your original plan
- arrange for demonstration of any new equipment
- give reassurance of no redundancy or loss of earnings (when possible)
- take steps to provide training.

Communicate and implement the change

The reasons for change and its impact on those affected, must be communicated by managers briefing down the line to all employees concerned, supporting this with adequate written information and/or instructions.

Follow up

Ensure that the change has proceeded as planned, and that the objective has been achieved. Further consultation, readjustment and communication may be necessary.

10 DELEGATION

Delegation is not easy. It requires courage, patience and skill. It is one of the most important aspects of any manager's job, and is an area where the manager frequently has greater freedom of choice than in almost any other. What managers choose to delegate, to whom, and at what stage, is almost entirely at their own discretion.

Delegation is not the same as 'giving out work'. There are certain duties which fall naturally into the lap of your staff, and the only action you need to take may be to decide which of them is to be given a particular piece of work to do, depending on that individual's workload, etc.

You delegate when you deliberately choose to give one of your staff authority to carry out a piece of work which you could have decided to keep and carry out yourself.

Note the word 'authority': we must continue to define our terms by distinguishing between responsibility, authority, and accountability.

- Responsibility, in this context, means the work that is delegated – the task, the job, the duty.
- Authority means the power or right to make decisions, and take action, to enable this responsibility to be successfully discharged.
- Accountability means 'carrying the can' for the responsibility concerned – being ultimately held to account for the success or failure.

Successful delegation demands matching responsibility with authority. To give someone responsibility without authority is unreasonable and doomed to failure. A traffic warden without the power to issue tickets would have to be exceedingly persuasive to have any chance of preventing traffic obstructions. So we must always ensure that we give our people authority

165

commensurate with the responsibility we entrust to them.

Accountability is a different matter. Managers are ultimately accountable for everything that goes on in their department(s). They can never shirk this: it is an integral part of the job of the manager. Managers cannot possibly make, or even know about, all the decisions taken but, as President Truman put it in a sign above his desk, 'the buck stops here'. So when you delegate, you do not shrug off your accountability, though how much you choose to delegate is up to you.

The advantages of delegation

Delegation thus involves taking a calculated risk. But its advantages are such that the manager who ignores them throws away a great opportunity. What are these advantages?

- Delegation enables you to concentrate on those aspects of your job which require your personal experience, skill and knowledge, i.e. the aspects where you really 'earn your keep'. Contrast the times when you feel 'What a useless day this has been – I've wasted my time with trivial things' with the occasions when you feel tired but satisfied with the day's work, because you have been really stretched or you have achieved something tangible.
- Much of a manager's job should be concerned with planning the future rather than organising the present. If you are not planning ahead, you will have to keep reacting to events instead of anticipating them, and your scope for initiative and enterprise will be severely limited. Delegating enables you to look ahead, to anticipate problems, to get one step ahead of your competitors.
- Delegation does wonders for morale. If you are a good delegator, your department is likely to experience lower absenteeism, less 'office politics', more willingness to work late when the pressure is high, and so on. If you are insular and secretive and keep all decision-taking to yourself, your staff will start becoming parochial and unco-operative too.
- Delegation is often the best of all possible ways of training your staff for greater responsibilities. When you need someone for an important task, or when a new opportunity crops up which you want to exploit, you are more likely to

have the right person available if you have groomed him or her by constant delegation than if you have to suddenly pitchfork someone into unfamiliar responsibility.

- To delegate and watch your people develop is perhaps the most satisfying experience you can have as a manager. They are your people and you have helped them grow. You may lose some of them, perhaps to greater responsibilities in another part of the organisation, but you will have helped to make their growth possible.

Difficulties and solutions

We have considered the advantages of delegation, but we must also face the difficulties.

Risk

All delegation involves risk. The first time you ask someone to carry out a new duty, you are probably more worried than he or she is. You are accountable – 'the buck stops here'. That person may make a mess of it, and you may have to sort it out.

The only answer to this problem is to accept it. All delegation involves risk, but taking calculated risks is part of a manager's job. You can do much to minimise the risk by:

- planning your delegation carefully
- showing the person that you have faith in his or her ability.

Confidence expressed is just as important as confidence felt. When your salesperson is losing his or her nerve and getting increasingly worried, you might say to him or her 'The time to start worrying is when I lose confidence in you. I have faith in your ability; you're going through a patch of bad luck at the moment'. This is enough to give the salesperson fresh heart.

Letting go

The second difficulty consists in letting go of certain duties which you, the manager, enjoy performing, even if they are not central to getting the results that matter. For example, the managing director who still has a large drawing board in the office, and spends several hours a week at it tinkering around with designs. We all suffer to some extent from this. These aspects which we hate to let go have been aptly named 'vocational hobbies'.

We have to be tough with ourselves, and ration them to not more than 5 per cent of our time. They are useful if kept down to that proportion, because, surprisingly often, our best ideas about important problems come when our minds are diverted from them. But, if these 'vocational hobbies' creep above 5 per cent, we are flagrantly misusing our time.

Thinking time

Then there is the problem of daring to sit and think. We all want to 'look busy', but constructive thought as opposed to idle day-dreaming is nothing to be ashamed of. Remember the wise advice given by the old craftsman to the young apprentice: 'Engage brain before operating mouth'. You have to accept the chance that one of your team will catch you apparently staring into space. When you are thinking you don't look busy, but in fact, you are really more 'busy' than at any other time.

Patience

The process of delegation is slow in the early stages, and not without setbacks. You must have patience, and not expect to see results immediately. Indeed, in the short term, you will become busier than ever by delegating, because you will be adding the coaching of your staff to your present workload. ('I would love to delegate this, but I just don't have the time.')

Keeping in touch

Some managers are reluctant to delegate because they want to feel 'on top of everything', 'in touch with the work of the department'. As a result, they take all important decisions personally and require frequent detailed reports, checks and data from their staff. At the other extreme is management by exception. In fact, if you want to be 'in touch with the work of the department' you will be more truly in touch by spot checks and discussing progress and problems with your staff regularly, than by inspecting all their work personally or having it fed to you for signature.

Losing out

The sixth difficulty about delegation is one we may be less than honest about. It is the fear that our staff will outstrip us and gain promotion over our heads, or that by delegating we will only accelerate the process of losing good people from our own department.

The answer to this lies partly in the real satisfaction of developing people, mentioned earlier. The organisation can also make sure that its personnel policy encourages managers to develop staff and see them go to other departments (quite a different matter from leaving the company because of frustration).

There is also the more selfish point that if you, as a manager, have a quite proper ambition to take on a greater responsibility, you will stand a better chance if you are not seen to be indispensable in your present job. Managers who immerse themselves entirely in the detail of their present job are the most difficult people to disentangle from that job. This is especially true if you keep a great deal of know-how and detail in your head. So delegating helps your own advancement – indeed some organisations go so far as to say that no managers will be further promoted until they have trained their own successors.

Performance

Perhaps the greatest problem of all is the natural feeling that 'he won't do the job as well as I do it'. And this may very well be true. The first time *you* carried out a duty which is now second nature to you, did you perform it faultlessly? This worry is closely linked with the risk factor already discussed. No one should delegate recklessly, but if you feel that someone will do a job well enough and has the capacity to learn quickly how to do it better, you should delegate it to him or her without delay. It is important not to confuse doing it badly with doing it differently from your own way. When you delegate something which you have always done yourself up till now, you can be certain that it will not be done exactly in the same way in future, for the simple reason that no two individuals are identical. The same end result can be achieved by many different routes. So the way to judge the success of delegation is not by methods but by outcomes. However, it is fascinating to see a more junior person tackle something which is new to him or her, and (dare we face it?) occasionally get even better results than ourselves.

What to delegate

All managers must delegate. But we all need a starting point to help us judge whether we could delegate more than at present, or more effectively.

A good first step is to look honestly at yourself and check for symptoms of failure to delegate enough. The questionnaire given in Appendix 16 on page 367, should be completed and the results carefully considered. This will give an indication of your present 'bill of health'. (In the unlikely event of your coming out unscathed, read no further, but apply for promotion immediately, and give your own manager this booklet as a Christmas present!)

Delegation plan

To delegate properly you must have a plan. A very effective approach is as follows.

1 Write down the main objectives of your job. If you already have a written job description, make sure it is up-to-date. By definition, 'main objectives' are not numerous, and do not go into great detail about means; they specify ends.

2 Go over your diary for the past month, and note how you actually spent your time. Jot down roughly how long you spent on each activity. Even better, if you have a colleague with some work-study experience, get this person to carry out a rough 'activity sampling' on you for a few days. This will reveal a pattern of what you actually do, under general headings like 'attend meetings', 'incoming telephone calls', 'discussion with member of staff (work problem)', 'discussions with member of staff (personal problem)', 'visit customer/supplier', etc.

3 Draw up a simple chart based on the information revealed – such as that shown in Appendix 18 on page 371. This provides

a comparison between stage one (your objectives) and stage two (your actual activities).

4 You are now ready to decide what can be delegated. Here, there are some limitations which immediately narrow your choice. These must be recognised, and it is best to list those features of your responsibilities which cannot be delegated even if you have someone itching for more responsibility, for example:

- tasks well beyond the skills and experience of your staff
- confidential, security, and policy matters which are restricted to your own level of seniority
- matters involving exercising discipline over the individual's peers.

In checking items against this list, make sure you are not using it as a means of rationalising your reluctance to delegate. For example, 'tasks well beyond the skills and experience of your staff': if you feel confident that an individual has the skill though not the experience in the area concerned, then it may still be possible to delegate such a task. After all, whenever an individual is promoted, you are backing your judgement about their skill. Similarly, when considering policy decisions, you must not confuse policy with custom and practice.

5 Having ruled out any items which clash with the criteria above, you will still be left with a range of possible tasks to delegate. The first two areas to look at are routine tasks, and tasks consuming a lot of your time.

- Routine tasks are good delegation material. What is routine to you, as the manager, will be new to someone below you, and by delegating it you will, at one and the same time, be stretching and developing your staff and giving yourself more time to concentrate on the results you are being paid to achieve.
- Tasks consuming a lot of your time provide obvious delegation opportunities. This is especially true if the reason they are time-consuming is either that you are not very good at them or you have simply run out of new

ways of tackling them. Someone else may come up with a better and quicker method. (If you put it to one of your people like that, these tasks will become an irresistible challenge.)

6 You are now ready to produce a detailed delegation plan for one or more of your staff. This will involve analysing their capacity for the type of work concerned, and providing such training as may be necessary. This crucial stage is dealt with in the following section on training.

Signing letters

An opportunity for delegation which many managers should consider, relates to the signing of letters. In many organisations, letters to customers or clients are actually drafted by a person at one level, but sent out under the name of the manager above. The justification usually given for this is that it makes the readers believe they are receiving the personal attention of the manager. But this is a charade, for when put to the test clients or customers rings up with a query, they are actually dealt with, not by the manager, but by the anonymous person who really wrote the letter all along.

Far better from every point of view, is to let staff sign their own letters, except for a minority which must carry the manager's name for special reasons. This makes the individual feel more personally responsible, more trusted and more recognised. The member of your staff should be identified by name, not merely by initials as part of a reference number, or even worse (as legal firms are prone to do) by an illegible signature with no reference at all.

The signing of letters is not a trivial matter. It is a delegation opportunity which is being missed day after day.

Training

Having reached the stage where you have identified certain tasks you wish to delegate, you now have to consider how and to whom they should be passed on. This can be done by analysing each of your staff in turn, thinking through these questions:

- what skills, qualifications and experience does he or she have: (a) which are currently being used; (b) which are not being used
- what type of work has he or she shown an interest in but has not yet done
- what type of work could he or she not do adequately, in spite of further training?

The answers to these questions should help you decide who is the appropriate person to take on each item of delegated responsibility. You can then complete a delegation programme, as in the example given in Appendix 23 on page 379.

You will want to discuss this with the person concerned. If you are already operating a system of target setting, this discussion can conveniently take place at the time of a progress review. The form your discussion takes will depend partly on your reason for choosing that particular person. You may want to:

- **stretch** him or her, i.e. discuss a duty you intend permanently to delegate
- **test** him or her, i.e. try out their response as a 'one–off', but without committing yourself to a permanent transfer of responsibility
- **shake** him or her, if they have become stale or lazy.

In accepting a newly delegated responsibility, the person must be clear about three constraints on the way it is handled. These are:

- objectives
- policies
- limits of authority.

These constraints are best understood through an example. Take the case of the departmental manager in an insurance company who wants to carry out a survey on claims against policies covering sickness while on holiday. She decides to delegate this task, which until now she has carried out herself, to a member of the department. She calls him in and briefs him as follows:

Manager 'We need to take another look at our holiday sickness policies. You've seen the recent figures and I'm not too happy about the trends. Now I'd like you to take on the responsibility for a survey covering the last three years.'

Job Holder 'Well, I've never done a survey on my own before – how should I go about it?'

Manager 'How you do it is up to you, very largely: what I want you to be clear about are the objectives of the survey and the limits on your authority in carrying it out. I've dictated a note about this – let's look over it together. The objective is to carry out a survey on claims against UK holiday sickness policies over the last three years, in order to: (a) compare our trends with our five leading competitors; and (b) produce recommendations for any changes in the premiums, together with estimates of the increased income and also possible fall-off in new policies and renewals as a result. Notice that this survey extends only to holiday sickness claims, not holiday accidents, and only to the United Kingdom, not overseas. All right so far?'

Job Holder 'Yes – that's quite clear.'

Manager 'Right. Now the limits. It shouldn't take more than three staff, including yourself; I would like your report by the end of the month, and the usual budget limitations apply. But for this project only, you can have a contingency allowance of £x for any travel you have to undertake during the survey.'

Job Holder 'I did some work with you on the last survey of accident claims – will this one follow the same pattern?'

Manager 'I expect it to – but you go about it your own way. By the way, any ideas you can come up with for special premiums for young families would be welcome.'

Job Holder	'Right – I've been thinking we might develop a clause about entire families holidaying together.'
Manager	'That's the kind of thing. There's one other point I want to remind you about: company policy on surveys involving members of the public. Do remember to conform to that – it's in your procedures manual. Number 37: you ought to have that number engraved on your heart!'
Job Holder	'How will Mr Shipman in Accounts and Mrs Parnell in the Legal Department know I'm going to be responsible for this?'
Manager	'Good point. I'm sending them a note – look, here it is. It makes it clear I have given you full authority for this project. Come back to me if you run into any problems, but now that you've helped on two or three reviews, I think you'll find this one quite straightforward.'

Notice that in her briefing, the manager has explained the objectives of the task clearly, has spelt out the limits on authority, reminded the individual about company policy, and has also given him confidence and backing by notifying other departments and stressing her own availability if needed. For more on how to specify authority limits, see below.

Many duties can be delegated progressively. Very few can be handed over *in toto* in a single step. 'Gently does it' will be the best approach in most cases. The sequence can be planned as shown in Appendix 21 on page 377.

It is important that, when you have delegated a task to an individual, you also notify the people who will be affected, especially those in other departments whose co-operation they may need to achieve their task. A brief note or a phone call will be enough.

Once the task has been permanently handed over to the person below you, make sure it is eliminated from your job description and written into his or hers.

To: Frank Edwards, Accounting Dept.
           Sarah Barnes, Marketing
From: Peter Marshall, Production Control

Launching of new product Z

This is to confirm that I am delegating the project to Jane Casey. She has full authority to take necessary decisions, and I know you will give her every assistance in her contacts with you about it.

Job descriptions, authority, and responsibility

A written job description, as we have already suggested, is an enormous aid to a manager, so long as it is a constructive, up-to-date document and not, as so often happens, a dreary catalogue of limitations on initiative.

Besides the job description itself, a booklet showing the extent of authority to take decisions can also be useful. As an example, BICC have produced booklets called *Statement of Responsibility and Authority* (SRA) for most of their middle management/supervisory staff. An excerpt from the SRA booklet of a general superintendent, who has several foremen reporting to him, looks as follows:

Responsibility	Authority Code D	A	R
1 Requisition employees – replacement	x		
– additional			x
2 Arrange for employee whose work is below standard to have further training	x		
3 Loan or transfer employee outside super-intendent's area of responsibility (making any necessary grade change)		x	
4 Authorise overtime:			
• for superintendents and foremen		x	
• to achieve production commitments			
– midweek	x		
– weekend			x
5 Issue warning in writing for disciplinary reasons	x		
6 Discharge employee for disciplinary reasons			x

Note: D = *Delegate* A = *Act* R = *Recommend*

When an SRA booklet is issued, the manager goes through it with the individual step-by-step to ensure that it is understood thoroughly by the person, and in particular whether any restrictions have been placed on the individual's authority during the training period.

Although SRAs can only deal in the main with 'predictable' (i.e. recurring) decisions, they have been found to reduce substantially the uncertainty often experienced, by supervisors in particular, about their ability to deal with problems on the spot instead of having to refer problems up to their manager.

Using an SRA

Managers and supervisors who have been involved in drafting and using SRAs, comment that they have served to clarify grey areas and speed decision-making. Interviewed several months after he had received his SRA, one older foreman commented: 'I wish we had had this long ago; it would have helped me to avoid many misunderstandings with the boss'. Recently appointed foremen explained that they now knew from the start exactly what their responsibilities were. They could therefore settle into the job much more quickly than their predecessors, who were never sure how the boss would react to any decision they made.

Typical of many managers was one who said that it was hard work and time-consuming to introduce SRAs properly '. . .but it worked! Because I have been able to delegate so much, I now have to reorganise my own time. I am no longer involved in the making of every decision, and I have more time to devote to the job of managing.'

The effect of SRAs on delegation has been considerable, and they have clearly highlighted training needs. In practice, the system can be developed and adapted by shifting the 'cross' into a different column as the job holder becomes more experienced, e.g. the newly appointed supervisor is likely to have a good many crosses in the 'Recommend' column, but as the individual gains confidence these may be moved across to 'Act' and even to 'Delegate'. Indeed, any system such as SRA should be checked at least annually to see what opportunities there are to push decision-making further down the line. The annual performance appraisal interview is a good time to do this.

You and your secretary

Delegation is especially important in the relationship between the manager and the secretary. An efficient secretary is a valuable member of any management team, and plays a key role in enabling managers to make more productive use of their time.

Most of the secretary's work involves delegated tasks from management, and there is very little limitation to what a secretary can take on, providing adequate training is given where necessary, and that the secretary has the time. Despite this, many secretaries complain that their managers are extremely poor delegators, delegating only routine boring tasks. This can lead to frustration and lack of career development. At the same time, managers argue that their secretaries are neither confident, nor flexible enough to take on more complicated responsibilities. This can all too easily develop into a vicious circle.

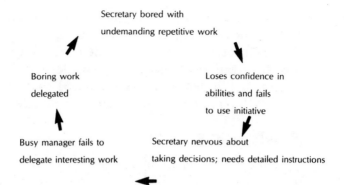

Secretary bored with
undemanding repetitive work

Boring work
delegated

Loses confidence in
abilities and fails
to use initiative

Busy manager fails to
delegate interesting work

Secretary nervous about
taking decisions; needs detailed instructions

Figure 10.1 *'Circle of frustration'*

Breaking this circle is essential; not only will your secretary benefit from more interesting challenging work, but you will also have more time to carry out your management role.

There are many basic responsibilities which should automatically be delegated to your secretary.

The Diary

This is a responsibility that should be delegated. Your secretary should always know your whereabouts, expected time of return, etc. so that your callers can be informed of your availability, and be able to contact you should any urgent messages need to be passed on. You should also delegate the arrangement of meetings, and let your secretary know immediately you have changed something in the diary, so that there is no possibility of double bookings.

The mail

Leave the opening and sorting of the mail to your secretary. This is one of the best ways for the secretary to be kept informed about your work, your contacts, and special projects you are involved with.

Filing

Paradoxically, many managers enjoy filing, while it is one of the secretary's pet hates. One of your secretary's responsibilities should be to maintain efficient filing systems and keep an index for each reference. Filing is one of those tiresome jobs that often get left, but you should clearly delegate the task. How many times, I wonder, have you mislaid that vital piece of information, which should have been put on file?

Travel arrangements

Delegating travel arrangements to your secretary should also be encouraged. This also applies to booking accommodation. It is also another way of ensuring that the secretary always knows where you should be.

Fact-finding

Gathering information for various letters and projects can be very time consuming, especially when you have tight deadlines to meet. Let your secretary do some of the ground work and fact-finding on various projects.

The telephone

A continually ringing telephone can distract anyone's train of thought. If your secretary answers incoming calls for you, inappropriate messages and callers can be filtered out. In her book, *Working with a Secretary: A manager's guide*, published by The Industrial Society Press, Corrine Devery highlights some of the common 'moans' from secretaries about using the telephone, including asking your secretary to ring a number for you then disappearing from the office.

Others

Many other responsibilities can be delegated, such as attending meetings in your absence, ordering office supplies, etc. In fact, the list is endless. Why not examine some of your everyday tasks and decide if any of these could be handed over? It's surprising what you'll come up with!

How to delegate to your secretary

You may be feeling pleased with yourself so far, because you *do* delegate many responsibilities to your secretary. The million dollar question is however: do you know *HOW* to delegate? Many secretaries complain that their managers are poor communicators, and delegate very badly. We have already seen in previous chapters how to delegate generally, but when delegating to a secretary, several additional points should be noted.

- One important thing to remember is never take the delegation for granted. This can all too easily happen when delegating to an assistant, because you are used to 'dictating' tasks daily that are always carried out to your requirements. It is dangerous to assume that everything is automatically understood. Equally, your secretary may be at fault for not asking enough questions. You should describe fully what the task is, highlight how it should be tackled, and discuss its *importance*.
- Encourage your secretary to contribute suggestions about the task: it often helps to hear things from a different perspective. Remember also to be patient. Delegation develops people, and your secretary should have as much chance as anyone else to try new things. New skills and experiences make for a more confident individual, and showing your secretary that you have every confidence in him or her can lead to a much better working relationship.
- It is also important to set realistic deadlines. You may not realise just how time consuming many routine jobs can be, especially, if you and your secretary work in separate offices. Don't get carried away and delegate everything. Make it a habit to discuss workload and try and work out a happy medium.

What you delegate to your secretary, and how much, obviously depends on the type of organisation you work in, the capability and flexibility of your secretary, and your attitude as a manager. A word of encouragement: it does take two to delegate, and if your secretary is unwilling or uninterested to take on delegated responsibilities, there is little you can do short of replacing him or her. However many of us are only too willing to be given greater responsibility and to take on extra duties. Set your secretary a challenge!

Delegation at senior levels

So far we have been dealing primarily with a manager in relation to his or her own department. There are some additional points which become relevant at the more senior levels, when you are a manager in charge of other managers.

Future planning

In all organisations, the higher the management level, the more you should be concerned with planning the future and the less with organising day-to-day matters. What employees look for from their top managers is a clear plan for the future. The plan may change, as circumstances change, but there is nothing worse than the uncertainty of feeling that '"They" don't know where they're leading us.'

So a salutary check to make, if you are a senior manager, is: how much of your attention is spent on today's problems, and how much on tomorrow's issues? Planning strategy is something which, by definition, cannot be delegated to more junior levels. Staff at all levels can contribute to the planning, but strategy decisions based on these plans have to be taken at a high level. So day-to-day operational management can and should be delegated by senior managers.

The external environment

The second characteristic of senior managers is to spend an increasing amount of time on external issues. For example, most managing directors rightly give much personal attention to relations with the media and the city, i.e. issues concerned with the company's reputation and image.

1992 means companies will need to spend still more time on international affairs. Concern for industry's impact on the environment is another example. All of these matters reinforce the point that senior managers need to spend much time on the external environment: political, legal, competitive, image-related.

They also should spend a significant proportion of their time physically out and about meeting decision-makers and seeing for themselves.

So the second check for you to make as a senior manager is – have you got this balance right?

Developing other managers

Many chief executives place the selection of tomorrow's main board directors amongst their most important activities. A good test for any board (or equivalent top strategy team in education, local government, etc.) is how far its members judge issues through 'functional blinkers', i.e. the finance person takes an accountant's view of everything, the marketing person knows much about marketing but little about anything else, etc.

A company employing several thousand people looked at the careers of its three hundred most senior managers and was horrified to find that only one in five of them had ever served outside their present function. In those organisations, discussions at board level can easily lack perspective and become insular rather than imaginative. Non-executive directors can help greatly, but what will really make the difference is for senior managers to move managers around across different functions in a controlled way – not as a permanent 'musical chairs' but as part of a conscious plan to broaden experience.

Broadening managers' experience

A useful device to help this is for you as a senior manager to arrange for one of your team to cover for a colleague *in another function* during a holiday or some other absence, or perhaps to arrange a straight exchange of jobs for a period. You will need to plan this carefully, and to give guidance, but with goodwill much can be learned. It should be made clear within the organisation that candidates for the most senior levels must have spent some time in at least three different functions during their career. The two professions most often needing this 'leavening' are finance and personnel.

So, in this respect, your responsibility in delegating is to be brave and imaginative. Use every opportunity to delegate new experiences to your managers, not just an extra helping of familiar responsibilities.

Walking the job

If you are sufficiently senior to have several levels of managers and supervisors below you, your delegation becomes even more an act of faith. You trust your people to respond to the responsibility and authority you have given them. But the ultimate accountability remains with you, so you need to see for yourself.

Some senior managers operate like hermits, forever closeted in their caves. One of the responsibilities of senior managers is to be visible. Not everyone can be charismatic and some managers find mixing difficult. But you have to consider the morale effect of being seen in person: 'the manager has taken the trouble to come and see *us*'. One very effective senior manager, responsible for 1200 staff at many different locations, arranges his time so that, on average, he is away from his office one whole day a week visiting customers, and one whole day visiting one of the many sites where his own staff are based. On these visits to his own people, he expects a short presentation on an issue *he* wants to hear about, plus a short presentation on an issue *they* want him to know about.

In this way he keeps in touch with two crucially important groups of people – his customers and his staff. To do this, he obviously has to delegate with confidence. But by seeing for himself, he receives plenty of feedback on whether his confidence is justified. If he finds problems, he will take them up with the intermediate managers. If all is well (and not just when there are spectacular successes) he will go out of his way to congratulate. As another top manager told me: 'I don't mind saying "Well done, keep up the good work" a thousand times a year. I don't ration my encouragement.'

Handling mistakes

We have seen that ultimate accountability still rests with the manager, and this contributes to our reluctance to delegate. It is worth repeating: delegation involves taking a calculated risk. And in spite of careful preparation, you will sometimes find that an individual has made a mistake with a delegated task. How should you handle such a situation? Your approach will depend on the reason for the mistake.

Reasons and solutions

If a member of staff omitted to consult someone in another department and irritated that person as a result, you should check whether you made it sufficiently clear who was to be consulted. If not, you should do the apologising, both to the colleague in the other department and to your own member of staff.

If it was clear who should be consulted, but he or she overlooked it, he or she must make peace with the offended party and go out of his or her way to help him in future. You will want to remind your member of staff, from your experience as a manager, how crucial is inter-departmental co-operation.

If newly acquired authority was abused, you should point out to him or her that delegation is a trust and that you will want to have confidence that it will not be abused. If the task concerned did not require a 'bull at a gate' approach when you were doing it, nor should it now that you have handed it on.

If the mistake was caused through lack of planning, some patient coaching by yourself is probably called for. Explain that you had gradually built up the skill to do in a flash what had originally needed considerable preparation.

Sometimes a task will grind to a halt for no obvious reason; this may be because the job holder lacks confidence. Talk it over carefully with the job-holder and try to pin down what precisely is causing the difficulty. Is it, for instance, a problem with figure work? Or that the task involves chairing a meeting, and he or she lacks experience in this? Whatever the reason, you may have to go back to the previous stage in the process of coaching (*see* Appendix 17 page 369) and build up his confidence by slow degrees.

Or perhaps you find that the person does not measure up to the new responsibility. You will then have to judge whether more training is required, or whether to cut your losses and take the task back, or give it to a different member of your team.

Throughout this process of analysing mistakes, it is helpful to keep two points in the forefront: first, everyone makes mistakes at some stage, and as long as they were not caused by sheer foolhardy behaviour, there is little to be ashamed of; second, mistakes can be used as opportunities to learn. As George Odiorne put it in *Management by objectives: a system of managerial leadership* (Pitman), 'When a man fails, don't hound him for it. Use his failures as a platform for coaching.'

Control and evaluation

Even when mistakes are not being made with delegated tasks, you have a responsibility for control. The spot check is perhaps the simplest method to use. After the job-holder has carried out the new task a couple of times, you can check on how it is going. If the task involves much liaison with another department, have a quiet word with the departmental head and ask how your person is handling it from his or her point of view. If the task involves written work, ask to see a copy of the report concerned. If it is running a committee, ask one of the committee members how the meetings are going.

However, spot checks can easily turn into regular reports, and the individual will quickly feel you have delegated with one hand while keeping a firm grip with the other. In particular, if the feedback on your job-holders' performance is favourable, do let them know this. 'Congratulation is the lost art of management', as has been said. We really cannot use the principle that 'no news is good news'. A job being well done deserves to be recognised, and a word of praise goes a long way in terms of morale and sustained performance.

Evaluating the results of delegation is also easily overlooked. If you have successfully delegated a task, you have a great opportunity to learn from this. Questions to pursue include:

- has the job-holder found a new way of performing the task, which can be copied elsewhere?
- is the job-holder capable of still further development?
- are there other tasks which you are handling yourself which you could now delegate?
- has success here stimulated others of your team to want more responsibility?
- can you learn anything about the training period needed to perform this sort of task?

- have you made sure about updating the job description to transfer the responsibility?

How much of your time has now been saved? And how are you using it? Can you improve your own coaching ability, so that other tasks can be delegated more easily from now on?

Having once delegated a task, it is only too easy for the time saved to be eaten away again, and you may end up with a disgruntled feeling that 'delegation doesn't pay'. Evaluating the results of delegation will reassure you that it does pay, and will help you to see how to make it pay still more.

Management by exception

Once the task really belongs to the job-holder and you have confidence to let him or her get on with it; once you have carried out a spot check and an evaluation, what next? Then you can rely on management by exception.

What management by exception is not, is vividly illustrated by a scene in a large London post office: each postman operating from that office filled in a report every day showing the proportion of letters delivered by the target time of first post in the morning. These reports came through to the Head Postmaster, whose desk was piled high with them. The Head Postmaster would plough through these massive reports so that he obtained an extremely accurate picture. But the proportion of letters delivered on time was consistently over 90 per cent; I dread to think what other aspects of his job were simply not getting done because of the time that manager took every day to read those reports.

Managing by exception is the complete opposite. You assume that the accepted standards are being met unless you are told otherwise. Here is where ' no news is good news' does apply. You are not bothered by masses of paperwork. Such reports as you do get highlight deviations (either for good or bad) from normal. You can concentrate your attention on the deviations, and rectify them where need be, rather than have to unearth them from among columns of figures.

The advantages

Now of course, one cannot manage entirely by exception. Apart from anything else, it becomes rather demoralising if the only reports you receive are of things going wrong! But a great many aspects in most managers' jobs could be managed by exception. Standards are set, those responsible get on with their duties, and you get rapid feedback when things start to go out of line. It is the difference between management accounting (where only the crucial figures are presented as the basis for managerial decisions) and traditional 'archaeological' accounting (where the past is dug up, mistakes are raked over, post-mortems held endlessly, while time marches on).

In many organisations, much time and effort is spent on checks and controls. Far less time is spent on reviewing the very standards which generate such checks. The technique of value analysis has convincingly demonstrated how worthwhile it can be to question accepted standards and methods. If we apply the same kind of ingenuity which is needed for value analysis to a review of our present standards, we will produce more realistic standards and management by exception then comes into its own.

Delegation, as we have seen, is not easy. Rather like abstract concepts such as peace and justice, everyone is in favour of it until they start to realise how much effort is needed for its achievement. Above all, it requires honesty to assess how you are using your time, and perseverance in the face of setbacks, once you have embarked on a delegation plan. The manager who fails to delegate is no real manager; the manager who delegates well is on the way to fulfilling a manager's key role, that of being an agent of change.

11 DECISION TAKING

Stages of decision taking

Our very future depends upon the decisions all sorts of people take every day at work. Decisions affect how others operate, what work is done, whether they even eventually have a job or, indeed, their health and safety. We must consider how we can best approach the decision taking process in a manner that will improve the quality of our decisions and, subsequently, the manner in which they are implemented. We must also understand that the process of decision taking involves people in a manner which contributes to the effectiveness of the decision and its implementation *without* undermining the vital leadership role of an individual leader.

The art of leadership is in making difficult things simple. In a similar way, a checklist for decision taking should be developed that enables ease of reference for most effective use. From the gathered wisdom of many managers and leaders our decision taking process can be based on five principle stages.

The five Cs of decision taking and implementation

1 *Consider*. The thinking starts now! Define the objective; consider the problem.
2 *Consult*. The stage at which you take initiatives to involve those affected.
3 *Commit*. Ensuring that appropriate action will be taken.
4 *Communicate*. The stage at which you explain what has been decided and why.
5 *Check*. The need for visible leadership in ensuring the decision actually works.

This is our foundation (*see* Table 11.1 on page 191) on which we can build more detailed actions. First, though, it is necessary to make three major points about these stages.

- it cannot always be a progressive step-by-step process. Sometimes it is necessary to go back a stage and repeat part of the loop. For example, following consultation with others and establishing further facts, it becomes clear that we need to return to the initial question or problem and reconsider the objective. However, we must be careful that this is not an eternal loop for ducking decisions!
- Consultation is not applicable in all situations. Through reasons of policy, time, or the extent of an emergency, the manager may well be in the situation of moving straight from the 'consider' stage to the 'commit'. This is all part of the vital thought process that must happen at the outset, so that the implications of omitting the consultation are understood, and appropriate actions taken to cope with this when at the 'communicate' stage.
- There is no recognition of negotiation in this five-stage process of decision taking. This is because negotiation is a separate stage when no one leader has the authority to take the decision. When that authority does exist, we must ensure that neither 'consult' nor 'communicate' degenerate into negotiation. It is vital that we either have one person taking the decision and being accountable, or a joint party negotiating. In either event, consultation before meeting at the negotiation table is important, as are the communication processes that would follow. During negotiation, however, we have more than one organisation system conducting these two stages (e.g. management seeking views and explaining outcome, whilst union officials or employee representatives would be doing likewise).

Regardless of the complexity of the decision it is vital to be clear at the outset who will ultimately take that decision. Managers are more enthusiastic about carrying out decisions that they have made themselves. Doubtless most of us know examples of marginal, or difficult decisions that have been turned into highly effective ones as a result of the commitment and enthusiasm of the person who took it. One lesson to be

Table 11.1 *Decision taking – key actions*

Consider	Consult	Commit	Communicate	Check
Ultimate objective	Others likely to be affected	A plan of action within time scale	Face-to-face in teams	Decision is being implemented Walk the job
ESTABLISH Problems Cause and effect Who is affected Time scales Constraints	ENCOURAGE Attendance Suggestions Listening Creativity Time to think	Take the decision Write it down Be committed and enthusiastic	EXPLAIN Sell the decision Check understanding	EVALUATE Understanding and acceptance Training Standards Quality Delegation Rewards Is it achieving the objective?
What, Why, When, Who, Where, How				

learned from this is that it is much more practical to delegate decision taking as far down the line as possible.

This is much easier said than done, since doing so involves trusting people and carrying the can for subordinates who make mistakes, as they inevitably will, from time to time. A decision-taking policy shows that there are enormous rewards to be gained from trusting people, and taking the risk, rather than *not* trusting them, with all the accompanying problems of time, failing initiative and morale, and enjoying the false luxury of being indispensable.

The actions that follow, under the five stages we have already identified, are as applicable to a senior manager taking policy decisions, as they are to the supervisor tackling today's problems. The major difference relates to the timescales involved in taking the decision, and in the extent of future impact. For those involved, however, the distinction is of scant interest – either the decision will be effective or it will not.

It is incumbent on leaders at every level to think carefully about the following actions and to be continually looking for ways to be 'in charge of their own destiny'.

1 Consider

The decision-taking process starts when it is apparent that some management action or initiative is necessary. The first action is to give yourself time to think. Consider if the real problem is being tackled and not merely the superficial symptoms of an underlying factor, or, indeed, whether intervention is actually necessary. Some problems solve themselves without the need for outside help. In some circumstances, the best possible decision to take *is to take no decision*. Next, however, you should consider what your aim is; what is it that you want to achieve? Finally it is sensible to establish what are the constraints within which action must be taken.

Establish

- What information do I need? How do I get it?
- Is the decision mine? Am I assuming too much authority? Am I undermining someone else's responsibilities?
- Who is likely to be affected by the decision?

- What other constraints are there likely to be? (E.g. policies, precedent, legal, financial, external influences.)
- Time-scales: what is the *latest* possible date or time by which the decision must be taken? If we decide too soon, we may deprive ourselves of information or relevant factors which have not yet come to light. If we delay, we may prevent others in the organisation from getting on with their jobs, thus wasting resources.

Finally, ask yourself: 'What would happen if no decision were taken at all?' (In this way, you may well save yourself a great deal of time and trouble.)

Checklist

- Has the *real* problem been defined?
- What is the decision intended to achieve?
- By when must the decision be taken?
- What other constraints are there?
- What would be the effect if no decision were taken?
- What information is needed?
- Should it be delegated?

---

2   Consult

Experience shows that group decision taking is not usually practical. Yet at the same time, all the evidence is that, when people are not involved in decisions that affect them, their commitment is difficult to obtain. The most effective way of involving people is to adopt the approach of *consultation before decision*. But the crucial word is 'before'. Consulting people *after* decisions have been made is rarely productive and frequently leads to resentment, as many managers have found to their cost.

In cases where consultation is not appropriate, it is vital to plan the communication stage well, and to make every effort to achieve acceptance of the decision. Where consultation processes have taken place, there is far greater understanding of the intentions of management, often creating an atmosphere of wishing to help on the part of the workforce.

It cannot be emphasised too often that managers have to get results through people. Others must carry out their decisions. Managers therefore need co-operation and commitment. To get these, they must convey to an increasingly better educated, articulate, and critical workforce, the facts of the situation relating to the decision.

But people perceive facts and situations from different standpoints. They see things differently; their feelings are involved; their interests are affected; their jobs and security may appear to be threatened and, above all, they often have the knowledge and experience which springs from having to carry out decisions and do the actual work. They therefore have much to contribute to the decision making process, but must clearly understand that the decision itself is the responsibility of the appointed leader.

Encourage consultation

Consultation can, in many instances, be limited to the immediate work group, as is often the case with operational decisions. But some tactical and strategic decisions affect far wider areas of an organisation, and this calls for the use of whatever formal consultation arrangement exists. The organisation may or may not be unionised, but, where unions are recognised, they must be included. A meeting should, therefore, be called with those involved, or their representatives, and the maximum amount of information made available.

Increasingly, decisions cut across conventional organisation boundaries. Lateral teamwork is becoming more important, and, frequently, it is of value to establish a multi-disciplinary team for specific problem solving activities. However, it is vital that *vertical* teamwork is strengthened *before* forming teams for generating ideas and suggestions that cut across the functional structure.

Working to timescales

The timing of consultation will often call for sensitivity and good judgement. There is a strong case for consulting as early as is practicable, so as to allow as much time as possible to weigh up the pro's and con's of the situation. But, on the other hand, the desirability of early consultation has also to be weighed against the need to avoid long, drawn out, and possibly destructive discussions of contentious issues, as well as raising hopes or apprehensions unnecessarily early. In any event, it is wise to set a time limit so that everyone knows when consultation will stop and a decision be taken.

Checklist

- Have all the people who should be consulted been identified?
- Has the information which should be tabled, including the constraints, been assembled?
- Have meetings been convened of consultative committees and trade union representatives?
- has the timing of consultation been chosen with care and a date been set for concluding the process?
- Have you attempted to think *outside* the problem by creating a task force and using creative techniques such as brainstorming?
- Are you fully prepared to listen to ideas and suggestions, without jumping to conclusions?

---

3   Commit

Having completed the first two stages, all that remains is to *take the decision*. One must weigh up the gathered views and opinions, evaluate the ideas and suggestions put forward, and review the facts. The result is a rational consideration of the risks, probabilities, and rewards.

In actuality, many managers are given an uncomfortable time by this process. Why is this so? Many reasons could be given, but the chances are that the answer is reflected in one, or more, of the following:

- insufficient time to think at stage 1; being under pressure, or simply failing to resist your own burning desire to get on and act

- failing to listen at stage 2; either not consulting at all, or doing it in such a way that you were not really receptive to the views, opinions and suggestions of others
- failing to assemble sufficient relevant data at stage 2; or assembling so much that the important issues were submerged under superfluities
- failing to face the issues within the timescale set for action, and not progressing beyond stage 2.

Far better instead to:

- review the information already assembled – which should include feelings as well as facts
- try to assess the extent to which the absence of some information will affect the quality of the decision
- list the operations and the arguments for and against
- give yourself time to think; if possible, sleep on it
- discipline yourself to decide within the set timescale.

Making up your mind

The decision, when arrived at, can sometimes be appropriately described as 'the least worst' decision rather than 'the best' decision since there are bound to be some disadvantages and some interests adversely affected. For this reason, decisions sometimes demand courage and resolution to face up to unpopularity and dissent. Once the decision has been taken, be committed and enthusiastic about the plan of action, however finely balanced the decision.

Checklist

- Review the objectives established at Stage 1.
- Classify them according to importance – what *must* we achieve? What would we like to achieve?
- List all options (and feelings).
- Evaluate options against objectives.
- Choose the best option and assess the consequences – if these are too great the second best option may have to be considered.

- Make a serious attempt to see the consequences of each option.
- Take the decisions – it may be the 'least worst'.
- Record the decision and the plan in writing.
- Be committed and enthusiastic.

Group decisions

Because decisions frequently affect an entire group of people, some managers are tempted to implement decisions because they will be popularly received by the group – but not necessarily because they are the right course of action! However tempting, it is worth remembering that:

- group decisions are frequently an outward and visible sign of consensus or compromise, for which few people feel any real enthusiasm – *UNLESS THE DECISION IS OBVIOUS*
- they frequently result from majorities outvoting minorities, but make no provision for the needs of the latter
- nobody remains accountable for what happens – if queries or problems arise, people feel free to pass the buck.

It is seldom worthwhile passing the decision taking process to a group. Teamwork is more likely to be weakened by providing the team with total responsibility.

4 Communicate

More decisions flounder because of poor communications than for any other single reason. Most managers all too frequently have experience of this, and it is appropriate to review the key points.

First, it is vital to secure peoples' commitment to decisions by communicating face-to-face. It is a selling operation, explaining the decision so that people have the opportunity to ask questions. This way, we all find it easier to understand and accept – even though we may not agree. If we only use the notice board, company newspaper, scan light, or a video, the decision is likely to fail. Any of these communication methods are invaluable back-up tools to the team meeting or equivalent forum, according to the nature and impact of the decision.

Second, it must be remembered that it is the job of whoever takes the decision to ensure that it gets communicated. Part of the problem at stage 3 may be hesitancy in taking the decision because of concern at facing the consequences of that decision. Managers who are leaders do not evade the importance of communicating face-to-face and ensuring that the decision is communicated down and across all necessary management lines.

Team briefing

Many of the problems of communication can be overcome by installing team briefing to ensure that the decision and the reasons for it are transmitted right the way down the line, from the level at which it is taken, to those whom it actually affects. It also ensures that the message is put over only by those who can be accountable for doing so. In this way, managers who check that even an unpopular decision is enthusiastically and properly put over – and it is enthusiasm that forms the springboard for a decision's success.

You can still insist that subordinates who manage others *put a message across* and do not fall back on weak apologies such as: 'It's not my fault, it was management's decision'. Team briefing is a good way of making sure that managers do actually *manage*, and that they are reinforced and consolidated in their rightful position as leaders of the work group (*see* Chapter 2, *Team briefing* and *The manager's responsibility for communication*).

Explain

The crucial points to communicate are the decisions and the reason for them, *plus* examples that will make the message real for the receiver. People need to understand when the decision will be implemented, who will be affected and how and, finally, what the procedure is for registering a complaint or grievance.

It is the added dimension of 'explanation' to information which helps reduce people's fear of change, and also effectively combats the grapevine, that rumour network frequently giving remarkably accurate information, completely distorted reasons, and, as a result, severe management headaches!

Checklist

- Have the methods of implementing a decision been planned?
- Have all those affected been briefed in teams, with facts and reasons, face-to-face?
- Are the channels for feedback fully understood?
- Have all those affected accepted the decision?

5   Check

Finally, there is a need to know whether the decision you have taken is actually working. Naturally, a great deal of information can be obtained through the normal channels of returns and statistics, not to mention the feedback from trade union representatives and from briefing groups. But there is no substitute for going out to see for yourself as well.

By going out and walking the job, managers can observe the operation for which they are responsible by talking with people. They can gauge a great deal, not just from what people actually say, but also from the way that they say it. They can develop their ability to observe the signs of effective team work, and can often catch the first 'wisp of smoke' from an impending crisis. Also, observing for themselves enables them to determine whether or not any corrective action is necessary. Above all, however, it enables people to see that managers are acknowledging their own responsibility!

If the decision is working then we need to know that, so as to identify good practices and promote a positive climate of motivation by 'catching people doing things right'. If the decision is not working, then we need to review potential weak areas:

- inadequate information
- poor judgement
- lack of courage
- inadequate plans for implementation
- a breakdown in briefing
- lack of enthusiasm on the part of management.

Evaluate

- whether people have understood the briefing and accepted the implications
- whether anyone needs training as a result of what is now being actioned
- that standards are being achieved
- whether quality can be improved
- whether authority can now be delegated for subsequent decisions
- whether any rewards are justified
- is corrective action needed?

Nowadays, we must take decisions by drawing upon other people's skills and experiences whilst still having the leadership responsibilities of deciding which course of action. Equally, we must have the commitment to see that course of action implemented, with all that is required in standards of quality of goods and services. Decision taking draws upon all our skills of communicating. It also demands making the time to think and getting others to think, whilst keeping to your timescales and not ducking issues.

12 EFFECTIVE USE OF TIME

This chapter attempts to help the busy manager get on top of some ever-present problems, such as:

- backlog of paperwork
- continual interruptions
- domination by the telephone
- instant reactions to urgent problems (regardless of their relative importance)
- falling asleep (on the train or at home) trying to catch up on some reading.

Lack of time is often used as a cover for inefficiency, lack of forethought, delays, or failures. It is no use muttering about 'theory' or 'an ideal world'. In reality we *have* to get things done in a far from perfect setting. Proper management of time is crucial to the success of organisations. Yet so much is left to chance. Where do the best ideas come from? How are decisions made? Do we use basic, taken for granted skills (like reading and writing) properly? Are our meetings short and productive, and do things get done on schedule?

Thinking time

There is a strong belief that we have to look busy all the time – or at least when the boss can see us. The idea of taking time off to stop and think produces uneasy feelings. Yet thinking must be a central part of productive work. To do it properly calls for concentration, self-discipline and proper allocation of time for the purpose.

Example

A senior official in a professional institute advises members to spend a period of every day in thought. She tries between 3 p.m. and 5 p.m. What about? About what exactly she is paid to achieve, and how her group can make a better contribution.

Example

The London manager of an international concern periodically climbs into a 'mental helicopter' and views the topic under discussion from a vantage point up in the ceiling. Her colleagues have grown used to her occasional trances.

Not all thinking is directed at solving work problems. The brain needs frequent short concentration breaks, and we can use some of the day's interruptions in this way. Neither does the mind switch off when we have found a solution. We can get much pleasure from spontaneous mental freewheeling and unwinding.

Example

A construction engineer asserts that, when he breaks away from 'banging my head against a brick wall', he experiences two remarkable effects: 'The pain goes, and my vision clears.'

So, not only should we set aside some time for serious work-thinking, but we should also tolerate, even welcome, play-thinking. The value of timely thinking cannot be overstressed.

The human brain

Our brains are much more efficient than we give ourselves credit for. We now know that the brain has a much greater ability than was previously believed. Tiny babies have an enormous capacity to learn and develop; far from being 'helpless little things' they grow intellectually at a pace far outstripping current advances in computer technology.

The athlete knows the value of regular training for the next race. The executive with middle-age spread will admit the possibility of getting back into trim with appropriate visits to the local sports centre (not forgetting changes in diet). The brain, too, needs regular exercise to attain a high level of efficiency.

We can think a lot faster than we can talk. The average person can speak at about 200 words per minute. Tests show we can habitually think at over 600 wpm. Perhaps this suggests we can gain an advantage by more listening and less interrupting. We could use the extra seconds gained, deciding from a range of possible replies, instead of relying on instinct.

It pays to listen properly. School leavers at work, who found it hard to respect their supervisors, levelled one criticism most often: 'They don't listen.'

Creative thinking

We habitually tend to think 'analytically', where logical deduction from known facts leads to a more or less indisputable answer. Most of us are good at this; it is the way we were taught. There are times, however, when we need 'creative' thinking, where imagination is brought into play because the facts do not permit logical deduction.

Creative thinking needs adjusting to. We hit barriers when we first try it. Self-imposed limits to new ideas get in the way: a belief that there is always one right answer; conformity, lack of effort in challenging the obvious; fear of looking foolish. 'That won't work,' we say, and another excellent idea has got away. Creative thinking relates things or ideas not previously related. It can be fun, too. Thoughts proceed in one plane then suddenly veer off in a new direction. The resulting release of tension often leads to laughter. Joke writers know something about this phenomenon.

A successful business thrives on creative thinking. It can stay ahead of the competition with better marketing, improved products and services, and higher motivation. A well-known pen manufacturer improved their performance once someone realised they were in the gift business: the market place took on a new size and shape.

Brainstorming

Brainstorming employs creative thinking to produce lots of ideas quickly. To get the best results, call together a small group of amenable people for about half an hour. Someone has to be able to write the ideas down very quickly – and legibly. Pose the question and encourage a flood of ideas. Once the stream dries up, stop and gaze silently at the chart(s). Allow the ideas to 'incubate' until someone begins to see the 'last piece of the jigsaw'. This is known as the 'AHA!' moment. Sometimes you can look at the silliest idea, pull it apart, and discover yet another usable idea.

The keys to successful brainstorming are:

- getting the problem right; the statement of the question
- consciously and deliberately separating the production of ideas from their evaluation
- letting people whose temperament or mood do not fit the occasion, slip away without loss of face.

For private thinking, there is no need for a separate office or a stonewalling secretary for protection. Many people simply avert their gaze from approaching visitors, put up a hand, or turn away for a moment. A good train of thought is hard to get back once interrupted. People respect our need for five seconds' grace.

Lastly, a word about trying too hard to remember little things. The extra effort seems to lock just the word we want on to the tip of our tongue. It can be very embarrassing to forget the boss's name just at the moment of introducing an important visitor. The infuriating fact that the answer pops up – unannounced and unwanted – at a future moment, gives us a clue to how to cope. Don't strain the brain.

Time utilisation

If we fail to plan, we plan to fail. Lack of time can become a very emotive issue to many people. Do we really know how we spend it?

In preparing to use our time more effectively, the first things we really need to know are the facts, not the feelings. A record of where our time is really spent is an important first step. There are a number of ways to investigate time utilisation: pre-prepared forms are useful as only 'ticks' or brief notes are necessary. Obviously, this takes a little time, but you can't save time by not spending it. The simplest and most commonly used method is a daily time log (*see* Table 12.1). Keeping this for a week is probably the best idea.

Other methods for investigating time utilisation are the content of work analysis (*see* Table 12.2), contacts analysis (*see* Table 12.3), work priorities diary (*see* Table 12.4) or the analysis of fleeting contacts (*see* Table 12.5). In all cases, the headings and layout may be changed to suit individual circumstances.

After analysing the facts that emerge from the investigation, one can then start identifying the real priorities for personal action. One action may be to discuss your time problems and solutions with your boss. Most bosses are much more likely to listen if you have done your homework and come up with suggestions.

Decisions

> ### *Example*
>
> One despairing warehouse superintendent complained that most of his decisions flowed down from an insensitive manager, or 'made themselves' by the pressure of events as the lorries came and went and the forklift trucks went up, down and along. Customers were infuriated with discrepancies. On investigation, it was difficult to find anyone doing anything really wrong. The men were taking short cuts, and some had got into bad habits, learned from their mates.

Table 12.1 *Daily time log showing major areas of time used*

Page . . . . . . Day . . . . . . Date . . . . . .

Day total . . . . . . hrs . . . . . . mins

Summarise weekly for overall picture

			Category of Activity						
Start time	**Finish time**	**Activity**							
		Hrs							
		Mins							

Table 12.2 *Content of work analysis, indicating what you are involved in and who involved you*

Brief description of subject	How was I involved? By whom?							Did I need to be concerned?		
	Self	Boss	Subordinate/s	Colleagues	Customers	Others		At all?	At what stage?	In so much detail?

Table 12.3 *Contacts analysis*

Length of time	Persons contacted	Brief description of topic

Table 12.4 *Work priorities diary*

Time	Brief description of activity	Should I have been doing it then?		Reason for stopping			
		A	B	A	B	C	D
		Yes	No	Finished	Unfinished but necessary	Unnecessary	
						Caused by others	Caused by self

N.B. A tick in columns 3B and/or 4D indicates lack of self-planning

Table 12.5 *Analysis of fleeting contacts*

Type of contact		Who was it with?	Who initiated it?		Was it an interruption?
A	B		A	B	
Personal	Phone		Self	Others	

When making a decision it is helpful to go to the trouble of *writing down* what it is we are trying to achieve: a statement of the problem. We rarely do this because we assume we know what is wanted. But once we get into the habit of isolating these things on paper, we stand to benefit from the powerful effect it has in sharpening our awareness and clarifying our thoughts. Often, what looks like the central problem turns out to be merely a symptom of something else. Once we are satisfied we have got the problem right, and when we have defined our objective, we are ready for some concentrated thinking. At this stage we generate several possible solutions and try to predict the probable outcome of each.

Now comes the time to decide and act. Choose and implement the most appropriate plan. Communicate it (share, rather than merely transmit). Check at regular intervals to see that the plan is working in practice, or whether it is necessary to re-plan or reorganise. Answer the question: 'Did the action achieve the objective?'

Remember: Consider, Consult, Commit, Communicate, Check.

Reading and writing

Time can be irretrievably lost by inefficient use of the skills we were taught when we were very young.

A first step might be simply to read less. Do we have to read every page of every document that comes our way?

We can do a lot about report writing and letter writing. Before diving into the body of the text, think (about the purpose, the readers, the action you want to result). As you write, remember the old 'ABC rule' (accuracy, brevity, clarity) And when it's first typed: read, check, edit, polish.

Good advice is to be found in *Report Writing* by T. Vidal-Hall and *Rapid Reading* by J. Grummitt (The Industrial Society Press).

Telecommunications

The telephone

It rings.
'Mrs Jones's office.'
'Can I speak to her please?'
'I'm afraid she's not in.'
'Do you know when she'll be back?'
'No, I'm awfully sorry, I don't. Can I take a message?'
'Ah – no, it's all right. I'll ring again later on.'

What has been achieved? Nothing. A recent survey produced the depressing result that 60 per cent of telephone calls failed to produce the information required on the first attempt. Also, less than one person in ten actually rang back after promising to do so.

With proper training and good leadership, a secretary can choose to handle such a call quite differently.

'Production: Lyn Taylor.' (The voice ends on an upward note.)
'Ah, Ferris here. Bradley and Stokes. Is Sarah Jones in?'
'I am expecting her back between 3 and 3.30 this afternoon. Is it something I can help with, Mr Ferris?'
'Well yes, I'm sure you could . . .'

By using our own name in this way, we encourage callers to give their names, too. This saves the awkward 'who's calling?' especially if the party on the other end thinks we ought to recognise the voice. Now that we know who's on the other end, we can decide how much to divulge. We can give the 'bad news' in a positive way. We have organised a time band during which Sarah Jones will be available to take and make phone calls. And, as 'god' is away, the caller might just as well parley with one of the angels.

Giving people every chance to work independently (rather than in someone else's shadow) is good: it saves time, and people like to be autonomous.

Example

One national public utility is giving its staff special training in answering customers' telephone calls. Ths idea is to deal completely with the enquiry even when it's not 'our department'. Staff listen carefully, write down the question, read it back and promise action within a specified deadline. Once the call is completed they can discover who the 'right department' is and pass it on with due urgency. No more transferring from one to another – less annoyance, better service, time saved.

Telephone operators have an unusual job which ought to be sympathetically understood by all extension users. The pressures vary between doing nothing and being rushed off one's feet. Everyone can help by spending a moment thinking about what life is like at the console.

Checklist

1 Decide who to contact, and think of an alternative if they are out.
2 Have a number, dialling code, extension/department written out in front of you.
3 Make brief notes of what is to be told or asked for.
4 Get together any papers you may need to refer to.
5 Make the call. Never let the ringing tone sound more than five times.
6 On reaching the person you want:
   • state who is calling
   • clarify the general purpose of the call
   • give the message or ask the question, and check understanding.
7 If you cannot get an answer at once, do not hold on. Offer to ring back after an agreed interval.
8 Ring back when you said you would.

Such a drill has helped to halve the cost of long distance calls, not least by cutting out long and expensive silences. When tariffs are lower in the afternoons, steer clear of the telephone during the mornings.

Computers

Computers will continue to play an increasing role in passing messages of all sorts. Do keep abreast of developments: encourage replacement of old with new devices. Try to introduce systems and procedures which fit national and international agreements – to save time (and money) later.

Paperwork

The best advice is to get rid of the paperwork as soon as you can.

Example

The legal adviser in a transport company claims, with a straight face, that she had a drawer in her desk labelled TDTDWT – 'too difficult to deal with today'.

A busy department head in a registered charity has a tray called GROAN meaning, 'get rid of, anywhere, now!'

Another manager keeps a big 'OBE' file where he collects things he knows will be 'overtaken by events'.

We may come to resent the onslaught of paper, but to the sender, each bit is an effort to communicate with us. Fewer people than we regularly curse actually set out to annoy. And those who are generating excessive paperwork to justify their existence are only crying out to be loved a little. A question frequently asked is, why do *I* have to deal with it all?

One way of tackling the job is to put each bit into one of three categories.

1 *Immediate action can be taken*. Do what is called for, make a note in the margin. Into the 'out tray' with it.
2 *Action can be started but not completed*. Do what you can, make a

note in the margin. Place in the 'brought-forward' file.

3 *Items for information, reading, circulation.* If it is short you can read it quickly. The more lengthy items can be gathered together and gone through at a planned 'reading time' each day. Do not sit on a circulation item: if you cannot finish it and pass it on within 24 hours make a note for it to be sent back to you when the others on the list have seen it. If you don't need to keep the item, throw it away.

Many replies to internal staff can be handwritten on the incoming memo. Get a photocopy made if you need to keep a record (compare this cost, in time as well as money, with dictation, typing, checking, signing and sending back a formal reply). Have a supply of little memos run off on the duplicator. You can clip these (have you got a stapler handy?) to incoming mail, or simply send them instead of typewritten internal memoranda.

Meetings

Meetings and committees have a bad reputation as a prime source of annoyance on account of the time wasted. But if they are well planned and run they can be the best, if not the only, way to: brief staff on policy, progress, points for action; uncover facts; produce new ideas; get people involved.

The basic skill of the chairman is in the deft use of questions to stimulate discussion, keeping to the point, summarising, tactfully rejecting irrelevancies, bringing quiet people in (*see* Appendix 26 page 384).

Participants

To make the best use of the meeting, participants will be:

- knowledgeable of the subject matter; aware of the purpose of the meeting; interested; conscientious (especially about preparing in advance)
- seated in place on time; equipped with the necessary papers and materials

- prepared to air their views strongly, making out a good case; able to keep to the point; ready to listen to other opinions; capable of being reasonably influenced
- disciplined and patient; prepared to contribute their best thinking and experience concisely and at the appropriate times
- reliable in accepting the decision reached and deferring to the control of the chairman, and in carrying out, on schedule, action assigned to them.

They will show skill in:

- producing new ideas
- helping to clarify and develop other people's ideas
- listening
- helping to keep the discussion to the point
- asking for clarification and summaries.

They will not allow emotions, inter-departmental battles or office politics to inject unwanted 'hidden agendas' into the meeting.

Delegation

Delegation is not 'allocating duties' or 'work scheduling'. It is about letting somebody else do something we would normally do. It demands giving away some of our authority to enforce action. It gives others freedom of action while we continue to carry the can. It is risky and painful. It can seem unnatural to people who have succeeded so far by doing things well themselves. It is an essential tool for effective use of time and is covered in detail in Chapter 10.

Other people's time

Middle managers spend about half their time on quite brief contacts, queries, confirmations, and progress chasing. These are unplanned and last from thirty seconds to five minutes. Formal interviews, meetings, correspondence, visits, and telephoning have to be fitted into what remained of the working day. Such impromptu encounters are neither unnecessary, nor useless interruptions, nor trivia. They are essential contacts without which the people on the shop floor are not able to get on with their jobs.

Example

One personnel manager was avoided as much as possible by her staff because she could not give a quick answer to an unexpected question. She always wanted to get involved in a long conversation.

Example

A night shift supervisor in a bakery had a way of taking himself off somewhere out of the way at the first sign of any trouble.

Example

A leading group of builders' merchants wanted to install a staff development programme along with an appraisal scheme. At the stage of analysing what the jobs were, some of the managers were astounded at the lack of common perception of what people were actually doing. The overlap between the job description drafted by the architectural ironmongery estimator, and what her manager wrote, amounted to less than 33 per cent (see Fig. 12.1).

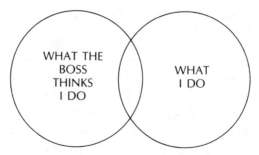

Figure 12.1 *An effect of lack of communication*

Management sins

Our actions are capable of having a more far reaching effect on those around us than we sometimes admit. Inept delegation can be self-defeating if all we are trying to do is solve our own problems at others' expense. Are *we* their biggest problem?

In the case of the last example above, the ensuing discussion brought new insight. The office was altered around. A direct line telephone was put on his desk. Much time was saved in staying in touch with manufacturers, architects, site foremen and retail branch managers. He got his own copies of professional journals instead of being 'permitted' to keep those that survived a long circulation list.

Most of us have been guilty at one time or another of getting in other people's way. As you glance down the following list of 'sins', remember, however, that we do have to do some of these things sometimes.

- transmitting information instead of sharing it
- keeping people waiting unnecessarily
- interrupting
- unaccounted-for absence
- destroying people's priorities with continued requests for work
- insensitivity to other people's unspoken feelings and ideas
- dropping in for a couple of minutes and wasting the whole afternoon
- forgetting important things, especially passing on informal decisions made over lunch or in the corridor.

Looking and listening

People may not like us popping up unexpectedly, but they moan if they never see us. The rule when going on our rounds is: have a reason for being there. It is awkward to be cast in the role of visiting VIP, and humiliating to be mistaken for the electrician. Equally, a 'detective' approach will merely generate 'alibis'. Show genuine interest, listen, take notes (put down what *they* want you to remember – you can always make your own notes afterwards). Let them have your reactions, or answers, within 48 hours, even when the answer is 'no'.

Listening has been called the 'lost art of our age'. We have already seen how must faster we can think than the other person can talk. Use the precious seconds. Submerge your own thoughts. Concentrate on what is being said. Show how you are willing to accept their viewpoint, and make an effort to understand. Hold back, wait; open eyes and ears and search for what they mean within what they actually say.

Consideration

When we are trying to uncover facts — at selection, appraisal, grievance or disciplinary interviews — it pays to remember that we can fail by:

- forgetting to remain neutral
- misunderstanding
- jumping to conclusions
- dealing prematurely with situations before knowing the full story
- rejecting the other person's explanation.

By indulging ourselves in this way we risk evoking fear, hostility, suspicious withdrawal or passive acceptance, which in turn can lead to sullen slavery.

Teamwork

We can waste a lost of time disapproving of other people's attitudes. It is not too helpful to berate young Alec about 'Your attitude, son'. Yet the young man is very willing to adapt what he actually does, minute-by-minute, to co-operate with his supervisor, and it is this that the older person should be trying to influence.

A harrassed 'team leader' in one of the practical exercises on an Action-Centred Leadership course was listening to the comments of other course members who had been observing her trying to lead four people to complete a task. 'We were only given twenty minutes!' True — if you only count 'elapsed' time. In fact, she had a total of $5 \times 20 = 100$ people/minutes. When this was pointed out, her exasperation disappeared.

People need managers who are expert and friendly: managers who respect their time and aspirations; leaders who can get the best out of all the people/minutes.

Roots and branches

Not many organisations operate entirely under one roof; we are members of teams dispersed throughout the land, and often the world. Some people get lonely, others relish the freedom. The opportunities for wasting time are legion.

Just because an organisation *does* operate within the one site, do not forget that the person two doors along the corridor can feel just as 'left out' as the wandering salesman. There are messages for us all in the experiences recorded in this section.

Example

A fast-growing building society recently introduced a policy of centralising systems (their new computer can show every investor's and borrower's account at a touch of the 'send' button) and decentralising decisions – each branch manager has the power to grant mortgages.

Example

Three-person teams plan deliveries to new customers from a northern brewery. A sales rep and two draymen walk the route, from the proposed parking position right through to the siting of the barrels, and discuss how to do it. It is not often that a delivery to an outlying club or a city-centre steak house is held up because of a last-minute snag.

Example

After the monthly briefing meetings of the senior managers in a shipping and forwarding business, each 'top person' climbs into a car and goes out to one of the regions, where the branch managers gather for their briefing. Then the branch managers return to do their meetings locally. The visiting senior manager goes out with a different branch manager in turn.

The multiple retailer stands or falls by the performance of the branch manager.

Example

One national chain reports immediately from head office on: the selling price account; the ratio of wages/sales; the branch's league-table position. They leave the local person to handle relations with customers, development, morale of the team, and the expansion of sales. Central specialists give support with buying, processing, book keeping, settlement of prices, point-of-sale display material, and administrative burdens.

Example

A leading ethical pharmaceuticals manufacturer sends representatives out to hospitals and general practitioners. Their jovial sales director says he never loses sight of one statistic: 'Young Appleby may only be 1 per cent of our sales force but, to the doctor she sees, she is 100 per cent of our company'.

Much time can be saved in planning journeys. Petrol and shoe leather can be saved if a visitor to an unfamiliar area reads the map intelligently and sequences calls to avoid covering the same ground over and again.

Example

A retail regional manager held a meeting with her district managers to discuss journey planning. She put up several maps and charted where several of the district managers had been the previous week. They were all amazed at the level of overlapping and extra miles driven.

Example

An area manager got an urgent message while visiting one branch to visit a branch 20 miles away, immediately. He jumped into his car and drove the 20 miles to find the problem was that one of the strip fluorescent lights had gone and needed to be replaced. The branch didn't have a spare. He sent someone out to buy one and waited until the boy returned so he could put it in!

Checklist

To be covered in discussions with regional/area managers.

- Compiling visit checklists.
- Setting a specific visit objective.
- Having a branch file.
- Organisation of car and briefcase.
- Planning, preparation, priorities.
- Studying the communication at meetings.
- Telling people where you are and can be got hold of.
- Having a base or 'anchor' branch – where all queries and problems are passed to. Some can be answered by the manager of the unit, with proper delegation and training. At least you just have one telephone call to make to find out problems and priorities.
- Spending longer in one location so you can really achieve something, not the twenty-minute 'hello – how are you – goodbye' visit! Spend one, or even two full days.
- Telling managers you're coming, and what you want to talk about, so that they are prepared.
- Analysing the trading pattern and staff coverage.
- Analysing branch layout and equipment; using string diagrams.
- Doing time–task analyses to find out how long things take.
- Managing your own boss!
- Having a written record to ensure follow-up on delegated tasks and points for action.

Finding more time

Most of us, given the time, would do more of what we are paid to do. We have seen what takes up so much time, seducing us away from what we should be doing. High on the list are the brief contacts, queries and the mundane day-to-day tasks. We get trapped into attempting to control failures when we should be monitoring progress. Too often we are no more than 'visiting firemen'. It would be nice to do the 'coping' at the start instead of trying to cobble it all together at the last moment (*see* Table 12.6).

Table 12.6 *Comparison of unplanned and planned use of time*

PUT THE LAST FIRE OUT		PUT THE NEXT FIRE OUT	
PLAN	ORGANISE	MONITOR PROGRESS	ACHIEVE

Elapsed time $\longrightarrow$

Textbook stuff? Not possible in the real world? Return to the beginning of this chapter and start again. And do it in the firm's time, too.

Seriously though, instant solutions are not available; offers of a panacea for saving time are mere quackery. But we have to start somewhere, on the little things.

Planning checklist

1 Set long-term objective.
2 Gather facts (opinions, feelings) relevant to the long term.
3 Sort out the facts into various appropriate headings.
4 Figure out the relationships, and the priorities, between the elements.
5 Draw up more than one long-term plan.
6 Try to forecast (this means 'guess'!) the probable outcome of each plan.

7 Select the plan that most closely fits the long-term objective.
8 Set each short-term objective in turn.
9 Gather facts (opinions, feelings) relevant to the short-term.

Long-term can be five years or one week; short-term can be one year or one day.

What to plan for?

There are some things we can't plan for: changes in legislation; breakdowns; delivery failures; industrial trouble in other organisations. These have to be coped with. But we can plan the mundane elements – the routine. We need to rid ourselves of the notion that 'routine' is merely 'boring'. It requires rational redefinition. The first key concept is its repetitive nature. Redefine it as 'regular' or 'recurrent' to take the nasty taste away.

The second key concept is that routine is 'necessary': the trouble here is that the word often goes into the phrase 'necessary *evil*'.

Routines were invented in the first place to ensure success of the total enterprise. For all the statements of objectives, the job descriptions and the checklists, the rule books and manuals of procedure, it is what we *do* that turns the dream into reality. Routines help us, step-by-step, to reach our goal. They are recurrent: they are therefore predictable. So they can be planned.

The common purpose

When each team member is doing his or her bit, that effort added to all the others, combines to take us on our way. It is the common purpose we are all going after that lends dignity to the process. We will know we're getting somewhere when the manager is purely accountable, i.e. when all the *others* in the team are responsible. It is then the manager's privilege to generate the activities of the rest, and to support them in what they are doing.

Time wasters are universal. Devices for saving time tend to be personal. Here are a few collected from life. Pick out and use any that appeal to you.

Example

In deciding which receptionists to keep on beyond their initial probationary period, supervisors in an international airline graded individuals by, amongst other factors, what the staff actually did on reporting for duty at the start of a shift. The 'good' ones got in early, took up their positions at the check-in desks, replenished the pigeon-holes with destination labels, filled the stapler, read through the daily list of flights, and the list of expected VIPs. The 'rejects' habitually got in dead on time, were never really ready for the customers and spent the whole 7½ hours in a state of barely controlled fluster, making too many uncorrected mistakes as they went along.

Example

The optician's assistant who could 'never find anything' was helped by one of the patients – a carpet layer by occupation – who advised her to put things down where they can be seen easily: light things on dark surfaces, dark on light.

Example

An office manager refers to the whole of the top surface of her desk as her in-tray. If it is clear, she feels free to patrol other offices, keeping in touch, helping individuals. Each of the drawers, too, has a specific purpose. The top right-hand one she uses as her out-tray. Her secretary, or any of her staff, can – without interrupting her on the telephone, or in a meeting with a visitor – empty this drawer. This is particularly useful when she has some unfinished task in there which someone else can take over while she deals with lengthy interruptions. Papers for the day's meetings, extracted from a brought-forward system, are placed each morning in another drawer reserved for the purpose. There is a drawer to tidy away all the little things: pens and pencils; paperclips; odd foreign stamps. The telephone, and the boss's intercom, are on a side table which has a shelf carrying a dialling code booklet and the manager's 'blue book'. This is a loose-leaf binder with all kinds of items connected with the job and the firm. Plans of how to get there, internal extensions and names, accountability chart, home telephone numbers of key personnel, last year's report and accounts are some of these items.

Example

Using a similar concept, a personnel executive at a major computer manufacturing company is able to appear to accomplish many things at once. People peering around his half-open office door can tell at a glance, by whether he keeps his head down or looks up, if they can interrupt him at that instant.

Example

An overseas director worked out with her secretary a flexible weekly timetable which is outlined below. Tuesdays and Thursdays were kept for booked appointments and meetings. Monday afternoons, she tended to withdraw to think. Wednesdays she tried to stay in the office doing tasks she didn't mind being taken away from – she was amenable to unplanned interruptions. Friday afternoon was the only time she would sign expense claims. (She wouldn't be drawn about Monday mornings, or Friday mornings for that matter!)

Table 12.7 *Example of a weekly timetable*

M		Thinking
T	Appointments and meetings	
W	Open door	
Th	Appointments and meetings	
F		'Authority'

Example

An insurance executive imagines large projects as slices of Gruyere cheese, into the 'holes' of which (short periods of waiting time during which he would be held back from the main job) he fits little bits of work.

13 A GUIDE TO EMPLOYMENT PRACTICES

The employment function

Every organisation will have an employment policy, whether this has been formulated deliberately or is implicit in the actions taken and attitudes adopted. Where there is little co-ordination, that policy may vary from department to department and create frustration and resentment. Employment policy, as for every other aspect of management, should be considered, agreed and implemented with care, to ensure consistency of action and approach.

Some of the questions that should be considered are as follows:

1 What kind of people do we wish to attract to the company? Are we interested in those who are looking for long-term careers, those who wish to widen their experience and then move elsewhere, or plodders who will carry out the more routine jobs conscientiously and competently but who do not seek, and are not capable of, more demanding assignments? If our need varies, have we thought out carefully what attributes each job requires?

2 What kind of salary structure is best fitted to meet our needs? Does this build in adequate recognition of individual effort? Do we aim to pay the average rate for our district and industry and will this enable us to recruit the right type of employee? Would it be economic to pay over the odds to attract higher calibre staff? Have we other attractions to offer so that a lower than average rate would be sufficient? What can we afford?

3 Can we, as far as we can foresee, offer relatively stable employment? Is this our aim, even if it means suffering some strains at a time of recession so that we may retain the skills and knowledge we have built up among our employees?

4 Do we believe that everyone, both staff and manual workers, should have the opportunity to develop his or her fullest potential? What if we cannot see a continuing progressive career for some?
5 Have we made it clear that there shall be no discrimination on grounds of sex, marital status or race? How do we ensure that this does not take place at any level of the organisation?
6 Are our working patterns too rigid or sufficiently flexible? Do we insist on a full day's standard hours or have we considered whether part-time work, shorter hours, flexitime, job sharing, etc., with the wider range of staff they attract, would contribute to, rather than reduce, our efficiency?
7 Are we willing to be committed to informing our employees about all matters that affect their work directly? What about indirect issues? How far and about what are we prepared to consult them?

Centralisation of responsibility

Whatever the size and structure of the unit and however much responsibility has been delegated, staffing arrangements – recruitment, transfers, promotions and dismissals – should be co-ordinated centrally, either by a specialist personnel department where circumstances call for this, or by a nominated senior member of management. The person or people concerned should have duties and authority clearly defined and know that they have the backing of top management in carrying them out.

Central co-ordination of this kind results in better human resource planning over the organisation as a whole. This in turn leads to:

- more efficient recruitment with consequent reduction in costs
- better career planning and development of staff resulting in a well motivated workforce and reduced labour turnover
- the establishment of policies and procedures which are applied consistently across the organisation.

Establishing staffing requirements

When future plans are considered and agreed, much time is spent in assessing a wide range of influences that will affect their viability. Technical and marketing considerations, finance and the like, are recognised as key factors in the success of the developments foreseen. Staffing requirements, though equally vital, are not always established nor are steps invariably taken to ensure that there are sufficient people with the right skills available at the right time.

If expansion is in mind, it seldom proves satisfactory to recruit large numbers of people at short notice and the problems can be very considerable, as:

- there may be insufficient people with the right skills in the local labour market, especially if a knowledge of new technology is called for
- recruitment standards tend to fall in the pressure to fill impending vacancies speedily
- rates of pay may have to be increased artificially if sufficient labour is to be attracted
- the recruitment of any substantial number of new employees makes it difficult to integrate them quickly or to give them adequate help in reaching a satisfactory standard
- supervisors will spend an undue amount of time looking after the new recruits to the neglect of other important aspects of their duties
- the higher turnover always found among those in the first weeks of their employment can lead to continuing disruption and low morale.

At times, technological change or a contraction of business may mean that fewer employees will be required or that the nature of the jobs will change over the years. Redundancies have very serious implications for the individual; they can also prove very costly for the employer. Here too, intelligent anticipation means that alternative options can be worked out and implemented while there is still time.

Some form of staffing planning in this area is therefore an essential of forward-looking management. While there are now many sophisticated methods and complicated formulae which can be used to calculate future supply and demand, there are a number of relatively simple steps which can be taken by those who do not wish or are not able to go into detail. The results will never be totally accurate whatever the method used. They should, however, provide a useful indicator to the position to be expected so that steps can be taken to overcome the main problems.

1 Analysis of the staffing requirements of the corporate plan

Nearly all organisations will have agreed plans for the future although the degree of formality, the detail incorporated, and the length of time covered will vary from one to another. Even those on contract work or whose output is greatly affected by external factors which change constantly and over which they have little control will try to foresee their overall pattern of development.

Current performance levels will show the numbers and jobs necessary to fulfil these plans if everything remains as it is. Future change, however, is inevitable and some of the factors which will affect the workforce are:

- changes in the nature of the product or service itself
- changes in the quality standards required
- changes in technology, materials, working methods and systems
- changes in the organisational structure of the company
- changes in the pattern of working hours, e.g. increased shift-working
- changes required to comply with UK or European legislation
- predicted national or local labour shortages in certain skills or categories
- market opportunities created by the European Community.

2 Calculation of potential resources

An analysis of those currently employed will probably exist already, but where not available this should be undertaken. Accurate information is essential and if your records are computerised, it will be easier to maintain an up-to-date database showing the profile of the workforce by skills and age.

3 Calculation of labour turnover

Before any meaningful staff planning can be carried out, it is essential to calculate the labour turnover. This can be done by using the standard formula to measure the separation rate:

$$\frac{\text{Number of leavers during the year}}{\text{Average number of employees during the year}} \times 100$$

Another formula which can be used in conjunction with the separation rate is one which shows the stability rate, i.e. the number of employees who are being retained. This is calculated as follows:

$$\frac{\text{Number of employees with 12 months' service or more}}{\text{Number employed a year ago}} \times 100$$

These two formulae should give an indication of the general level of labour turnover, although it may vary somewhat with economic changes or if, for example, there were a large intake of new labour.

Where labour turnover is at an unacceptable level, this should be tackled as early as possible for it is very costly. The number of leavers should be examined in meaningful units, for it is only by highlighting an excessive turnover in, for example, a particular department or a specific age group that the problem can be identified. The whole background can then be carefully examined to determine what has gone wrong and how far this can be remedied.

It is useful for employees who are leaving the company to be interviewed by a member of management or of the personnel department to ascertain their reason for leaving. It should, however, be borne in mind that some employees may be reluctant to offend or imply criticism of those for whom, or with whom, they work. On the other hand, they may be quick to see faults where few in practice exist. Careful interviewing and the exercise of good judgement is necessary when carrying out this exercise if the areas of dissatisfaction are to be discovered.

Some of the areas which should be examined in cases of high labour turnover are:

- the recruitment process, including the sources of recruitment and methods of selection
- the induction of new employees
- training given and promotion prospects
- financial rewards and employee benefits, in particular the way in which these recognise personal merit and their relevance to different sections of the workforce
- supervision given, whether this is too authoritarian, lax or inappropriate to the people controlled
- job content and the opportunity it gives for satisfaction to those engaged on it
- communication and consultation and the sense of involvement in the organisation that these should bring
- physical working conditions
- departmental efficiency.

Once the problem has been identified, steps should be taken to rectify it.

4 Planning for expansion

The first step is to establish exactly what the requirements are by numbers and skills and then consider:

- to what extent these can be met by existing resources
- what training and development is required to enable existing employees to acquire the necessary skills
- whether there is a pool of suitable labour available in the area
- what steps need to be taken to recruit staff from outside the immediate area if necessary
- what training for new employees will be required and how long it will take.

The more thought and planning that goes into this kind of operation, the more successful it is likely to be.

5 Handling cutbacks

Any situation that could lead to cutbacks in the workforce should be handled with care and sensitivity as redundancies can be extremely damaging both to the individuals affected and the morale of the remaining workforce.

Accurate forecasting should enable reduced demand for products or services to be identified at an early stage so that redundancy can be avoided or at least reduced by stopping recruitment and allowing the numbers to reduce by natural wastage. The value of a redundancy policy will be recognised in these circumstances as it will provide a framework within which to operate and reduce the risk of unfair practices.

Should redundancies become inevitable there are certain legal requirements to be followed, including consultation with any recognised trade union and notification of the Secretary of State for Employment within certain time limits. It is important to check all the legal requirements relating to redundancy and ensure that they are followed, as failure to do so could result in employees bringing successful claims before an industrial tribunal. Employees should be informed of forthcoming redundancies as early as possible and the method of communication should be planned to ensure that all those involved are told simultaneously.

The provision of early retirement on attractive terms may ease the problem of large-scale redundancies, as many people may volunteer for this option. The availability of a counselling service may also help people to adjust to the situation, particularly long-term employees.

In the event of a closure or relocation of a business or department, where it is important to retain employees to the end, it may be necessary or desirable to offer a bonus payment to those who do not leave before the appointed date.

Recruitment and selection

Agreeing establishments

It is obviously essential to keep a tight control of the number of staff in each department and staff establishments should be specified, based on the corporate plan and the annual budget.

Procedures should be set up for reviewing staff establishments, e.g. when major changes occur, and ensuring that no additional staff are taken on without proper authorisation.

Job descriptions

Once a vacancy has been agreed it is important to have a detailed description of the duties to be undertaken so that the full requirements and responsibilities of the post are clearly understood by the interviewer. Job descriptions have a variety of uses – for job evaluation, training, career planning and the like – and each use will carry its own special emphasis. As far as recruitment is concerned the following information should be included:

- job title, grade or salary, department
- hours of work
- place in the organisation structure – to whom responsible
- number and job titles of subordinates
- objectives of job
- main responsibilities and tasks
- occasional tasks or special responsibilities
- working conditions.

However carefully the description has been drawn up, it may become inaccurate as the months pass. It should therefore be checked at regular intervals, and especially when a vacancy is to be filled, to make sure that there have been no variations.

Person specifications

Once the job is established, the next step is to get a profile of the right person to fill the post. In the event, the 'right' one may not necessarily be the ideal one for we often have to compromise in recruitment standards. Accordingly , the requirements may well be divided into two sections – essential and desirable – so that it is clear where it is possible to be flexible and where a given qualification cannot be varied.

A very common framework for the specification is one based on the seven point plan recommended by the National Institute of Industrial Psychology. This covers the following areas (p. 234).

- *physique* – health and appearance, including age if relevant
- *attainments* – education, qualifications, experience, etc.
- *general intelligence* – including ability to benefit by training, and apply knowledge
- *special aptitudes* – manual dexterity, numeracy, etc.
- *interests* – which may reveal strengths and aptitudes
- *disposition* – acceptability, reaction to stress, initiative, motivation
- *circumstances* – mobility, ability to work irregular hours, etc.

The details should be given in specific and not in general terms for such phrases as 'a good education' will be interpreted in different ways.

Sources of recruitment

Internal sources

All vacancies should be advertised internally before or at the same time as they are advertised externally. Filling a vacancy internally makes good use of existing knowledge of the organisation and its methods of operation as well as possibly saving the expense of external recruitment. It also shows employees that they are given first consideration and every opportunity to widen their experience within the organisation.

External sources

The following is a list of external sources which may be used when recruiting staff:

- advertising – newspapers, journals, notice boards, television, radio, cinema, careers publications, house-to-house distribution of leaflets
- job centres, careers officers, disablement resettlement officers
- schools, colleges, polytechnics, universities and other educational bodies
- employment agencies, recruitment consultants
- ex-service organisations
- professional bodies and trade unions
- organisations connected with groups with special problems – the blind, deaf, ex-prisoners, etc.

- ex-employees
- casual inquiries and applicants who have previously applied to the organisation.

Applicants will be attracted to a company if they know something worthwhile about it beforehand. Try to maintain general interest throughout the year by arranging school visits, work experience schemes, holding open days. Get write-ups of special functions, interesting contracts and personal achievements into the local press. Develop contacts with local organisations, education authorities, employment and other committees.

Advertising

Advertising is a very costly exercise so it is important to choose methods and media wisely and to monitor costs and results. Time, too, is expensive so that the advertisement itself should be designed to discourage those manifestly unsuitable and make the selection process less onerous. To get the most effective advertisement, consider the following points.

- Choose the most suitable papers carefully. Study past experience or take advice from an advertising agency. Balance the value gained overall from the national press (the most expensive), the specialist journals (a little less so), and the local papers which normally carry lower charges.
- Decide on the presentation – single or double column, display, semi-display, run on. Give thought to the layout, making quite sure that the job title itself is given full prominence. Where jobs are many and potential applicants few, economy on space can respresent a false saving though there may well be a maximum effective size.
- Give as much important detail as practicable without overloading the space available and taxing the readers' patience. Always indicate the salary range unless this presents an insurmountable problem or is genuinely negotiable.
- Avoid meaningless generalisations such as 'good working conditions', 'an attractive starting salary', etc.
- Remember that not everyone will know of your organisation, what its business is, whether it is a large unit offering good

career prospects or a smaller one with all the advantages of a friendly, close-knit working group. Give some general indication of the background.

● Make it clear what action the applicant should take – call for an interview, telephone for a form, or write a letter of applications. State if there is a date after which application will not be considered.

Presentation of advertisements

Advertisements will be noticed and read by a wide range of people, including those who are not actively seeking work. It is important therefore that they reflect the right company image.

To be effective, an advertisement needs to give a clear description of the job, the type of person required (with particular reference to experience and qualifications) and the salary and benefits package offered. Care must be taken to ensure that the wording of any advertisement does not imply that the company will discriminate against any applicant on the grounds of race, sex or marital status. Employers should also guard against indirect discrimination in the method of recruitment they adopt, e.g. by advertising in papers which have a readership predominantly of one sex or race.

Agencies which specialise in recruitment advertising will usually handle business without charge to an employer as they receive commission from the newspapers and journals on the space they reserve for clients.

Monitoring effectiveness

The effectiveness of each advertisement should be checked by recording:

● the cost of each advertisement
● the total number of applicants from each advertisement
● the number of short-listed applicants from each paper
● the source of recruitment of the successful applicant.

Recruitment officers should also be aware of:

● the most effective position and layout of advertisments
● the best day of the week to advertise.

Making a shortlist

Unless the response to an advertisement is very small, it is not practicable to interview all the candidates. A comparison of the job description and person specification with the applications will show who are strong contenders and who do not warrant consideration. The criteria for shortlisting should be spelt out carefully so that there is no basis for a subsequent claim for discrimination at this stage. The use of an application form will ensure that comparable details have been taken into account and no important information inadvertently omitted.

Arranging the interview

When applications have been received:

- acknowledge all letters promptly
- consult with other staff involved in the appointment
- arrange interviews as soon as possible so that those who appear suitable do not lose interest or accept other appointments (remember that yours is unlikely to be the only vacancy for which they have applied)
- make sure that anyone else who will be invited to take part in the follow-up interview will be available at the time suggested and has seen the relevant correspondence
- try not to be too rigid about interview times, remembering that junior staff may well find it embarrassing to take time off and that senior staff will often have other commitments which they must honour.

The interview

Much has been written about the employment interview, and rightly so, for bad selection can have far-reaching results. Moreover, recruitment is a very expensive business and a single replacement may involve an expenditure of several hundred pounds if all the direct and indirect costs are taken into account.

The interviewer's objective is to assess the suitability of the applicants and select the right candidate. To do so it is essential that he or she knows and understands all the details of the job in question.

Before the interview, the interviewer should study the job description, person specification and application form and make a list of any points to be clarified or followed up at the interview. The interviewer should also prepare a list of questions to ensure that nothing important is overlooked.

Use of tests

Various tests have been devised as an aid to selection but these should:

1 be administered only by someone trained in their use and interpretation
2 always be supplemented by a face-to-face interview
3 be evaluated and checked against the ongoing performance of those appointed.

The most usual tests are those to assess job performance (and these can more easily be given by an amateur) or to determine intelligence, special aptitudes or personality. An allowance should be made for any distortion caused by the candidate's nervousness, origin in a different culture, or by any facility gained by those who are accusomted to this form of testing.

Interview assessment form

Many companies use a special assessment form so that interviewers are obliged to record their impressions immediately in a standard way enabling a comparison to be made between applicants factor-by-factor. Interview assessment forms should be kept for at least six months in case any unsuccessful applicant claims they were discriminated against on grounds of sex or race.

The offer of appointment

The offer of appointment should be made as soon as possible after the decision is made, to ensure that the selected candidate is still available. Once a verbal offer has been made and accepted, a legal contract exists. However, all offers of employment should be confirmed in writing setting out the terms and conditions relating to the appointment. Appointments may be subject to satisfactory references and medical examination and both of these should be cleared quickly so that the applicant does not resign from one job only to find that the offer of another has been withdrawn.

Statement of terms and conditions of employment

A written statement of terms and conditions of employment must be given to all employees who work for 16 hours a week or more, within the first 13 weeks of employment. (Similarly a statement must also be given to those who work for eight hours a week or more and have over five years' service.) These statements must contain the following information:

- the name of both parties involved
- job title
- date of commencement of employment
- original date of commencement where this is different, e.g. where an employee has transferred from another part of the same company or associated company
- rate of pay and method of calculation; the interval of payment
- hours of work and conditions relating to overtime
- holiday entitlement and holiday pay, both annual and public
- sick pay and rules on sickness absence
- details of pension arrangements, if any, and whether they are contracted out of SERPS
- the length of notice required on either side
- disciplinary rules and procedures and the person to whom an employee may appeal in the case of disciplinary action
- the person with whom a job grievance may be raised and the procedure to be followed.

Reference may be made to other documents, e.g. collective agreements, employee handbooks, pension fund booklets, etc. If individual copies of these documents are not provided they must be reasonably accessible and the employee should be told where they can be inspected.

Although by law, written particulars of the terms and

conditions of employment may be given to the employee up to 13 weeks after the commencement of employment, it is preferable to provide these at the time the offer is made as this prevents misunderstandings at a later date.

Employee handbook

An employee handbook is an invaluable medium for telling employees about the organisation which they have joined and for setting out the main conditions of employment and rules to be observed. If numbers are small and money limited, it need not be an elaborate publication. It should, however, be carefully thought out and friendly in tone.

In addition to the terms and conditions of employment, the handbook should contain background information about the organisation – its history, products and structure – and more detailed reference to any employee benefits mentioned in the statement of terms.

Information should also be given about other benefits – staff restaurant, medical services, long service awards, etc. It should also contain any company policies, rules and procedures, particularly the company's disciplinary procedure, so that these are as widely known as possible.

Work rules

If there is no employee handbook, these rules should either be issued individually or brought to the attention of employees in some other way, e.g. by posting them on notice boards. If the latter, these should be in a central position which everyone will pass, and be well lit and uncluttered so that the essentials stand out clearly. As people often do not read notices on notice boards, however, the rules should also be discussed in some other forum, particularly during induction.

References

Opinions vary about the value of references, especially personal ones, but they do at least serve to confirm the facts that the candidate has given. In routine jobs they may well do little but highlight any special ability and qualities; they may also, by their silence, draw attention to certain limitations. References for senior members of staff, however, can be more revealing for they may discuss more fully the extent of responsibilities and mention any special achievements and growth in knowledge and ability while with the company.

References may ask for answers to direct questions: job title, dates of joining and leaving, ability and conduct, timekeeping and attendance. Those asking open-ended questions will give more opportunity for the referee to bring in aspects of the applicant's experience and qualifications which are believed to be important. Nevertheless, where organisations are completing references for large numbers of staff, this kind of answer may also become automatic. If there is any doubt about a point, or a more informal opinion would be valuable, it is helpful to telephone the person to discuss the backgrond.

There is no compulsion on employers to give references but these are *privileged* documents and there can be no successful action for libel if the information was given without malice and was believed to be true at the time. Claims, however, can be made by the new employer if loss was caused by a misleading statement.

Personnel records

The importance of adequate and meaningful personnel records is now widely accepted. A good and well-maintained system is essential for:

- planning future labour force requirements
- wage and salary administration
- pension administration
- training and development
- administering sick pay and controlling absenteeism
- producing government statistics
- providing management information.

Employee details

Records should provide information which show the individual's career pattern and provide details on which statistical information can be based. They should therefore cover:

- personal details: name, address, telephone number, marital status, ethnic origin, whether registered disabled
- educational and professional qualifications
- records of posts held with dates and salary progression
- training received.

Computerised records

Computerised records, which are becoming more and more common, have obvious advantages, particularly when it comes to producing statistical information. However, when introducing computerised personnel records for the first time, it is essential that a careful analysis is carried out first to determine the needs of the organisation and personnel staff should be closely involved in this. Care should be taken to ensure that the system selected meets these identified needs.

Data Protection Act

The Data Protection Act 1984 gives employees the right to request a copy of any information about them that is held on computer. This includes any opinions that are recorded, but not intentions. Employers must comply with a written request to supply information within 40 days of receipt. Employees may have any inaccuracies amended and claim compensation for any damage caused by inaccurate information, loss of personal data or unauthorised disclosure. The provisions of the Act do not extend to manual records or to computer records which are held for payroll purposes only.

Manual records

Manual systems should be chosen to suit the needs of the organisation and should be flexible enough to cope with future change. They should be convenient to use, easy to update and avoid duplication of information. A number of companies specialise in the supply of personnel systems and records and are usually prepared to adapt their printed forms to suit the needs of the customer.

Application forms

A carefully designed form will help in the initial screening of job applicants and ensure that answers are given, in an agreed order, to key questions. It will also provide the basis for an employee's file.

The contents of the form can be many and varied but should concentrate on those things which have bearing on recruitment. Personal questions which may cause embarrassment are always best avoided and left to be raised at an interview if one is arranged.

Sufficient space for the answers is important. Senior staff in particular may be given the opportunity to expand their views on certain topics or to answer more open-ended questions. As in the case of advertisements, the form will give an impression of the standards and status of the company to a wide range of people and care should be taken over the wording and layout. The quality of the paper and printing will also make an impression.

Confidentiality

The confidentiality of personnel records has long been recognised and access should be strictly limited to those authorised to use them.

Policies

There are a number of policies and procedures which are either required by law or, if they are not statutory, are nevertheless desirable for the promotion of good employee relations. The main policies and procedures which should be considered are as follows.

Health and safety policy

Chapter 14 explains the requirements for a health and safety policy.

All health and safety policy statements should spell out the employees' responsibility for their own health and safety and that of other employees and/or visitors to the workplace and their duty to co-operate with management in ensuring that all health and safety requirements are complied with.

Health and safety policies should be regularly reviewed and updated.

Equal opportunities policy

The Codes of Practice issued by the Commission for Racial Equality and the Equal Opportunities Commission recommend that employers should draw up an equal opportunities policy which should be communicated to all employees. Most equal opportunities policies:

- state the organisation's commitment to the principle of equal opportunity
- undertake not to discriminate against any employee or applicant on account of race, colour, sex or marital status, in terms of recruitment, training and development, or promotion
- identify a senior manager with overall responsibility for seeing that the policy is carried out
- emphasis the responsibility of all levels of management and supervision to ensure that the policy is adhered to
- remind employees of their responsibility not to discriminate against or induce others to discriminate against other employees or job applicants on account of race, colour, sex or marital status
- state the procedures for monitoring and reviewing the effectiveness of the policy on a regular basis.

Redundancy policy

This should preferably be drawn up when there is no imminent risk of redundancy occurring. While it is management's responsibility to initiate the policy, recognised trade unions should be consulted about its provisions and if possible assist in drawing it up. A redundancy policy should contain:

- a general statement of company philosophy on redundancy and the measures to be adopted to avoid it
- criteria for selection

- procedures to be followed
- details of compensation.

Retirement policy

It is no longer legal to have different retirement ages for men and women. Companies should inform all their employees what the normal retirement age is, whether or not retirement is compulsory at that age and if not, the conditions for continuing to work beyond normal retirement age.

Extended leave policy

Some companies, especially those with large numbers of employees who originate from overseas, receive frequent requests for extended leave of absence to visit friends or relatives abroad. In these circumstances it is advisable to draw up an extended leave policy so that such requests are dealt with on a fair and equitable basis.

The policy should apply to all employees, regardless of their sex, age, nationality or country of origin. It should state the maximum period of extended leave that will be granted, whether it is paid or unpaid and any conditions, such as length of service, required to qualify for it. It should also state the permitted frequency of applications, e.g. not more than once every three or five years. The policy should also state who has the authority to grant extended leave, the procedure for applying for it and the penalties for failure to return on the appointed date.

It should be noted that automatic dismissal of an employee who fails to return from extended leave on the agreed date is likely to be found unfair by an industrial tribunal. Similarly, doctors' certificates from overseas should not be disregarded. A thorough investigation should be carried out to ascertain the full facts of the case before any disciplinary action is implemented.

Termination of employment

Periods of notice

The Employment Protection (Consolidation) Act 1978 lays down minimum periods of notice on each side which must be given to terminate employment.

For the employer:

- not less than one week for an employee with more than four weeks' and less than two years' continuous service
- not less than two weeks' for an employee who has more than two years' and less than three years' continuous service
- one additional week's notice for each additional year of service up to a maximum of 12 weeks' notice for 12 years' continuous service or more.

For the employee:

- one week's notice if they have four weeks' service or more.

These are minimum periods laid down by statute and do not preclude employers from making their own contractual arrangements with their employees, providing they are not less favourable than those stipulated by the Act.

Employees who give notice

It is a wise precaution to insist that employees give notice in writing as this prevents any misunderstandings.

Employees are normally expected to work their period of notice. In certain circumstances, particularly if an employee is going to work for a competitor, the employer may wish him or her to leave immediately, in which case payment in lieu of notice must be made. If an employee requests to leave before the expiry of the notice period, the employer may agree to waive the requirement to work out the notice in which case no payment in lieu is due.

Dismissal

Under the Employment Protection (Consolidation) Act 1978 there are five fair reasons for dismissal. These are:

1 a reason related to the capability or qualifications of the employee
2 a reason related to the conduct of the employee
3 redundancy
4 that the employee could not remain in the position in which he or she was employed without contravening a statute
5 some other substantial reason of a kind to justify the dismissal of that employee.

In assessing a case for unfair dismissal, an industrial tribunal will take into account not only whether the reason for the dismissal was fair, but whether the manner in which the employee was dismissed was fair. It is therefore very important that the employer goes through all the stages of the organisation's disciplinary procedure before dismissing an employee, as failure to do so could result in the dismissal being found unfair by an industrial tribunal.

Detailed records of all points at issue and of warnings given should be kept, in case the employee brings a case for unfair dismissal. Claims for unfair dismissal must normally be made within three months of the date of dismissal and employees must have had two years' continuous service and have worked for 16 hours per week or more (eight hours or more in the case of an employee with five years' service or more).

Written statement of reasons for dismissal

Any employee with six months' service or more (to be increased to two years in the Employment Bill, going through Parliament at time of press) has the right to request a written statement of the reason or reasons for dismissal. This information must be provided within 14 days of the request and failure to do so could result in a penalty of two weeks' pay.

Termination records

Records should be kept on all employees who leave the organisation. These will be required if another employer requests a reference or if the employee reapplies to the organisation at a later date.

Termination reports should record:

- dates of joining and leaving the organisation
- job title
- rate of pay on leaving
- reports on ability, conduct, time-keeping and attendance
- whether suitable for re-engagement.

14 THE MANAGEMENT OF HEALTH AND SAFETY

Why manage health and safety?

Health and safety, like other aspects of an organisation's activities, such as production, cost control or quality assurance, need to be effectively managed if the aims and objectives of the organisation are to be realised.

The minimum aims and objectives in relation to health and safety should be to ensure, so far as is reasonably practicable, that employees and members of the public are not exposed to unacceptable risk as a result of the organisation's activities. These objectives are legal obligations under the Health and Safety at Work Act 1974.

The crucial role of managers

Although most health and safety legislation places the duty of compliance firmly on the body corporate (ie the company), this duty can only be discharged by the effective action of its managers. Time and again studies by the Accident Prevention Advisory Unit have shown that the vast majority of fatal accidents and those causing serious injury could have been prevented by management action.

1 During the period 1981–1985, 739 people were killed in the construction industry. Ninety per cent of these deaths could have been prevented. In 70 per cent of cases positive action by management could have saved lives.[1]
2 A study of 326 fatal accidents during maintenance activities occurring between 1980 and 1982 inclusive showed that in 70

---

[1] *Blackspot Construction: A study of five years fatal accidents in the Building and Civil Engineering industries:* HMSO, 1988.

249

per cent of the cases positive management actions could have saved lives.[2]

3 A study of maintenance accidents in the chemical industry between 1982 and 1985 demonstrated that 75 per cent were the result of management failing to take reasonably practicable precautions.[3]

Since 1981, although the total number of fatal injuries at work has remained more or less constant, there has been a substantial rise in reported major injuries which must give cause for concern. Combined fatal and major injury incidence rates have risen by some 31 per cent in manufacturing, 34 per cent in agriculture and 45 per cent in construction[4] and at the time of writing there is no sign that this trend has been arrested. Every year around 500 people are killed and some 400,000 accidents at work causing more than three days absence are reported to enforcing authorities. Available evidence suggests that many non-fatal accidents still go unreported.

It should not be forgotten that more people die from occupational diseases than from accidents at work.

Accidents and occupational ill health cost more than money

Every accident and case of occupational ill health involves not only a cost to the individual, family and friends in terms of pain and suffering but also financial costs borne by the individual, the employer and the exchequer. It is difficult to be precise about the costs of accidents as there is no agreed basis for calculating them, but a study in 1981[5] estimated that the resource costs in 1978/79 of occupational accidents were between £700m and £1,400m (recalculation at 1987 prices puts this figure at £1370m–£2740m) and that of prescribed industrial diseases diagnosed in 1978/79 at £56m (£109m at 1987 prices).

[2] *Deadly Maintenance: A study of fatal accidents at work:* HMSO, 1985.

[3] *Dangerous Maintenance: A study of fatal accidents in the chemical industry and how to prevent them:* HMSO, 1987.

[4] *Health and Safety Commission Report 1985–86.*

[5] P. Morgan and N. Davies, 'Costs of Occupational Accidents and Diseases in GB': *Employment Gazette*, P477 November, 1981.

DuPont[6] have recently reported that a disabling injury in the chemical industry (involving loss of at least one shift) costs $18,650. In the USA, an average chemical company with 1,000 employees could expect to have nine lost workday injuries and, given the estimated profit margin of 3.75 per cent, would need $4.5m in sales to offset these injuries.

Although the total cost of personal-injury accidents may be difficult to establish, some estimated costs in terms of damage to plant and equipment and production losses resulting from large-scale incidents have been published. For example, at Flixborough in 1974, the direct damage to the plant was estimated at £20.5m or £77m total reconstruction cost of plant and surrounding property (£77m and £290m in 1987).[7] In addition to the dreadful human toll, the direct and indirect financial consequences of the Piper Alpha disaster are likely to dwarf these figures.

There is no doubt that occupational accidents and ill health do impose substantial costs on industry, and costs are of vital importance to managers. Management of health and safety can therefore be considered as essential to an overall loss control programme.

There are other reasons why firms need to manage health and safety. The public is now increasingly aware of the interface between industry and the environment and industrialists need to acknowledge this concern. Failure to manage health and safety can have important commercial implications. An international company has so far been unable to obtain planning permission for a new plant in a particular part of the United Kingdom following a major incident in one of their chemical plants abroad. This was despite the fact that the chemicals involved in the proposed new plant bore no relation to those present in the plant where the incident occurred.

In the United Kingdom, the law requires health and safety to be managed to ensure, so far as is reasonably practicable, that employees (and non-employees) are not exposed to risks to their health and safety. A major company was recently fined £750,000

[6] *AM Paint Coatings J.*, 20 April 1987, 16.

[7] Fred a Manuele, 'One Hundred Large Losses – A Thirty Year Review of Property Damage in the Hydrocarbon-Chemical Industries', *Loss Prevention Bulletin* No. 058, August, 1984.

for failing to comply with their duties under the Health and Safety at Work Act 1974. Other costs associated with the incident ran into many millions of pounds. Small firms are often particularly vulnerable to the costs of accidents and work-related ill health. The loss of a single key worker is often more acutely felt in a small firm than in a large one; it may be harder to replace damaged plant, and the resultant higher insurance premiums may make all the difference between profit and loss.

In addition to the legal obligations on the company, individual managers have legal obligations both in terms of their positions as employees and also in their specific roles as directors, managers, secretaries or officers of the company. Failure to comply with these obligations is an offence, and indeed some managers and directors have been prosecuted under the Health and Safety at Work Act. Similarly, in incidents where the safety of the general public is affected, the actions of managers and directors and perceived failure to manage health and safety are likely to be open to public scrutiny. The public inquiries into the disasters at Zeebrugge and King's Cross are but the latest examples.

The benefits of managing health and safety

Conversely, there are real benefits to be accrued from managing health and safety. There is ample evidence[8,9] that companies which have made a conscious decision to manage health and safety have reaped positive rewards as a result of their efforts in terms of reductions in accidents and ill health, consequential claims reductions, improved compliance with the law and better working conditions. Improved standards of health and safety have spin-offs in terms of better employee relationships, lower absenteeism and increased efficiency, better public image and bottom-line profitability. It is no accident that the firms with the best safety records in the UK are often numbered amongst the most profitable.

[8] *Success and Failure in Accident Prevention:* HMSO, 1976.

[9] *Managing Safety: A Review of the Role of Management in Occupational Health and Safety by the Accident Prevention Advisory Unit of HM Factory Inspectorate:* HMSO, 1981.

Where to start

The safety policy

Section 2(3) of the Health and Safety at Work Act 1974 requires every employer (except where there are less than five employees) to prepare and, as often as may be appropriate, revise a written statement of the general policy with respect to the health and safety at work of employees and the organisation, and arrangements for carrying out that policy and to bring the statement and any revision of it to the notice of all his employees.

This written statement is generally referred to as the 'safety policy' and has a vital role to play in managing health and safety. It should be the reference document for the management of health and safety within the organisation. Advice is available on writing safety policies.[10] The basic elements are:

1 specifying objectives
2 organising to achieve the objectives
3 specifying the arrangements for carrying out the policy
4 monitoring of the effectiveness of the organisation and arrangements and the results they achieve, and revising policy accordingly.

Securing commitment and communication

Success in managing health and safety can only be achieved by having a clear corporate commitment. This commitment should not be merely words in a written document but should permeate the organisation; it is sometimes termed 'the safety culture'.

The lead must be given by the most senior executives within the company who must demonstrate that their commitment to health and safety is translated into positive action at successive levels throughout the organisation. They must ensure that health and safety has a high profile and take a personal interest in it. Without this leadership success is unlikely to be achieved.

---

[10] *Effective Policies for Health and Safety:* HMSO (3rd impression), 1986.

The Sheen Report[11] on the *Herald of Free Enterprise* capsize gave a useful exposition of the nature of duties and action expected of directors in dealing with health and safety. This theme has been continued in the Fennell Report[12] on the King's Cross Underground fire.

Once a clear lead has been established by senior managers, then middle and junior managers must also play their part. The company's rules and standards for health and safety must be observed by all staff. Subordinates soon perceive what managers regard as important and act accordingly. Managers must consistently illustrate by example that they give health and safety a high priority and not forget that, often, what a manager does not do or say is equally as important as what he does do or say. For example, a manager who walks past unguarded dangerous machinery without commenting, who fails to take action when he sees employees not wearing appropriate protective equipment or fails to take part in fire drills is implicitly accepting sub-standard conditions. This is readily perceived by the workforce who will carry on working dangerously, particularly if it makes life easier for them. Should an accident or incident occur, the manager can not then claim that the fault lay with the employees merely because they did not follow instructions.

Effective communication throughout the organisation plays a vital part in promoting the 'safety culture'. The safety representative and safety committee system should be effectively utilised as part of the communication process.

Getting organised

Who does what?

Seeking to achieve objectives in health and safety is no different to achieving production or sales targets – it requires proper organisation. Most successful organisations demonstrate the following features:

[11] *Herald of Free Enterprise* Report of Court No. 8074. Formal Investigation, paragraph 14: HMSO, 1987.

[12] Investigation into the King's Cross Underground fire: HMSO, 1988.

- Unbroken and logical delegation of duties through line management to the supervisors who operate where the hazards arise and most accidents happen.
- Identification of key personnel, accountable to top management, who ensure that detailed arrangements for safe working are drawn up, implemented and maintained.
- Definition of the roles of line and functional management. Job descriptions should identify specific roles to avoid expensive and potentially dangerous overlapping. A concern for safety and health should be seen as an essential part of good management. Job descriptions should include health and safety and be agreed with the holder of a particular job, to ensure that he understands what he has to do. It is equally important that they define the limits of a particular role. For example, responsibility for taking direct action will normally lie with line management rather than with the safety officer or adviser. The safety adviser's role will probably include monitoring the effectiveness of safety procedures and the provision of information for senior management.
- Arrangements for adequate support by relevant functional management, not only by the safety adviser, but also, according to need, by the works doctor or nurse, the works engineers, designers, chemists, and so on. Where processes involve complex, technical hazards or particular occupational health considerations, an appropriate level of specialist advice is essential. Sometimes it may be necessary to buy this in from consultants.
- Nomination of persons with the authority and competence to monitor safety performance both individually and collectively, by unit, by site or by department.
- Provision of the means to deal with failures to meet the requirements of the job as it has been described and agreed. Once a manager knows what he has to do and the means have been established for measuring what he has done, he must be held accountable for his management of safety and health in the same way as he would be for any other function. The organisation must indicate unambiguously to the individual exactly what he must do to fulfil his role; thereafter a failure is a failure to manage effectively.
- Making it known in terms of both time and money what resources are available for safety and health. The individual

must be certain of the extent to which he is realistically supported by the policy and by the organisation needed to fulfil it.

Assessing the risks

The nature of the hazards in the workplace must be identified and the related risks assessed. A good starting point is to identify the legislation applicable to the particular process or operation and then assess compliance with it. Published guidance on the legislation and on recognised standards may be consulted. The Health and Safety Executive produces a variety of publications,[13] as do the British Standards Institute, some trade associations, and safety organisations.

Sections 2, 3, 4 and 6 of the Health and Safety at Work Act 1974 can also form a useful basis for making an assessment by listing topics (e.g. systems of work, supervision, training, safe place of work, working environment) which need to be addressed.

Health risks should also be assessed to establish the adequacy of existing occupational health provisions and to identify unmet needs for expert advice. The assessment should include the prevention of occupational ill health, health aspects of job placement and rehabilitation, arrangements for first aid and treatment services and the use of the workplace as a focus for health-promotion activities.

The Health and Safety Executive has published advice on reviewing occupational health needs[14] and on essentials of health and safety at work, aimed at the smaller firm[15] which may be of particular assistance to managers.

Setting control standards

Having established the nature and extent of the hazards and assessed the risks, they should be eliminated where possible. Where they cannot be eliminated, measures need to be taken to

---

[13] Health and Safety Executive Library and Information Services Publications in Series: List July 1988.

[14] *Review Your Occupational Health Needs: Employer's Guide:* HMSO, 1988.

[15] *Essentials of Health and Safety at Work:* HMSO, 1988.

control them. The minimum control measures can be identified by reference to the legislation and recognised standards mentioned previously. The existing control measures can then be compared with the required standard and upgraded as necessary or, where they do not exist, be introduced. The control measures adopted should then be formalised into standards and procedures to enable them to be monitored. These should also cover the aspects of occupational health provision mentioned above.

Standards should be agreed in consultation with the people directly involved. A realistic approach taking account of how people actually work is required. Groups of employees often devise methods of working which are very different from those which managers believe they use. Sometimes these do not have any health and safety implications, but often they will. Where such implications are established then particular effort, mainly in time and persuasion, will be needed to convince people that a change is needed if they and their fellow workers are to be safeguarded.

Procedures must be clear, unambiguous and capable of being understood by the recipients. It is essential that they are relevant and kept up-to-date. All too often procedures do not keep pace with changes on the workshop floor and become irrelevant. Non-routine operations such as maintenance work also need to be included. Serious and fatal accidents are often associated with maintenance activities.

Although there is a general need to ensure that procedures and standards are written and adopted, it is important to ensure that both managers and employers are not overwhelmed with paperwork, as this may produce an adverse reaction.

A useful approach is to have a safety/procedure manual as a source of reference, with checklists and edited procedures for use as working documents.

Monitoring for effect

Managers are accustomed to evaluating performance against targets in their everyday work, and measurement by whatever means is an essential element in achieving stated objectives. Health and safety are no different.

The primary aim of measurement is to ensure that the standards achieved at the workplace conform as closely as possible to the objectives of the organisation. The secondary aim is to provide information to justify either a change of course or a revision of the original goals. By comparing the actual results with those originally hoped for, corrective action may be taken as necessary.

Accident incidence rates

How is health and safety performance measured? Perhaps a manager's first reaction is to look at the accident statistics for his own department or company, either in terms of total number of accidents, or incidence and frequency rates:

$$\text{the accident incidence rate} = \frac{\text{total number of reported accidents}}{\text{total number of employees}} \times 1000$$

and

$$\text{the accident frequency rate} = \frac{\text{total number of accidents (time lost} > \text{one shift or day)}}{\text{total number of man hours worked}} \times 100{,}000$$

These can then be compared over time or with the performance of others engaged in similar activities. The Health and Safety Executive publishes incidence rates for the major industrial classifications. Although accident rates are one indicator they do not tell the whole story. The unreliability of historical accident data as a guide to future performance has been recognised for years. Accident reporting criteria can be subject to influences which have nothing to do with safety performance, e.g. different individuals react differently to injuries of a similar nature, and there are geographical variations. There is no clear correlation between such measurements and work conditions, the injury potential or the severity of injuries which have occurred. Managers need to be aware of these limitations when looking at their own accident statistics and not be lulled into a misplaced sense of security merely because no accidents have been reported recently.

Safety audits

What is a realistic measurement of safety performance? Measuring means making a comparison with a standard. In health and safety terms this means making assessments of compliance with standards and procedures introduced to maintain health and safety performance with agreed objectives. Hence the importance of having standards and procedures which are clearly defined and written down, making them amenable to audit. Audits can help to assess the standard of managerial control by identifying sub-standard conditions and initiating remedial action; the achievement of good standards by managers and staff can be recognised and performance evaluated over a period.

Some companies have devised their own audit schemes involving scoring systems whereby points are awarded under various topic headings. Other companies prefer more qualitative audit systems. There is no hard and fast rule except that monitoring is necessary. What gets measured gets done. A number of proprietary health and safety monitoring schemes are now available in the UK. The benefits of any scheme, be it proprietary or in-house, are dependent upon the level of commitment by senior management and all those involved in its implementation. It is for each undertaking to determine which scheme is best suited to its needs and, in the case of proprietary systems, this involves making choices on costs and potential benefits.

Accident/incident investigation

Why investigate?

Although the majority of companies investigate accidents which involve serious injury, managers should be alert to the possibility that the difference between a serious or even a fatal injury accident and a non-injury accident can sometimes be measured in terms of inches or seconds. Relatively minor incidents may therefore require thorough investigation based on their potential to have caused injury or plant loss. The severity of the injury therefore should not be the only criterion for a thorough investigation. Accident investigation helps to identify weaknesses in safety systems or in the way they are being applied.

Managers should be aware of the concept of accident triangles which describe the approximate relationship between the numbers of fatal and major-injury accidents, lost-time accidents, property-damage incidents and near misses. The following ratios have been reported.[16]

For every one fatal/major injury:

- there were ten lost time accidents
- there were 30 incidents involving property damage
- there were 600 near misses.

Human factors

Company accident-report forms often include sections to describe the circumstances of the accident and for managers' comments. Examination of such reports often reveals phrases such as 'did not comply with instructions', 'was not paying attention' or 'injured person was careless'. Managers' comments often take the form of 'told to take more care', 'more training required' and 'guard repaired'.

There is sometimes a tendency to consider that if an accident occurs then it is more likely that the injured person was the agent of his own misfortune and only had himself to blame, or that the accident was the result of 'human error'. All too often ascribing an accident to human error is seen as sufficient explanation in itself, precluding further attempts to look for the underlying causes of that error.

It should be recognised that people do not make errors merely because they are careless or inattentive. Usually they have understandable (albeit incorrect) reasons for acting in the way they did. Most accidents have multiple causes and it is important that managers recognise this fact and look beyond the immediate cause of the injury. Invariably they will find that the incident itself was the culmination of a number of failures in management control and that the action/inaction of the individual(s) immediately involved was only the last link in the

[16] Frank E. Bird Jr and George L. Germain, *Practical Loss Control Leadership:* Institute Publishing, 1986.

chain, and that the 'human error' cause was foreseeable and therefore amenable to control. The investigation of accidents and incidents should therefore look beyond the immediate cause of the injury to the fundamental causes. By analysing the incidents in this way and categorising causes, useful information and trends can be obtained. This enables resources to be targeted effectively.

Training

Training is an essential ingredient of any successful safety policy and the lack of training is a major contributory cause in many accidents. It is perhaps the main source of human error.

Senior staff

It is particularly important to ensure that the key personnel who have special health and safety responsibilities within the organisation are properly trained. In the experience of APAU, health and safety training for managers, particularly those in senior positions, is often neglected; they are often the last people to recognise or admit to the need.

Supervisors

Similarly, supervisors have a vital role to play in ensuring health and safety yet often they receive little or no specific training. Particular regard needs to be given to the need to train them in hazard identification in order that action can be taken to remove hazards from their areas of control. Safety training should be an integral part of job training and of job specification.

New starters

New starters to any job are particularly vulnerable and likely to have accidents. All new starters need to be trained in the essentials of health and safety relevant to their work before being put in a position where they are at risk or can become a hazard to others.

Checklist

The following questions are intended as an aid to managers. They are not exhaustive but are intended to cover the main issues addressed in the text.

Where to start

- Do we have a safety policy statement? When was it last revised?
- Is it comprehensive? Does it specify the organisation (i.e. people and their responsibilities) and arrangements (i.e. systems and procedures)?
- How is the policy commitment to health and safety promoted throughout the organisation?
- How do individual managers demonstrate their own commitment?
- How is a 'safety culture' promoted?

Organisation for health and safety

- Is the delegation of duties logical and successive throughout the organisation?
- How are people made aware of their responsibilities?
- Is final responsibility accepted by the relevant director?
- Are the health and safety responsibilities of senior managers specified in job descriptions?
- How is the safety performance of managers measured? Is it an ingredient of their annual review?
- Are the roles of key functional managers clearly defined?
- How are managers made aware of the requirements of health and safety legislation relative to their own departments?
- How is compliance with legal requirements assessed?
- Has a competent assessment been made of all hazards associated with the company's activities?
- Has an assessment been made of occupational health needs?

Monitoring for effect

- Is there a comprehensive established system for monitor-

ing compliance with standards and procedures?
- Are there sufficient staff with adequate knowledge and facilities to carry out the monitoring?
- How well do we comply with the law on health and safety?
- How far have we met our own policy objectives?
- What is our own accidents and ill health record? Is it acceptable?
- What deficiencies have we identified? How are they to be remedied? What more needs to be done? Now? Within the next year?
- Are the results of monitoring made available both to the managers concerned and to senior managers?

Accident/incident investigation

- Are there clear criteria for reporting and investigating accidents and incidents?
- How well are they understood?
- How are near-miss incidents investigated?
- How far does the accident-investigation system seek to identify fundamental causes and failure in management control?
- Is information obtained from accident investiation analysed to establish trends? Do we make good use of it?

Training for health and safety

- What is the system for identifying training needs?
- Does health-and-safety training cover all levels from senior management to new entrant?
- What 'special risk' situations requiring training exist?
- Are sufficient people trained to cope?

15 ABSENTEEISM

In a climate of increasing need for economic efficiency, absence and absenteeism from work is now the focus of considerable attention. Managers need to acquire the skills to understand what kind of absence is occurring within their organisations and to devise effective methods for getting the employees back to work at the earliest date, relevant to the circumstances.

Before a company can decide if it has an absence problem it has to have information. This enables it to make judgments about the size of the problem and to decide what action should be taken to improve the situation. This chapter therefore aims to:

- investigate the costs of absenteeism to the organisation
- examine the methods of monitoring absenteeism and their costs
- identify the causes of absenteeism
- identify practical ways of reducing the level of absenteeism
- consider the legal and practical framework.

Measuring the cost of absenteeism

Before it is possible to consider or implement any policy to control absenteeism, it is necessary to consider:

- what form does it take?
- how many employees are involved?
- how much does it cost?

What form does it take?

When looking at absence, holidays are normally ignored as these are authorised. There are, however, a number of other forms that absence takes:

- sickness – certified; self-certified; suspension on medical grounds
- statutory time off
- strikes/industrial action
- special leave absence – sabbaticals
- personal/domestic
- lateness
- unauthorised/casual leave.

Absence must be measured in both terms of duration (severity) and episodes (frequency). One measure alone can be misleading, as a single calculation cannot describe the situation adequately. Most firms produce some sort of lost time rate and this method of calculation is preferred by accountants, as time can be easily costed. Frequency rates, however, are more valuable references in planning absence controls.

The three main methods of calculation normally used are as follows:

1 *Lost time rate*

$$\frac{\text{Number of days lost through absence}}{\text{Average number of employees} \times \text{working days}} \times 100$$

2 *Number of employees affected*

$$\frac{\text{Number of employees with one or more absence spells}}{\text{Average number of employees over the period}} \times 100$$

3 *Average length of absence*

$$\frac{\text{Total days lost in period of absence}}{\text{Number of spells of absence}}$$

The 'average number of employees' is taken as the average number employed over the period for which the absenteeism statistic is being calculated.

The 'average number of working days' is worked out by calculating the number of possible working days over the period for which the absenteeism statistic is being calculated.

Example:

The national absence rate of 5.05% per annum found in an Industrial Society survey, *Absence rates and control policies*, (1987) was calculated according to the following formula.

$$\frac{\text{Total number of days lost through absence during year} \times 100}{\text{Number of employees} \times 230 \text{ working days}}$$

The resulting figure is the absence rate in percentage terms. The figure of 230 working days was arrived at by the following calculation:

52 weeks × 5 working days	260 days
Less 8 statutory days	− 8 days
	252 days
Less 22 days' holiday	− 22 days
	230 days

How much does it cost?

Once the levels of absenteeism have been calculated it is possible to start considering the costs to the company. These come from a number of different sources, some of which are obvious. For example:

- the cost of sick pay schemes
- the costs of providing temporary cover
- increased overtime costs
- loss of production.

There are, however, hidden costs which, if taken into account, amount to a considerable expense. These can include:

- increased pressure on administrative time as a result of changing rotas or administering sick pay
- increased pressure on supervisor's time
- interruption to work flow.

Few companies attempt to cost their absenteeism, but those that do normally become more concerned with controlling it. The Industrial Society did some work in the early 1970s to try to establish how much, on average, one day's absence cost. The figure that emerged was £70 per day.

Causes of absenteeism

In order for absenteeism to be controlled, it is necessary to understand why it occurs. Although sickness is generally the stated reason, there are often a number of underlying reasons which contribute to the company's problem. Long-term absences are usually due to genuine illness and should be dealt with in accordance with the procedure outlined in Appendix 29. It is the reasons for persistent short-term absences which have to be examined if major reductions in absenteeism levels are to be attained.

Each organisation will have varying circumstances and it could be a combination of reasons which are causing individuals to take time off. However, these tend to fall into three main categories:

- the company
- the individual
- the environment.

The company

Reasons for absenteeism which are related with the company are usually a result of dissatisfaction with the job or with management. Job related reasons include:

- an employee finding the job boring or repetitive
- poor organisation and inefficient systems
- lack of equipment.

Dissatisfaction with management can be as a result of it:

- being perceived as unfair
- being too autocratic

- being perceived as incompetent
- not treating employees as individuals
- being unable to make decisions
- being too aggressive
- being afraid of confrontation.

The individual

Reasons related with the individual can include:

- personality clashes with managers, supervisors or colleagues
- being incapable of doing the job
- being over-qualified for the job and therefore finding it boring or frustrating
- being unable to cope with the pressure
- being lazy or workshy.

The work environment

A problem arises in this area when absenteeism becomes part of the culture of the organisation. For example, an employee's contract of employment states that they are entitled to six week's full pay for sickness per annum and employees take this to mean that they can take this time off as a right, regardless of whether they are genuinely ill.

Variations

These factors influence absenteeism to varying degrees, depending on the individual organisation and the personalities of those involved. However, research has shown that, although the root causes of absenteeism are probably the same, the problem is more serious in certain sections of the workforce. The Industrial Society survey of 1987 found the following differences.

Regional differences

There is still something of a north–south divide in absence rates. However, the southeast has an absence rate higher than the mean and the northwest's rate is below the mean. The southwest has the lowest absence rate (2.38 per cent). The midlands (6.40 per cent), northeast (5.76 per cent), Scotland (5.44 per cent), and the southeast (5.43 per cent) are above the mean. The northwest (4.60 per cent), eastern region (3.91 per cent), Wales (3.89 per cent), and London (3.31 per cent) are below the mean.

Industry differences

The mean absence rate was lowest in the financial services sector (2.52 per cent) and highest in the transportation/communication industry (8.97 per cent). The other sectors which have low absence rates are construction (2.71 per cent), agriculture/forestry (2.93 per cent), distribution (3.91 per cent), and other services (3.23 per cent). Extraction/chemicals (4.17 per cent), and energy/water (4.29 per cent), are nearer to the average rate. Higher absence rates are found in 'other manufacturing' (6.03 per cent), and engineering (6.50 per cent).

The survey also found that the larger the organisation or the site, the higher the absence rate. The average rate with sites with 1–99 employees is 2.40 per cent. The rate increases to 5.06 per cent at sites with over 1,000 employees.

Management, staff and manual differences

In all types of absence – medically certified, self-certified, and uncertificated – manual workers are absent almost twice as much as staff, who themselves are absent almost twice as much as management. Supervisory absence fits almost exactly half-way between staff and management absence. Among manual workers, absence is greatest on Mondays.

Differences between males and females

Male staff have less medically certificated absence than females. Of female respondents in the survey, 56 per cent had an average medically certificated absence at nine or less days per year. The corresponding figure for males is 70.2 per cent.

There was also a difference in self-certificated absence. The female employees of 25.9 per cent of the respondents were absent more than seven days, while the male employees of only 17.1 per cent of the respondents were absent.

Full-timers and part-timers

In both the medically certificated and self-certificated categories, there was less absence amongst part-timers than full-timers.

Roles and functions in controlling absenteeism

In order for absenteeism to be controlled effectively, it needs to be clearly identified who has the responsibility for managing it.

One of the factors which influence an individual's decision to stay away from work is whether or not their absence will be questioned or even noticed. Direct control therefore needs to come from someone close to the employee, ideally their line manager or supervisor. The personnel department has the responsibility for ensuring that the standards of absence control required by the organisation are maintained and that the agreed procedures are implemented consistently throughout the company.

The personnel function

As a support service, the personnel department should provide line management with information to enable them to deal effectively with absenteeism. This should include:

- regularly monitoring overall absence rates to enable managers to make comparisons between their and other departments
- analysis of the causes.

Personnel departments also have a role in providing specialist advice and counselling to line managers. This can include:

- dealing with specific individuals
- looking at working practices (e.g. flexible working patterns, attendance bonuses)
- interpreting trade union agreements that control absence (e.g. possible disciplinary action if over a certain percentage)
- providing training in absence control.

The line function

As has been stated, the direct responsibility for controlling absenteeism lies with the line manager or supervisor. An employee needs to know that management are aware of absence records and that disciplinary action is taken when they are unacceptable. Managers should keep records which enable them to monitor their absenteeism and to identify any trends (e.g. higher than average absences on a Monday).

The role of the trade unions

Where there are trade unions, they should be involved in the drawing up of any procedure for dealing with absenteeism, in order to ensure their commitment. Generally, trade unions are very supportive in this area, recognising the disruption that persistent absenteeism causes to its members.

The contractual framework and ACAS guidelines

Whenever a person is employed under a contract of employment, then the employer undertakes to provide work and a salary, and the employees undertake to make themselves available for work. If an employee becomes incapacitated (temporarily or on a longer-term basis) then, in effect, there is a failure to meet these obligations. Consequently, there is a potential breach of contract. However, it is implied that the employee will be away from time to time, but once the incapacity is such that they are unable to fulfil the terms of the contract, then the employer is in a position where they are able to dismiss.

Under the legislation concerning dismissal, one of the fair reasons specified is on the grounds of capability. This can mean qualifications and mental capacity, but also includes situations where the ill-health of an employee is the reason for dismissal. There are two types of ill-health to consider:

1 long-term chronically sick employees
2 persistent short-term absences.

Long-term sickness

Long-term ill-health can be a fair reason for dismissal under the heading of capability, provided a proper procedure has been followed. This procedure cannot be a series of warnings as per the disciplinary procedure, as obviously warnings are inappropriate. However, two important cases have given guidelines on how to handle this problem. They are *Spencer v. Paragon Wallpapers* **[1976]** and *East Lindsey District Council v. Daubney* **[1977]**.

Spencer v. Paragon Wallpapers [1976] IRLR 373

Mr Spencer had been suffering from a bad back for two months when the company, who needed everyone at work, approached his doctor to see when he would be fit to return to work. The doctor indicated that it would not be for another four to six weeks. In view of this and the fact that the company had operational needs, Paragon decided to dismiss Mr Spencer. This dismissal was found to be fair because, in these particular circumstances, the employer could not be expected to wait any longer.

The implications here are, that if you have an employer doing an exclusive job, then there will be a fairly immediate effect on your productivity if they are absent. You therefore have a greater capacity to dismiss than if they are one of many.

East Lindsey District Council v. Daubney [1977] IRLR 181

Mr Daubney was a surveyor and on 29 April 1975 he suffered a mild stroke and remained certificated sick until 30 September 1975. In July 1975, the Personnel Director asked the District Community Physician to indicate whether he felt that Mr Daubney's health was such that he should be retired on grounds of permanent ill-health.

After an examination, it was reported that he should be retired and so Mr Daubney was dismissed. At no point was Mr Daubney consulted and, although efforts had been made to seek medical advice, both the Industrial Tribunal and the Employment Appeals Tribunal (EAT) felt that this was only part of the story.

They felt that discussions and consultations should have taken place, as these will often bring to light facts and circumstances of which the employer was unaware and which will throw new light on the problem. It may also be possible that the employee wishes to seek medical advice on his or her own account which, brought to the attention of the employer's medical advisers, will cause them to change their opinions. The dismissal was therefore found to be unfair.

A procedure for dealing with long-term absence through ill-health which takes these findings into account and follows the guidelines given in the ACAS advisory handbook, is given in Appendix 29.

Short-term persistent absences

This type of absenteeism is usually as disruptive as it is unpredictable. As a result, the courts have taken a different view of this type of absence and tend to consider it as a mischievous abuse of generous sick pay schemes, and therefore, a matter of conduct.

There are, again, two leading cases that set out the procedures to follow if a company is considering dismissal on these grounds. They are *International Sports Company Limited* **v.** *Thompson*, and *Rolls Royce Limited* **v.** *Walpole*.

International Sports Company v. *Thompson* [1980] IRLR 340

Mrs Thompson's doctor was given the task of certifying her absences which average 25 per cent (against the acceptable level of 8 per cent agreed with the union) and came up with 'dizzy spells, anxiety and nerves, bronchitis, virus infection, cystitis, dyspepsia and flatulence'. Over a period of nine months, she received a string of warnings but her level of absenteeism remained at 22 per cent. The company doctor was consulted but he realistically expressed the view that no useful purpose would be served by his seeing Mrs Thompson because he could see no common link between the illnesses and there was nothing that could be subsequently verified.

The Industrial Tribunal found the dismissal unfair. The company appealed to the EAT who reversed the decision.

Provided a fair review of the absences takes place and the appropriate warnings are given, an employer is justified in dismissing if absences persist.

Rolls Royce v. Walpole [1980] IRLR 340

Mr Walpole was sufficiently young and fit to play rugby regularly and yet, during his last three years of employment, his rate of absence was 44, 35 and 44 per cent respectively. On 23 September 1977, he injured his hand at rugby, causing further absence. He saw his manager on 21 October, who said that if Mr Walpole's doctor agreed, he should return to lighter duties. Before seeing his doctor, Mr Walpole played rugby again and injured his shoulder, extending his absence still more. He was dismissed.

The EAT found the dismissal fair and they coined a phrase which is used in virtually every unfair dismissal case: that it was 'within the range of reasonable responses', to dismiss.

It can be seen from these two cases that persistent absenteeism is considered much more as a disciplinary matter which has more to do with conduct than with capability. Again, the ACAS advisory handbook lays down the procedure to follow and guidelines are given in Appendix 30.

Controlling absence

In order to develop effective policies and procedures for controlling absenteeism, there are a number of areas which need to be considered. A judgement can then be made as to whether they are appropriate for inclusion into the organisation's overall strategy. These include:

- questioning the employee on their return to work
- counselling
- offering attendance bonuses
- reorganising working time
- the procedure for first reporting absence
- harmonisation of sick pay schemes
- use of the disciplinary procedure
- publication of absence statistics
- visiting the absentee.

Questioning the employee on return to work

This should be a key step in any absence control procedure. The fact that the interview takes place shows the employee that the company is concerned with the individual and that their absence has been noted. This should discourage those that were not genuinely sick from taking time off in the future.

This interview is also an opportunity for the manager or supervisor to discover any underlying reasons for the absence. Care must, however, be taken that these interviews do not become a formality and their effectiveness needs to be monitored regularly.

In a large organisation with a medical department, it may be appropriate for the employee to be seen by the staff sister. The advantage of this is to give the employee a chance to provide additional information that they were unable or unwilling to give to their manager or supervisor. This is particularly relevant when it is the management that is at the root of the problem.

This procedure should not, however, take away the responsibility for absence from line management. It should be viewed as an additional resource in the management of absence.

Counselling

If an employee has a problem, whether at home or at work, he or she is more likely to take time off. If the company is able to offer counselling or advice through an employee assistance programme, they may be able to help resolve the situation.

As companies realise the effect that absenteism has on their profitability, they are beginning to offer additional services to their staff. In some organisations this includes things like marriage guidance and alcohol abuse advice.

Attendance bonuses

Some companies take the view that attendance bonuses are unnecessary, as employees should not be paid twice for coming to work. Others see such payments as an effective way of maximising production or giving a high profile to the subject.

Attendance bonuses do not have to be paid in cash. Other incentives can be offered, such as additional days of holiday.

The disadvantages of paying employees these bonuses are that:

- they can be a reflection of weak management
- they can penalise the genuinely sick
- they encourage those who are genuinely sick to report to work
- the novelty tends to wear off, with subsequent claims to have the bonus consolidated into basic rates.

However successful bonus schemes do exist and there are alternative ways of applying the principle. For example, instead of paying an attendance bonus, other rewards such as productivity bonus or profit share could be withheld from employees with poor attendance records.

Re-organising working time

Introduction of flexible working hours can help to avoid casual absences. Many companies cited in IDS Study No. 301 (entitled *Flexible Working Hours*) reported that this was a major advantage. It enabled employees to have the time to go to the dentist, or to take time off to meet a relative from the station or airport, or it encouraged an employee who has overslept to come to work.

Company procedure for first reporting absence

The procedure should make it clear who they should notify that they will not be attending work and by when. Research has shown that if this is the employee's line manager or supervisor, they are less likely to feign illness than if they can get away with leaving a message with the switchboard or a colleague. If this is established as part of an agreed procedure, non-compliance can then render the employee liable to disciplinary action.

Harmonisation of sick pay schemes

The quality of sick pay schemes within organisations undoubtedly affects absence rates. Some companies feel that the introduction of harmonised schemes will lead to higher rates of absence amongst manual workers as they take advantage of the improved entitlements. Introduction of such schemes has therefore been accompanied by tighter absenteeism controls and, where possible, involved the unions.

However, the answer to the control of absenteeism is more likely to lie in finding out the underlying reasons and motivating the staff than in examining sick pay schemes.

Disciplinary procedure

The disciplinary procedure can be invoked when dealing with short-term persistent absenteeism. However, this should be done in accordance with the guidelines given in Appendix 30.

Some companies have devised formal definitions of unacceptable absence that act as trigger points for taking action. These are useful for two reasons:

- they guide supervisors and line managers as to when warnings should be issued
- application of the disciplinary procedure is consistent.

Publishing absence statistics

The advantage of publishing absence statistics is that it illustrates to employees that absence is taken seriously. The aim is to impress upon employees that their attendance affects the companies productivity and profitability.

Absence statistics can be presented in graph form and pinned to the wall in departments or issued at departmental or briefing group meetings. The key to success is to present the information in a way that is meaningful to the target audience.

Visiting the absentee

Several studies have shown that visits to the employee at home can have a marked effect. The way in which the visit is done, however, is important, as the impression can easily be given that the company is spying, giving rise to resentment of the system. Any policy on sick visiting must, therefore, be applied consistently and include clear guidelines on whose responsibility it is to carry out the visit.

Although visits are usually used with the long-term sick, the effect has been shown to be more valuable if shorter absences are included in the programme.

Absence records

Accurate monitoring and recording of absences is essential to any policy of absence control. Although the actual method of recording will vary depending on the individual requirements of the organisation, the basic purposes of keeping records should be the same:

- to provide information from which to assess whether a problem exists
- to provide information from which analysis can be made of the patterns and types of absenteeism
- to ensure that action can be taken promptly when an individual has a poor record and that any procedure is applied consistently throughout the organisation.

The information required to collate absenteeism statistics can come from a number of sources, including:

- self-certification forms
- absence record cards
- medical notes and records
- statutory sick pay returns
- clock cards
- computerised records.

The 1987 Industrial Society survey found that the most common methods used for discovering absence problems were absence record cards and self-certification forms, medical forms and statutory sick pay. Less popular were computers and time checks.

However, detailed statistics cannot be produced manually without many hours of work. Companies should be looking at ways of computerising their records to enable them to produce meaningful information on absenteeism patterns. This will help to identify and then deal with problems.

The information should:

- give overall absence levels for the organisation
- categorise the reasons, i.e. sickness, maternity, industrial action
- give comparisons of absence levels between departments
- give statistics over a rolling 12 month period to identify whether absence levels are deteriorating or improving and the extent of annual, seasonal and weekly trends.

The responsibility for maintaining absence records will depend on the organisation and needs of the company. Line managers should have responsibility for controlling absenteeism within their own departments and should therefore keep records. However, if the system is computerised it might be more appropriate for the records to be compiled centrally on the basis of information received from each department. Even in this case, line managers can still keep their own records of individuals' attendance within their department.

Positive action to reduce absenteeism

Accountability

- Define who is responsible for monitoring absence.
- Ensure that line managers understand that they are responsible for controlling absence in their teams.

Interviews

- Ensure that line managers interview their employees on their return to work to determine the reasons for their absence.

Records

- Ensure that line managers keep adequate and meaningful records.
- Ensure that patterns of absence are looked at monthly and annually.

Communication

- Ensure that employees are aware that management are concerned with absence.

- Where appropriate, involve the trade union in order to build commitment to dealing with the problem.

Sanctions

- Ensure that employees understand the consequences of abusing the system.
- Be prepared to take the disciplinary route when dealing with short-term persistent absence.

16 EFFECTIVE DISCIPLINE

Objectives

What does discipline set out to achieve? Working in reverse, we will start by summarising the overall objectives of a system of rules. These could be stated as helping to achieve the objectives of:

- the organisation
- the customers
- the employees
- the public and environment
- the future.

Some of these items may well appear to be extraneous to the normal run of discipline matters, so let us develop them a little.

- *The organisation* – could include attendance, work rate, stability, profitability, presentation, public relations, etc.
- *The customer* – service, price, quality, delivery, value, presentation, etc.
- *Employees* – safety, hygiene, welfare, security, wages, etc.
- *Public* – safety (environment), social responsibility, company image.
- *The future* – research effort, long-term security, use of people's creativity, etc.

These are a few of the items which could be considered when setting out to structure a disciplinary code within an organisation. That is not to say that there must be a rule or rules for every aspect as listed, but that the effect of the code of conduct upon these items must be considered.

This is the wider aspect of what discipline sets out to achieve. The approach should be simple. It has been found to be very effective if the workforce is helped to understand the overall objectives and if the workforce knows that success in achieving these objectives affects their future security and prosperity. This is what managing a more informed workforce effectively is all about.

To be effective, a code of discipline (or law) must be seen to be fair, reasonable, logical, and easily understood, and it must be readily acceptable to the majority. To achieve this standard, people must know *why*, as well as *what*, in order to get the correct action.

There are, of course, certain legal minima which must be included in contracts of employment to satisfy such legislation as the Health and Safety at Work Act, the Employment Act and the Employment Protection (Consolidation) Act. The company's rules are drawn up to suit the specific industry, product and environment. These could be listed under the following headings:

- protection and safety – of the person, the company and its resources, products, customers and shareholders
- creation or regulation of codes of behaviour to give parameters within which people can operate to their mutual satisfaction
- outlining minimum standards which will ensure the well-being of the company and its employees
- prevention of inefficiency or losses
- presentation of the company as one of good standing in the community.

To achieve all these things, it should not be necessary to publish an enormous volume of rules; it *is* necessary, however, that everyone understands the objectives. This would indicate that good communication, maintained training, and acceptable relationships at all levels are prerequisites to good discipline.

It has already been discovered that legislation without commitment is not the key to better behaviour, but a workforce which is united in achieving its objectives has often proved successful. Be sure before you set out what your objectives really are.

Effective discipline

At this stage it becomes necessary to expand on the two types of discipline normally recognised: the accepted and the imposed.

Infringement

It should be established that there are 'penalties' for infringement of both of these types of discipline. For breaking rules or the law, one may be fined, imprisoned or suffer other forms of punitive action. For breaking accepted codes of behaviour people can be isolated or 'sent to Coventry', all co-operation save the minimum required may be withdrawn or, as once described by one supervisor, they may be 'roasted on the gridiron of public opinion'. These actions may be 'just' according to one's beliefs, but they may not always equate.

Probably the most common breach of the law is to do with road traffic legislation. A person fined heavily for speeding may not be regarded as being guilty of misconduct by his or her colleagues – indeed he or she may be given sympathy or regarded as some sort of hero. On the other hand, a blackleg, informant, or someone with really bad manners, though not technically 'guilty', can be brought under such pressure by his or her colleagues that he or she is forced to leave the organisation.

Communicating the reason

There are occasions when these two forms of discipline clearly equate. On these occasions, the person will be found 'guilty' by the law and his or her colleagues. When the accepted and the imposed are both acceptable to the majority, the rule or law is obviously considered reasonable. Thus, to be effective a rule must be considered reasonable by the majority. If it is not, it will probably become an accepted practice to break the rule. When a rule is considered unreasonable, it is not necessarily that it *is* unreasonable; it is almost certainly not understood and often considered to be restrictive.

For example, rules against smoking on an oil refinery are accepted, understood and often policed by the majority. However, rules against smoking in a foundry could be considered to be unreasonable. It may be that there *is* a reason, but unless everyone understands *why* it is almost certain to be ignored and may become the subject of grievance.

Here is an example of an apparently restrictive rule in force over the use of a grinding wheel. A young apprentice was told not to use the grinding wheel for grinding brass and copper laminate. He was not told why and, as he had discovered a way of speeding up his job, thought it was merely the foreman dreaming up restraints. As soon as the foreman's back was turned he used the wheel for this purpose. Shortly after the apprentice finished the job, a fitter used the same grinding wheel to sharpen a large high speed drill. Within seconds, the clogged-up wheel jammed on the drill and disintegrated. The result was the loss of an eye. No punishment could have brought back the eye or made the apprentice any more distraught. Between his sobs he was heard to say: 'If only he had told me why!'

Even if a rule is obvious it should be explained: if it is in any way complicated it *must* be explained.

The very best disciplinary rules should be acceptable as well as being imposed. Some would say, if it is acceptable you do not need a rule at all. However, rules are usually for the minority and some framework for conduct is necessary, if only to build standards and procedures on. At the very least, a set of *agreed* procedures should be in existence.

The rule book

When considering the effectiveness of rules, one must consider the rule book. Most organisations have a rule book or set of procedure notes – the latter amount to the same thing but might be considered slightly more democratic. What creates most problems is the needless longevity of some of these rule books. What should be considered to be the lifespan of a rule (or a law)? Obviously (though not actually) a rule should only exist if and when there is a need for it. All too often a rule once made is seldom repealed.

Added to this, there is the annual crop of additions to the rule book. These additions come about due to modern and changing technology and are often very necessary. Recognising that life is fast-moving should make it obvious that some rules cease to be necessary and, in fact, may well become restrictive due to their continued existence.

For example, a very large organisation called in a mediator when a large section of the workforce had gone on strike after a worker had been suspended for smoking in a non-smoking area. It should also be stated that a new manager had recently been appointed and had been instructed to tighten up on the seemingly slack discipline. The occurrence had taken place outside in an open space, under a very large NO SMOKING sign. There had been two previous cases and the offenders had been severely warned. At the mediation meeting, attended by the individual, his representatives, the manager and his director, the first question asked by the mediator was: 'Why is that particular place designated a no smoking area?' This was probably the last question expected and no immediate answer was forthcoming. After some debate, the meeting was adjourned with no decision, but with the workers' agreement that they would return to work while enquiries were made.

Some two days later the mediator was telephoned to be told everything was all right; the men were back, all was well. 'Why was it a no smoking area?' After a pause he was told: 'Well, in 1942 we used to store high octane fuel at that spot, so the sign was put up'. 'When did you stop storing it there?' 'Ah – well – in 1944 actually'. So for thirty odd years the sign had been repainted regularly and the reason for its being there had never been queried.

The whole rule book of that organisation was subsequently revised and eventually shrunk to less than a quarter of its original size. The amount of conflict was reduced by considerably more than that amount.

The one-sentence rule for effective discipline is – make it objective, reasonable and easily understood, and involve all those concerned with its structure and maintenance. Finally, avoid those things that will almost certainly be unacceptable and ineffective.

Rules and regulations

Acceptable rules and regulations (or at least procedure notes) are necessary if only to legislate for that minority who seem incapable of working under an accepted code of behaviour. General objectives and a few of the items to be avoided have already been discussed. It has also been observed that, for the rules to be effective, they must be acceptable, reasonable and clearly understood. Bearing these things in mind, the structuring of rules and regulations will now be discussed.

Creating a structure

Commitment of the workforce to the organisation's objectives is an old established method of getting maximum effort. Involvement and participation have been the 'in' words for a few years now. Therefore, if all levels of the workforce are involved and participate in the structure of a system of rules and regulations, maximum commitment can result, and this will give a good initial start towards acceptance and understanding.

The rules committee should include representatives from both first line management and unions, if they exist; the training department should be involved and the personnel department representative should act as either chairperson or secretary. A similarly structured group should be involved with rules revision.

Types of rules

What rules and regulations are necessary? There are two basic types for any organisation. First, there are the common rules which are those required by law; they include contracts of employment, the Health and Safety at Work Act and its attendant Regulations, industrial relations, and employment protection legislation. Some organisations find it advantageous to publish these separately as they *are* the law, can be amended quite separately, and are not subject to much debate. It should be noted that some of these statutes may vary according to the type of industry: trades such as food and paint spraying have their own specialised regulations which are often difficult to comprehend. They should be carefully interpreted in a simple format. It is essential to find a method of training staff on these, as well as the local requirements.

Second, there are organisation rules. The rules committee should have a clear understanding of the objectives these rules are required to meet, before they waste time waffling along on an unknown track. Once they understand clearly what is required, it should not take long to start structuring the basic framework on which they can build required procedures. Normally it takes four or five meetings to define the necessary basics which can be edited to a logical set of notes to establish the rule book.

The most successful rule books are those which state the objective immediately after the individual rule, and also include recommendations for acceptable behaviour which are not necessarily rules. One well-known food company has a rule book comprising only 14 pages. Seven of these are dedicated to the objectives of the rules, i.e. what is to be achieved. One page is an agreed statement made jointly by unions and management giving their commitment to both rules and objectives. One page outlines disciplinary and appeals procedure and only four contain the rules, leaving a blank page for notes. The book size is only 5″ × 3″. This has been in use for several years and no problems have yet been encountered.

Brevity

Many lessons can be learned from national legislation – mainly don'ts! *Don't* make excessive rules – think carefully whether five or six separate items can be covered by one good short rule; involve those people covered by the rules or expected to adhere to them. *Don't* try to cover every aspect of interpretation – this usually only leads to more confusion and more loopholes. Brief and clear is the ideal, so the workforce can understand. *Avoid*, like the plague, marginal rules or rules that are only to cover up shortcomings. Above all use commonsense and logic.

Selling the rules

Having got the rules established and written they must be 'sold'. There is absolutely no reason why the committee that was involved in their formation should not also do the training; they can answer any questions which arise and should know the reasons behind each rule. Management and unions together should be involved in implementing and applying rules, as it is advantageous for these influential groups to appear on a

288 HANDBOOK OF MANAGEMENT SKILLS

platform in accord. The fallout which can thus be obtained is worth all the investment in time. Talking jointly about matters upon which they agree considerably, smooths the path on items upon which they may appear to disagree initially.

If carried out in a calm, logical and well structured manner, formulating a rule book and disciplinary procedures can be a very constructive and worthwhile exercise.

Ensure, however, that the 'forgotten legions' of first line management, i.e. foremen and supervisors, are included at all stages. It will probably be down to them to maintain discipline so their commitment is paramount.

Disciplinary procedure

This lays down the procedure to be followed in the case of unsatisfactory work or conduct on the part of an employee. When drawing up or revising a disciplinary procedure, reference should be made to the ACAS Code of Practice on Disciplinary Practice and Procedures in Employment, and the ACAS advisory handbook *Discipline at Work*.

The ACAS Code of Practice lists certain essential features of a disciplinary procedure. These include:

- provision for individuals to be informed of the complaints against them and to be given the opportunity to state their case before decisions are reached
- the right to be accompanied by a trade union representative or a fellow employee of their choice
- the right to appeal.

In addition, a disciplinary procedure should contain:

- the number of warnings that an employee can normally expect before being dismissed
- the procedure for holding disciplinary hearings
- how long warnings should remain on record
- a list of offences likely to lead to summary dismissal
- procedures for dealing with shift workers, night workers or employees at isolated locations where members of management are not readily available
- procedures to be followed if it is necessary to discipline a shop steward.

ACAS will normally assist with drawing up or vetting disciplinary procedures free of charge.

Once a procedure has been drawn up it is essential that it is followed. Failure to follow procedure may result in a dismissal being found to be unfair even if the reason for the dismissal is fair.

Disciplinary action

Having drawn up a set of rules, trained everybody, ensured understanding, and with the best will in the world done all the 'right things', what happens when a person flagrantly disregards a rule? The time has come to consider disciplinary action. There are many possible actions, all of which appear to be in regular use. Before discussing these, let us first consider what is the underlying objective of any action taken against a proven culprit.

Objectives of action

These seem to cover every aspect of human reaction: punish, set an example, discourage repetition, expose the person – and 'get the person's co-operation and bring him back to an acceptable standard'. This latter case may well sound trite and akin to the psychiatrist's couch but, considered further, it is exactly what is required from any employee – to work to an acceptable standard of performance.

A breach of the disciplinary code means that part of the standard of performance is unacceptable; therefore a return to that standard is the objective. That is not to say that some disciplinary action should not be included, if only to aid memory. However, bearing in mind the ultimate objective, let us consider sanctions in regular use and their effects upon an individual. In this discussion, we are considering the occasional transgressor, not the hardened and regular offender who, failing all attempts to correct, can only be dealt with in one way.

Dismissal

The ultimate sanction – which may well be linked with legal action in some instances. With current legislation, this is likely to be either the last resort after several warnings, as per procedure, or for one of the well known offences which give no second chance. Examples of these latter offences are smoking in a refinery or a coal mine, theft, assault, etc. Dismissal should not be taken lightly, nor without first making the fullest enquiries as to the reason for breach of the rule; always ensure a precedent is not being created, or that similar offenders have not been treated differently.

Also make sure that the employees' representative is involved in the procedure if further problems are not to be encountered. Always consider the legal, moral and motivational aspects of dismissal. Dismissal should be very much the last resort.

Suspension

This is still commonly used. In some instances it is illegal if it is without pay, as part of the current legislation spells out that an employer may not remove or reduce an employee's ability to earn as indicated in his or her terms of employment. If, however, there is an agreement in existence to use suspension as a sanction then suspension can be used. The major factors against suspension without pay are as follows: you may need the person's services; they may leave anyway; they may obtain alternative temporary employment – often at a higher rate; they may well be demotivated enough to withdraw any co-operation and become an irritant to the rest of the workforce. Although in common use, suspension has many side effects that have been given insufficient consideration. Suspension with pay, pending enquiries, or for the individual's well-being or safety (i.e. if incapable of performing duties satisfactorily), is usually understood and acceptable.

Black marks; written warnings

Again, in common use and can be constructive if used correctly. However, if used carelessly, the results of this type of disciplinary action can be extremely poor. Any form of warning *must* be preceded by a full discussion so that the situation is understood. There must be a prescribed period after which that black mark or warning is withdrawn from the record. If, however, the person understands that the situation can be retrieved by continued good behaviour, it can be a good and constructive form of action. There are exceptions to this last statement, where it may be necessary to keep records. It should also be noted that written warnings should normally follow, in recommended procedure, an informal or non-recorded warning, often described as an informal warning.

Transfer

Once again, a well-worn and common disciplinary action. Usually, it can mean not only a move, but a move to a job of lesser status. The consideration behind a disciplinary transfer is often insufficient. At one end of the scale it can be described as buck passing, at best, it removes a problem from one area only to put a disgruntled employee in another. Even having accepted the transfer with reasonable grace, the person may not be welcomed in the new environment. This can be extremely traumatic and may lead to the individual leaving. If carried out in a constructive manner, and if it allows a square peg to be fitted into a square hole, then the action is not only justified, but constructive to both the individual and the organisation.

Demotion

Can be used right across the organisation, from demoting a foreman back to the bench, to the demotion of a director. The effect upon the individual is about the same. Even when demotion is caused by redundancy, it can hardly be described as a motivator. Quite often, demotion and transfer occur at the same time: this at least allows, on some occasions, a small opportunity to save face. It has often been said that it is kinder to dismiss than demote. The positive side of demotion, like transfer, is when it meets the need of both the individual and the organisation. Instances of this are when people have worked themselves into a position where they cannot cope and may be endangering their health. By common consent, or at least after counselling, there may be a vacancy which the person can fill very satisfactorily. Sideways moves to non-jobs should be avoided. Management also needs to bear in mind claims for constructive dismissal.

Fines

This, like suspension without pay, can be illegal under certain circumstances. Not being paid when late, or cutting a bonus for under-production is a monetary punishment and acceptable. Holding back increments is also acceptable, providing there does not exist a legal agreement to pay. Minimal or no performance review increase is also commonly used and could be described as a fine. All of these, like a black mark, should be retrievable as and when performance improves. However, to be effective, this should be well understood by the person; the period involved should also be known, as should the method of obtaining help if necessary. Many other possibilities exist and are used.

Interviews

One very important piece of procedure in any disciplinary action is the *discipline* or *grievance interview*. *All disciplinary action should be preceded by a face-to-face and frank exchange of views.* Even when the individual has been caught red-handed in the most heinous crime, it is important to find out *why*; what was the root cause, the objective, and even the logic (if any) behind the action. The discipline interview can be the single most important action carried out in the whole discipline procedure. To be effective it must be carried out well and structured very carefully.

Disciplinary and grievance interviews

As has been stated, all disciplinary action should preferably be preceded by an interview to establish the what and why. Of all actions in the cause of good discipline, the well structured and controlled interview can be the most constructive and effective. There are obvious differences between discipline and grievance interviews, but the basic rules remain the same. It should be remembered that, often, the removal of a grievance will avoid having to interview the same employee on the subject of discipline.

Disciplinary interview checklist

Below is a checklist and the method to follow when conducting a disciplinary interview.

1 Purpose

- To inform, and correct, mistakes or bad behaviour, and to prevent this happening again.
- To establish understanding of the standard required and bring the person back to this standard.

2 Preparation

- Gather the facts (consult others, records, rules, procedure, previous record, etc.).
- Do not prejudge issue – guard against bias.
- Plan the approach according to the individual concerned.
- Ensure privacy and no interruptions.
- Allow adequate time.
- Establish the offence.
- Clarify the sanctions available and the authority possessed.
- Notify the time, place and reason for the interview.
- Notify others concerned that the employee will be absent.

3 Conduct

- Put the person at ease.
- Establish and advise of offence: be specific.
- Allow the person to state case (listen). This may involve

asking open-ended questions (what, when, where, how and who).

- Keep calm (do not argue or use bad language).
- Establish the cause of the problem.
- Be constructive in showing how improvements can take place.
- If possible get interviewee to suggest how improvements can be made.
- Ensure understanding of the standards required.
- State action to be taken by both parties.

4 Follow up

- Record the interview (unfair dismissal).
- Check: future behaviour – attitude, performance.
- See necessary help is given if required; check informally with the person concerned to monitor progress.
- Praise and encourage improvements.

Always remember your objective, which is to return the person to an acceptable standard of performance, and ensure the interviewee also understands this objective. Although interviewers must be aware of action available to them, the most vital aspect is getting the interviewee to understand and act to correct their own performance.

Grievance interview checklist

1 Purpose

- To enable individuals to air their grievance.
- To discover and remove the cause of dissatisfaction and establish the background.

2 Preparation

- Endeavour to establish circumstances causing dissatisfaction (particularly attitudes, feelings).
- Consult with the people concerned, check previous record/ history.
- Be aware of company policy which may affect action which can be taken.

- Ensure privacy and no interruptions.
- Allow adequate time.
- Check that others concerned know where the person will be during the interview.

3 Conduct

- Put the person at ease – establish rapport.
- State the purpose of the interview.
- Allow the individual to state the grievance/problem.
- Get feelings as well as fact – feelings frequently are paramount, facts minimal.
- Listen attentively.
- Do not evade the issue or belittle it.
- Probe in depth to ensure all relevant details are known.
- Investigate facts.
- Do not commit yourself or the organisation too quickly.
- If possible, get the individual to suggest solutions.
- State proposed course of action – if known at this stage. If no decision has been reached, then state the nature of future action.

4 Follow up

- Investigate the facts/information if necessary.
- Decide on the action in light of investigation, and communicate to the person concerned.
- Check that results are as required – relationships, attitudes, performance.
- Record only if necessary.
- Make sure the person is seen informally later, if only for a few seconds.

Points to consider

During discipline interviews, the employee's representative is entitled to be present. However, it is often more constructive to carry out the initial interview on a one-to-one basis. Employees should be clearly told that if at any time they may wish to have their representative present, they can do so, but until that time, a better understanding may be established on a face-to-face basis. Should a worker's representative be present, the interviewer would be well advised also to have a back-up.

The grievance interview can often prove constructive by just listening. Care should be taken, however, not to allow too much time to the organisation's 'professional moaner', nor to react to non-established problems. The grievance interview, however, can often be an early warning system.

People have often queried the approaches in setting up discipline interviews. To get the best results, adopt an informal attitude, certainly at first/verbal warning stage. The atmosphere may need to become formal if the disciplinary action has to continue to formal/final warning stage. A discipline interview is not different to any other. If both parties are on tenterhooks and wish to get the thing over, nothing useful will result. On the other hand, careful and considerate handling pays dividends. For example, one well-known organisation discovered unused talent and established an exceedingly useful member of staff (now the works manager). His words at a discipline interview were: 'That's the first time anybody has ever listened and agreed to help'. The lesson learned was that if a person's creativity and talent are not fully harnessed for the use of the organisation, it may still be used – against the organisation.

Causes of breaches of discipline

It is probably true to say that there are a million causes for breaches of discipline, all with different accents. However, an analysis of a fairly large selection of these breaches established only three root causes, as follows:

- for gain – 20 per cent (including all aspects of 'gain')
- due to frustration – 75 per cent
- other – 5 per cent (miscellaneous events).

Of the organisations surveyed, it was found that in any one year, 4 per cent or less of the employees were involved with action under the heading of 'disciplinary'. As approximately 75 per cent of these occurrences were due to frustration, some further study was made to establish the events leading up to this frustration. In most cases it followed a definable pattern: starting with some kind of misunderstanding, each event in the series had a reaction which in turn resulted in undesirable side effects. The route is normally as follows:

- *misunderstanding* followed by
- *simple problem* or *complaint* which, if not dealt with, leads to *resentment*
- *actual grievance* which, if not dealt with, leads to *aggression* or *regression*
- *dissatisfaction* which, if not dealt with, leads to *depression*
- *frustration* and *fixation* which, if not dealt with, lead to *apathy*.

It was found that a majority of the people with queries were not discussing them with their bosses, and often, after discussion with their colleagues, the wrong answer was found. If the problem was large enough to make it imperative to ask the boss, various types of reaction resulted.

Q 'Have you got a minute?'
A 'Does it have to be now? I'm very busy.'
  'See the wages people, it's their problem.'
  'Personnel can sort that out.'
  'That's not your problem.'

These and many other similar answers, all lead into grievance and a 'couldn't care less' attitude. They are also signs of either an irresponsible or an overworked boss. In any event, one must always remember that, to individuals, their 'minor' complaint is of the greatest importance. It must be dealt with as quickly as possible – often just listening to the problem significantly reduces its effect. Unresolved problems will lead either to labour turnover or discipline situations.

One complaint often voiced by first line managers is that their authority has been reduced to virtually zero. It may be that they give their authority away by directing all their problems to senior or specialist management. Here, the case for a set procedure being adhered to is paramount. All problems must first be dealt with by the immediate boss and must only be passed on if they are insoluble at that level.

Managers should:

Diagnose

As a general rule, humans are not instinctive animals, but experienced and knowledgeable managers will develop a sixth sense which will warn of any impending crisis. These managers make a study of the individuals under their control and probably will have developed a good relationship with the workers' representative. Thus, successful managers will find time to walk the job and will not allow pressures to bog them down in the office. They will also be good delegators, successful motivators and, probably, well liked by the workforce. All of this will amount to a happy and effective workforce where disciplinary problems are less likely to occur.

Anticipate problems

No amount of rules, regulations or procedures can substitute for the application of commonsense. With the pressures of modern working life, the urgent often takes priority over the important, which leads eventually to the important cropping up as urgent when it gets out of control. Systematic priorities and good anticipation, together with the ability to shed the streams of excess information, all help to make the best use of time and avoid crises. Most important in the field of discipline is the encouragement of people and their representatives to discuss problems in the embryonic stage: to get maximum effectiveness from this one must always be prepared to listen and act. As ever, prevention is by far the most effective cure.

Leadership and discipline

One way by which to raise the morale, and therefore the standard of behaviour of people at work, is by good and effective leadership, which must include the involvement of the workgroup and the individuals in that group.

Effective leadership in itself will create within the team a supportive atmosphere, which means that a self-discipline is created and the team will tend to monitor its own standards. Part of an individual's task as leader is to ensure that communication is good and that their workers thoroughly understand the objectives and their necessary contribution towards the achievement of these objectives. Further still, by involving the team and individuals in distribution of tasks, the leader can get a high level of commitment from the people, which again will contribute to good discipline and high performance.

An effective leader will almost certainly give and receive respect to and from the team. Workers with high regard for their leaders are much less likely to carry out acts against the organisation than people who work in an environment where the work-group leader merely dishes out work and discipline. It has often been observed that, where the work-group is of a reasonable size which the leader can manage, and where the leader has the authority to carry out the total leadership role, the incidence of breaches of discipline is low.

A good leader is an accepted leader and will always endeavour to help, advise and listen to team members. Individuals will get reassurance and the leader will show enthusiasm for their ideas. In such circumstances it is rare for people to rock the boat. In return, the team will support the leader and output will be high. Good leadership is almost a prerequisite to good discipline, since a bad leader will often be rewarded by a troubled discipline scene.

As in all things, a practical, honest, and simple approach offers the best return in matters of discipline. Additionally, good management will pay dividends in the field of discipline. Foremost are the following.

- Does everybody know and understand what the disciplinary code sets out to achieve?
- Have all levels been consulted in setting up the procedures?
- Does the procedure set time limits and is it geared for swift solving of grievances/problems?
- Have all the managers had a basic grounding in leadership techniques? Good leadership is paramount to good discipline.
- Have unions, if they exist, been fully involved and are they instructively committed to a good standard of behaviour?

Attention is required at all times to ensure continual good

discipline because, like most things, maintenance and the ability to spot latent problems are essential. Understanding is a key which opens many doors and, as soon as mutual respect is established, so too are the roots of a good disciplinary atmosphere.

17 SALARY MANAGEMENT

Small organisations usually have an informal salary structure which reflects the flexible approach required in a growing business. However, when expansion takes place and employee numbers begin to grow to over fifty then it is time to adopt a more formal approach.

This booklet describes how to go about establishing a salary structure for staff grades based on sound and well-tried principles.

Objectives of a salary policy

In overall terms the aim of a formal salary policy is to ensure that employees are paid in accordance with the value to the company of the work they perform. This aim should be incorporated into the salary policy which should be tailor-made to meet the needs and objectives of the organisation as a whole. An example of a salary policy is given in Appendix 33.

Responsibility for salary management

The responsibility for sound salary management lies with line management. In small organisations the senior line manager or director will have overall responsibility for the policy but in larger firms the detailed aspects of salary administration will be co-ordinated by the personnel officer.

It is very important that all members of line management understand the aims and content of the salary policy because it is their responsibility to explain it to staff and operate it correctly within their own departments.

Communicating salary policy

Equally important as the preparation of a salary policy is the need to communicate it to everyone concerned; indeed there is no reason why every staff member should not have a copy of the actual policy.

By far the best way of passing on information is for departmental managers to call a briefing meeting with all their staff to explain in general terms what the policy covers and how it will operate. Care should be taken to ensure that each employee's questions are answered sympathetically and honestly without going into detail on individual cases.

A successful briefing session will dispel fears. Failure to do so will result in the grapevine taking over with often disastrous consequences.

Job description

Every organisation has both formal and informal aspects regarding who reports to whom and how work is done. When developing a salary policy, however, it is necessary to have a clear picture of the content of jobs and the formal reporting arrangements. This is not a difficult exercise and in most small organisations can be completed in a few months. Job descriptions are easy to complete and invaluable because they have many uses. For example, they can be used for job evaluation, on-job training, appraisal of staff, and, of course, recruitment.

A job description is a basic statement covering such items as:

- job title
- department
- to whom responsible
- job titles of subordinates
- overall purpose of the job
- duties and responsibilities
- limits of authority.

Furthermore, don't forget the *date of preparation*.

The completed job description must be agreed by both the job holder and relevant supervisor. A short, punchy style of writing should be adopted and the golden rule is to keep it short and simple.

An example of a job description is given in Appendix 34.

Job evaluation

Many organisations avoid introducing job evaluation because they feel it is either too costly or too sophisticated. This need not be the case. Two methods can be considered as practicable: ranking and classification.

Ranking

Ranking involves studying all the job descriptions and placing them in order of importance. Note that it is the job which is being evaluated and not the person doing it. Here is a 'plan of attack'.

- Set up a committee of, say, three people who have a good knowledge of all the jobs being covered.
- Select about 15–20 jobs as being a good representative sample of all the jobs being covered. These are the benchmarks or key jobs and form the basis of job evaluation.
- Write job descriptions for these key jobs.
- Separately rank these jobs and seek agreement with other committee members.
- Design a job questionnaire (*see* Appendix 35).
- Brief all employees on the value of well-written job descriptions and explain how they should complete them (*see* Appendix 36).
- Ensure that all descriptions are agreed by the respective supervisors.
- Call the committee together to slot in the jobs according to the benchmarks to reach an overall rank order.

An extension of ranking known as 'paired' or 'forced' comparisons should be considered. Each job is compared with every other job and a decision made as to which job is the more important. It is rather like filling in a football coupon.

If the job is more important, insert 2; if equally important, insert 1; if less important, insert 0. For example, in this chart an accounts clerk is considered less important than a receptionist and more important than a messenger.

Table 17.1 *An example of paired or forced comparisons*

	A	B	C	D	E	F	G	H	J	K
Accounts clerk (A)	x	1	0	0	2	0	0	0	1	0
Invoice typist (B)	1	x	0	0	2	0	0	0	1	0
Receptionist/telephonist (C)	2	2	x	1	2	1	0	1	2	1
Wages clerk (D)	2	2	1	x	2	1	0	1	2	2
Messenger (E)	0	0	0	0	x	0	0	0	0	0
Costing clerk (F)	2	2	1	1	2	x	0	1	2	1
Director's secretary (G)	2	2	2	2	2	2	x	2	2	2
Shorthand-typist (H)	2	2	1	1	2	1	0	x	2	1
Stock clerk (J)	1	1	0	0	2	0	0	0	x	0
Sales clerk (K)	2	2	1	1	2	1	0	1	1	x

(An 'x' is entered where a job is being compared with itself.)

Reading from the left, compare each job in turn with every other job shown along the top (signified here by initial letters).

Once this is done, a matrix is drawn up showing the jobs in rank order, for example:

A word of warning: thirty is the maximum number of jobs which can be ranked manually, so do not attempt to include more than this number.

Job classification

Job classification is, like ranking, a non-analytical method of job evaluation. It is a method of separating jobs into natural groups according to a pre-determined classification system. For an example, *see* Appendix 37. To develop your own classification scheme you will need to:

1 rank 15–20 benchmark jobs
2 decide natural breakpoints between groups of jobs
3 define in words the common features which the jobs in a particular group share
4 rank a further 15–20 and slot them in with the first group
5 refine the wording used for each classification as necessary.

Table 17.2 *Rank order following paired or forced comparisons*

Director's secretary	2	2	2	2	2	2	2	2	2
Receptionist/telephonist		2	2	2	2	1	1	1	1
Wages clerk		2	2	2	2	1	1	1	1
Costing clerk		2	2	2	2	1	1	1	1
Shorthand-typist		2	2	2	2	1	1	1	1
Sales clerk		2	2	2	1	1	1	1	1
Invoice typist							2	1	1
Stock clerk							2	1	1
Accounts clerk							2	1	1
Messenger									0

The advantages of this method are:

- quick and simple to operate
- can be reasonably defended in an appeal situation
- can cover a large number of jobs.

The disadvantages of this method are:

- not suitable when jobs have a complex skill content and range
- has a limited life of about four years.

Operating the scheme

Job descriptions are written task-by-task. Each task is allotted a grading by matching the task descriptions with the grade description. When grading is completed, the number of grades accorded is totted up and a decision made by the committee on the overall grading, for example:

Grade	A	B	C	D	E
Number of tasks allocated to grades	2	8	3	–	–

The decision is made on a whole job basis as to whether the job is, say an A, B or C grade job. Some schemes allow for an approximate percentage of the job holders' time spent on each task as the determining feature, but on this basis it is terribly easy to add 2 and 2 to get 5!

Drawing up grades

Whether the ranking method or the classification method of job evaluation is used, the aim is to arrive at groups of jobs or grades containing broadly similar-sized jobs.

In general, jobs will tend to fall into broad groups, but there are bound to be a few jobs which will cause some soul-searching. The grading completed, the jobs on either side of the grade must be scrutinised carefully to ensure they are in the right group. In the event of appeals being raised it is likely that they will spring from this grey area.

Five grades ought to suffice, up to and including supervisory level. To have more will mean that differentials between grades will be narrowed and staff will see little financial advantage in taking on more responsibility. In addition, the personnel officer may be faced with an excessive number of requests for upgrading each time there is a slight increase in responsibility or change in job content.

Analysing the results of job evaluation

Once the job evaluation has been completed and the jobs have been grouped into grades it is time to think about salaries. The use of graphs is invaluable at this stage when creating a new salary structure. By presenting the information visually, anomalies will stand out and a clearer picture will emerge of the current position.

As an aid to determining the new salary structure it is very helpful to create a scattergram. An example is given in Appendix 38, but here is how it is done.

1 On a graph, plot each job holder by basic salary and grade. This will give you the scatter on your current salary structure.
2 Draw a curved line through the centre of the scatter so that there are roughly the same number of points above as below

the line. This 'line of best fit', as it is called, will illustrate your salary practice now. It represents the current mid-points of each of the new grades.

3 Salary ranges can now be added with the maximum and minimum salary levels drawn between 12 per cent and 25 per cent above and below the lines. Jobs falling above the maximum and below the minimum are, of course, anomalies in the new structure. Appendix 38 shows a typical salary structure.

We now have a formal salary structure based on job evaluation which reflects accurately the current organisation structure. The next step is to decide how this matches up against the outside market for a similar range of jobs.

Surveying the outside market

There are a number of ways of finding out how your current salaries compare with the external market.

- By purchasing professional salary surveys such as those published by Reward Regional Surveys or the Institute of Administrative Management. Both these organisations can provide information on up-to-date salary trends in any part of the country.
- By telephoning your opposite number in other organisations in the area and exchanging information.
- By sending to selected organisations a job description from each grade and asking for a comparison. (It is wise to telephone personally to enquire if the organisation is willing to take part.) This must be followed up by sending to the participants details of the survey but excluding actual organisation names.
- By inviting four or five opposite numbers in your area to form a Pay Policy Comparison Club with the first meeting on your premises. An agreed agenda should be drawn up stating jobs to be discussed in order that salary and benefits information is forthcoming.

When considering salary survey information, care must be taken to ensure that as far as possible you are comparing like with like. Some salary surveys rely heavily on job titles when gathering their data and it is well-known that different organisations often pay very different salaries to jobs with the same title.

On balance, using selected job descriptions and gathering information on these from other local organisations is the most reliable method of obtaining salary data for your location.

Deciding final salary structure

So far we have:

- Established a grading structure and allocated all the jobs to a grade using sound job evaluation methods.
- Established what our current salary practice line is and added maximum and minimum salary levels for each grade (*see* Appendix 38).
- Surveyed the external market place and gathered information on how we measure up in terms of market rates.

If the salary survey data indicate that your salary rates are low compared to rates paid by other similar organisations, consideration should be given to adjusting your salary ranges to ensure you are competitive. You may, for example, decide to adjust your salary ranges so that the mid-point of each range is equivalent to the market median (defined as the point in a range of values at which 50 per cent of the sample is higher and 50 per cent is lower). Cost considerations will, of course, be a major factor in deciding your new salary structure and thorough costing of proposals must be carried out first.

As a general rule, organisations which pay their staff at the lower quartile level (defined as the point at which 25 per cent of the sample is lower and 75 per cent higher) may experience difficulty in recruiting and retaining good quality staff. The cost of moving salary ranges up to match market rates must be balanced with the high cost of labour turnover which is often a result of low pay. Appendix 38 shows an example of the final salary structure.

Salary anomalies

Once salary ranges have been finalised it will be found that the majority of staff will be on a salary within the new grade boundaries. However, there may be a number of staff who are either over- or under-paid. Those under-paid should be brought up to at least the minimum for the grade. Apart from explaining the situation to those staff who are over the maximum for their job grade, the following should be considered:

- promotion to higher grade work
- rearrangement of job content in order that some higher-grade work is included
- salary standstill until the new maximum overtakes the individual's current rate.

Rate-for-age

Some organisations find it useful to retain a rate-for-age scale to enable young employees to progress on a formal basis as they gain work experience. Rate-for-age reviews can be made quarterly or six monthly and combined with a full review of progress in the job. It is preferable to ensure that young adults are paid at least the minimum of the grade applicable to their job by their eighteenth birthday.

Employee benefits

It is worthwhile mentioning that, when constructing a new salary structure, consideration must be given to the adequacy of existing employee benefits. When conducting a salary survey, employee benefits must also be taken into account.

While staff accept employee benefits as a fact of life, different social groups within the organisation and, indeed, within the area, will view different benefits with varying degrees of interest. Young people are more attracted to an organisation by the promise of a realistic salary than the offer of a generous sick pay or pension scheme. Assisted house purchase, membership of a hospital scheme and share option schemes are likely to appeal to management.

In designing the salary structure, therefore, it is important to consider how much influence employee benefits have on the *total* salary package, i.e. the *real* cost of employing staff.

Table 17.3 *Classifications for performance*

	Performance
Category	Definition
Unsatisfactory	The employee has not performed to the minimum standard required in the job.
Incomplete	The employee has performed well in most areas of the job but there are areas which need substantial improvement. (This category can also be used for those who have not been in the job very long and who have some way to go before becoming fully proficient in all aspects.)
Effective	The job holder has reached and maintained the level of performance required by the organisation. This is experienced worker standard. All tasks and objectives have been achieved.
Superior	The employee has exceeded the standard level of performance required. There will be significant achievement of results in areas beyond the basic requirements of the job.
Exceptional	The job holder's performance is such that outstanding results have been achieved in the most important aspects of the job. All targets have been exceeded.

Performance appraisal

Performance appraisal is a two-way exchange of information between boss and subordinate about the job and the job holder's performance. It provides valuable information on the employee's training and development needs and assists in assessing potential for future jobs. It is also an essential method of reviewing an employee's concerns and aspirations as well as jointly deciding priorities and targets for the future.

More and more organisations today are linking pay directly to achievement and abandoning systems whereby everyone receives the same salary review regardless of performance.

One method of differentially rewarding employees is to place their overall performance in the job into one of five performance categories.

Great care should be exercised to ensure that all managers and supervisors responsible for appraising the performance of their staff are being consistent in their interpretation of the performance categories. Several meetings will need to be held before and after the appraisal discussions to ensure that a consistent and equitable approach has been adopted. It is likely that the majority of employees will be in the 'effective' category with only relatively few who are above and below the standard performance level.

Once the classification of performance has taken place, differential salary awards can be made to those in each category. Whereas it may be appropriate to give a 5 per cent increase to those in the effective category, employees whose performance is classed as superior might receive a 7 per cent increase. Careful costing must be carried out before the final amounts are decided.

How much the organisation can afford to pay will be the overriding consideration when determining the final distribution of amounts.

Departmental budgets

Every department should have a budget and, within this, there should be an agreed figure for salaries. This should be decided one year in advance and should take into consideration staffing requirements, promotions and increases in staff complement. The budget should also take into account a figure to be set aside for salary increases. This can either be an agreed lump sum or, more usually, a percentage of the departmental salary budget.

Salary review procedures

It is usual in most organisations for staff to have an annual review of salary except for trainees and those under 18 years of age who may receive more regular reviews.

Salary reviews should be carefully planned with adequate briefing of managers and supervisors on the guidelines for the review, the timing, and the communication of the results to staff.

Documentation will be required on which managers can make

their salary recommendations (*see* Appendix 39). Once all the recommendations have been made the results should be reviewed to ensure the guidelines have been correctly followed. It is usual for the final figures to be agreed at director level before staff are informed of the results of the review.

Once employees have been advised of their increases, managers must gather feedback on reaction to the review. Not everyone will be happy at the outcome, but if the communication process has been thorough staff should understand the reasons behind the review.

Management salaries

Most of this chapter has been devoted to salaried staff up to supervisory level. However, the same principles apply to management staff, although the type of job evaluation system used for management is often more involved.

And finally . . .

Remember how important the job description is as a management tool. Keeping job descriptions up-to-date is essential because they are the key to many decisions regarding staff. The following diagram illustrates this.

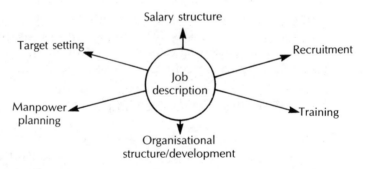

Figure 17.1   *The job description as a management tool*

18 INDUSTRIAL RELATIONS

Despite recent arguments against collective bargaining and in favour of direct employer/employee contact, and despite a decline in some areas of union membership, collective negotiations between employers and employee organisations continue to play a key part in industrial relations.

This chapter is about the relationship between management and unions or staff organisations. It is intended for managers who may now, or at some future time, be required to work with representatives of the workforce. It seeks to cover the key issues involved in such work: recognition, consultation, discipline, training, and negotiation.

What follows applies equally to blue and white collar organisations. A key area for growth in union membership has been, and is, the white collar area. This growth still tends to be regarded with surprise and some dismay. In fact, the reduction in the differentials between manual and staff employees, the marked change in the ratio of staff to manual workers employed, the tendency towards greater concentrations in one place of staff employees, and the general increase in size and complexity of industrial, commercial and public service undertakings, have all made the relative growth of white collar organisations inevitable.

In facing up to such a new areas, managers should use their part experience to establish positive fruitful relationships and to avoid the mistakes which have been made in the past in traditional areas of industrial relations.

It is accepted that, today, organisations which people join to represent them at work, have a variety of names, and their representatives a variety of titles. The term 'union' and 'steward' are used throughout this booklet for ease of reference, and because we believe that the same 'good practice' can apply in industrial relations whatever the employees' collective organisation is called.

313

Management's attitudes towards unions

Do we need to have unions? There could be a wide range of answers to the question, but managers' views generally fall into one of two categories.

1 Those who think that industry would run very much better if there were no unions, and managers were left to get on with it by themselves. Managers who hold this view generally believe that the right thing to do is to oppose the unions, or at any rate actively discourage them. Managers in this category tend to think of all the individuals in their organisation as members of a team, all with the same clearly defined common purpose. If they are not pulling together, they ought to be. No matter how hard they try to keep up to date with what they think or do about industrial relations, at heart these managers tend to resent the existence of the unions.
2 Those who take the more positive attitude. Not only do they accept the existence of collective bargaining, they also believe that there is an important job for the unions to do (not that they are necessarily doing it) and it is up to managers to take the initiative and make sure that it gets done.

Those who take the latter attitude recognise that conflict between management and the unions is as possible as conflict within management, for example, between sales executives who are trying to satisfy customers, and production executives who are in the throes of installing new machinery. But having identified and accepted areas of conflict, they are able to agree joint procedures for the orderly resolution of disputes and grievances. They are also in a better position to eliminate or reduce conflict in areas where it *can* be avoided – and there are many. This does not mean, however, that one should restrict oneself to 'fire fighting'.

Two sides?

Is industrial relations necessarily about conflict between management and unions? This is an old chestnut and it is as well to get it out of the way.

In the sense that they have different roles to play and different functions to perform, management and unions do form two sides. In the sense that they have a common interest in the success of the organisation, there are not two sides. Although it is in the interests of both management and unions that the organisation should develop and grow, when it comes to deciding how the benefits of growth and development should be shared, their interests are not the same, nor will they necessarily agree about the best method of promoting a successful organisation. Essentially, the role of the unions is to look after the interests of their members (in the long-term as well as the short-term), while management has to judge what is in the best interests of shareholders and/or customers, as well as employees. The fact that their interests are bound to clash when it comes to deciding who gets what share of the cake, all too often obscures the point that management and unions need to co-operate in order to increase the total size of the cake, and *must* co-operate if the economic objectives of the organisation and all the people in it are to be achieved.

Employees' attitudes towards unions

Much could be said about people's reasons for joining unions. Suffice it to say that, for over sixty years, collective bargaining has been an accepted method of determining wages and conditions. Today, a substantial proportion of the workforce is covered by collective agreements between employers (or their associations) and unions. In joining a union, an employee is simply becoming part of a system that is accepted by the majority of employers and recognised by the state.

Security is, increasingly, one of the main reasons for joining a union. Mergers, take-overs and closures being commonplace, employees see membership of a union as a means of safeguarding their interests. This can happen just as easily where management–employee relations are good and terms and conditions of employment are above average. Employees recognise that there are economic forces to which employers sometimes have to give way, in spite of themselves.

In the case of younger employees, their conception of loyalty is different from that of older generations. They are more questioning, more aware, and keen to be involved in the process that determines their terms and conditions. Membership of a union may meet this need.

With senior people, in technical and managerial roles, membership means having a greater potential influence over the affairs of the undertaking, and feelings of insecurity or isolation may be alleviated by the knowledge that one can turn to the union for information and advice.

Unions today are also, increasingly, providing services for their members, e.g. training, insurance, travel bookings, and are responding to particular interest groups, e.g. women at work.

The role and function of unions

Basically, the role of a union is to represent its members. Within an organisation, employee representatives are elected. Full-time officials may be either elected or appointed (since the Trade Union Act 1984, the Principle Executive Committee of the union has had to be elected by secret ballot). Either way, the unions provide a means for collective expression of views, reactions and requirements, both to management within organisations and to employers' associations.

In all but the very smallest organisations, the practical arguments for having a representative system are strong. With the best will in the world, management is unlikely to get a true picture of employee attitudes and aspirations if it relies on individual contact and consultation. A representative system helps to ensure that employees' interests are taken into account, and this may well be a major factor in the satisfactory achievement of change. When employees' interests clash with those of management, a representative system is an effective way of ensuring that justice is done, and seen to be done.

There is a tendency to think of unions as being concerned only with securing higher wages and better conditions for their members. While these are key objectives, unions are also concerned to represent individual members and to provide a forum where people can discuss concerns about their employment.

Over the years, unions have done a lot to improve physical conditions at work, including industrial health and accident prevention. They have also contributed much to greater efficiency, higher productivity and better use of people.

In a wider context, unions, as representatives of the work force, are involved in many aspects of national and regional life, from local arts associations to sitting on government statutory bodies.

Their views are sought by employers and employers' associations, and listened to (although not always agreed with) by Government.

Union recognition and membership

Pre-recognition policy

Most managers accept that once they have recognised unions, there are a number of practical things they can do to create and maintain good relations.

Policy towards unions in situations where there have previously been no unions, or where there are the first signs of union activity, can be a much more delicate and difficult matter. Managers cannot be blamed for wanting to put off having to deal with unions for as long as possible, particularly if they feel that they have got along perfectly well without them in the past. At the same time, it is foolish for any manager to ignore the fact that collective bargaining is widely accepted as a method of determining employees' terms and conditions, or to suppose that at some point there may not be a move towards union representation among employees. If employers accept that, at some point, recognition of unions may be likely, it follows that they should act positively and constructively when it is apparent that employees are beginning to take an interest in unions. In organisations where management–union relations are damaging, it is often because management failed to influence and guide the relationship in its infancy. The management–union relationship *does* impose constraints, but these constraints can and should be productive.

Policy towards union recognition and membership should be related to the overall objectives and policies of the organisation and should be determined at board level (or equivalent).

Handling a claim

Management is usually aware when a union is beginning to recruit. The first formal approach is likely to come from a full-time official of the union, who will either claim bargaining rights, or ask for recognition of union, stewards, or both. The most sensible response is to establish as much information as possible about the union involved, and then arrange a meeting as quickly as possible with the union official. Before this meeting, it is unwise to make any statements to employees that might be premature. However, *all* levels of management should be informed.

At the meeting with the union official, it will be established as precisely as possible exactly which employees the union claims to represent, by grade, category or department. That clear, a realistic percentage figure of employees already in the union can be assessed. At the same time, the percentage figure at which management would agree to formal recognition should be discussed (this percentage might, of course, already have been reached). At this stage, it is reasonable to talk in terms of majority or substantial support for the union. This could be done by carrying out a ballot or a survey of the attitudes of employees.

Pending full recognition, some managements grant *representational* as opposed to bargaining rights, that is to say they grant a union the right to represent a member with an individual grievance, but they do not concede the right to negotiate wages/salaries and conditions of service.

The decision to recognise

If management is satisfied that it is dealing with the most appropriate union (or that the union is adequate, and there is no viable alternative) and if the percentage of union members is too low to justify recognition, but sufficient to indicate substantial interest in union representation, e.g. 20–25 per cent, the following first steps are usually found to be most effective.

- Agree with the union, times and facilities for recruiting members *at the place of work*.
- Prepare a brief formal statement, referring to the discussions

with the union, indicating that recognition will depend on additional (or majority) support, but encouraging the employees concerned to join, expressing a constructive management view of collective bargaining, safeguarding the genuinely held views of conscientious objectors to union membership, and stating that the union will be recruiting members on the premises at such and such a time.

- Explain policy to all members of management right down to first line supervision and discuss it fully. Not everyone in management will necessarily agree with the policy, but at least they should understand and support it.
- Issue the formal statement to all employees and explain it to them verbally. If there is a consultative committee, it should also be discussed there.

Assessing at what point recognition should be granted is not easy. Having indicated initially to the union that a majority of the employees concerned should be in the union, some managers argue from experience that it is better to settle for a lower percentage.

In the developing union situation, there will be a few activists, a few who are strongly anti-union, and a large band of 'don't knows'. The activists work on the 'don't knows' and membership goes up to the 30–40 per cent mark, where it tends to slow up and sometimes to stick. This can be a dangerous time. Insistence on 51 per cent may cause needless antagonism, and haggling acrimoniously over the precise number of people in the union is not a good start to the management–union relationship. If, on the other hand, management recognises sooner rather than later, it is in a much stronger position to get the terms it wants in the recognition and procedural agreement. Other unions may also be prevented from attempting to build up membership in the vacuum that is left if there is a 'hang-fire' period at around 30–40 per cent. The evidence is that frequently, *after* recognition has been argued and employees learn that the union has its negotiating rights, membership increases significantly, particularly if management is actively encouraging employees to join the union, in order to facilitate orderly industrial relations.

Drawing up the agreement

Assuming that management has reached a stage where it will be possible to concede recognition, a second and even more vital stage begins. This consists of discussing and agreeing with the union all those matters that provide the framework for industrial relations which are embodied in the recognition and procedural agreement (*see Model Procedural Agreements*, published by The Industrial Society Press). These should include:

- policy regarding union membership
- definition of the areas for negotiation
- definition of the employees covered
- the responsibilities of union representatives and the facilities, including time off, for them to carry out those responsibilities
- the provision of written credentials for union representatives
- a clear and workable procedure for settling issues, disputes, and grievances
- disciplinary procedure.

All this involves a lot of hard work and hard talking. But it is time well spent. Managements that are rushed into an inadequate recognition and procedure agreement have missed a golden opportunity to get their industrial relations off on the right foot. While the agreement should be as comprehensive and precise as possible, it is the tone and spirit of the discussions leading up to the signing of the agreement that can determine the long-term future of industrial relations in the organisation.

Encouragement to join unions

Constructive industrial relations depend on maximum participation by union members in the system of collective representation and negotiation. Although an individual can opt out of union membership, it is important that management should welcome employees joining an appropriate recognised union and taking part in its activities. It is perfectly permissible for management to encourage employees to join recognised unions, and managers who argue that this is the unions' job have missed a number of salient points.

- If all, or the majority, of eligible employees in the 'unit' are in the union, there is a better chance that men and women of the right calibre will emerge as union representatives. The 'right calibre' does not mean 'management people', who serve no-one's interests. Good shop stewards are those who understand the respective roles of management and unions and can effectively represent the real views of the majority of employees.
- Officials and stewards with a high membership behind them are less likely to feel that they have to play to the gallery. If membership is low, they may have difficulty in making agreements stick because they do not have the authority to carry through their part of the bargain.
- Low or fluctuating membership and ineffective or unpopular representation may lead to a proliferation of unions. Full and active membership of recognised unions makes for stability in inter-union relationships.

Supervisor and management union membership

While managers may adopt a positive attitude towards the unionisation of manual and white collar workers, they sometimes find it harder to accept the idea of supervisors or managers joining a union, often because they feel it is disloyal. Supervisors *are* part of management, but they may also feel a need for collective representation in matters such as pay, promotion, status and the extent of their authority. This is felt particularly when differentials narrow between them and the people they manage, or when changes in the organisation are being considered that are likely to result in redundancy, or to reduce promotion prospects, or (more so nowadays when they feel they have less identity with what is happening within the company) where their subordinates, through unions, have influence, and they may wish for a slice of the action. If the latter point is dominant, then there is a need for senior management to investigate, as union recognition alone will not solve the problem.

Supervisors or managers who are promoted from within, often remain in the union. Many remain members in name only, but if they are anything more than this and continue to be members of the same branch and to be represented by the same stewards, they may face conflict with doing their job properly. Managers should try to negotiate that supervisors are not members of the same branch or section as the people they supervise, and insist that they are not represented by stewards drawn from the employees over whom they have supervisory responsibilities.

These two points are accepted policy in a number of unions which have special organisations for supervisors.

Stewards

The influence, and therefore the importance, of the steward has grown with the increase in power of the work group. Plant bargaining, often taking the form nowadays of self-financing productivity, has in many cases put the steward in the lead position, where the full-time official, who has widespread responsibilities, simply has not the time to get involved in every local negotiation.

New techniques and methods, legislation – like health and safety – require new skills and greater flexibility among employees, thus making plant-level bargaining and consultation more important than ever before. It is therefore crucial for management to have effective, responsible stewards who understand the issues at stake, can present a case logically and reasonably, and report back to their members clearly and persuasively.

The role of steward is far from easy. He or she has the role of both employee and elected representative, as well as representing the union to its members. In dealing with an individual grievance, the shop steward must think not only of the individual but also of the majority.

Management–steward relationship

It is important, however, that neither stewards nor management should see the role of steward *only* in terms of negotiation and the settlement of grievances. Stewards must be seen as representing their members in *all* matters that affect them. Management should keep them well informed of plans and future developments and should consult them whenever appropriate. Attention should be given to the advice in the ACAS *Codes of Practice*.

Effective representation can make an enormous difference to the efficiency, productivity and morale of an organisation. What can management do to influence the type and quality of the men and women who are elected as stewards, and to make sure that they are properly equipped to carry out their work?

In addition to taking a positive attitude to unions in general – which should, among other things, help to ensure that in everyone's eyes no stigma is attached to becoming a steward – there are four main areas in which management can act.

Qualifications and elections

Management should take up the question of stewards' qualifications with the unions. A minimum period of service with the company – not less than one year – might be agreed (this may have to be waived in special circumstances, e.g. new sites) and a minimum period of union membership should be laid down. Without these qualifications, employees should not be eligible to stand for election. Great care should be taken when discussing these points.

The number of stewards to be elected and the areas or groups they represent should be agreed with the unions.

Assistance and facilities should be given if ballots are to be conducted in secret, e.g. a secure place for ballot boxes. Election dates and details should be given publicity on noticeboards; this also encourages high polls and the widest interest in elections.

Recognition of stewards

Stewards should have written credentials which should be issued jointly by management and the union. These should be signed by a senior member of management, by the appropriate union official, and by the steward. The credentials should state the steward's rights and responsibilities and specify:

- period of office
- the department/section which the steward represents
- the above mentioned rights and responsibilities.

The purpose of credentials is not merely to acknowledge that a particular individual has been elected. They also show that management recognises the steward's job as an important and responsible one, and are a useful way of encouraging better employees to stand.

Sometimes it is not possible to get union agreement to the use of join credentials. When this happens, management should provide stewards with a formal letter acknowledging their election. The union should be consulted about the content of these letters. They serve the same purpose as credentials. In practice, both credentials and letters can be withheld or withdrawn by management, but only when there are absolutely clear-cut reasons to justify it, e.g. constant refusal to follow procedure.

Stewards should be given copies of all the relevant agreements, rules and schemes (the negotiating procedure is particularly important) together with any verbal explanation that may be necessary.

In addition, a senior manager should meet a newly appointed steward as an indication of the importance the company attaches to the job of the steward.

The first line supervisor should also make a point of acknowledging the appointment of a steward and discuss the ways in which they can co-operate. For instance, arranging regular short meetings to discuss departmental development. Senior management must be given these points and support and encourage the steward to take all issues through the first line supervisors.

Facilities for stewards

Stewards must receive average earnings while carrying out their industrial relations functions within the company.

The circumstances in which they can leave their normal job in order to carry out their duties as stewards should be defined. They should get permission from their manager on each occasion and, in all normal circumstances, permission should be given.

Training

Defining stewards' responsibilities and rights and giving them copies of agreements is one thing, but making sure that they understand them is another. Formal training in the following is necessary for this:

- *the role of stewards*, e.g. in relation to overall management and union functions and responsibilities; their role and responsibilities as a representative
- *union affairs* – the aims, policies and organisation of their union
- *company affairs* – organisation; policies on employment, wages, work study, pension, promotion, etc.; non-negotiated fringe benefits; job evaluation scheme, etc.
- *company–union agreements* – details of negotiating and discipline procedures, etc.
- *skills* – negotiation, listening to members, etc.
- *joint affairs* – health and safety committees, equal opportunities, and financial information.

Both management and unions are becoming increasingly aware of the need for training for stewards, and it is a joint management–union responsibility to ensure that it is provided. Any time off work necessary to undergo training must be paid for at average earnings by the employer. Management and unions should therefore get together over this.

Who actually carries out the training in each of the areas listed above is not as important as seeing that it is done. Union affairs are clearly a matter for the union. Company affairs and company–union agreements are the concern of management, in collaboration with the unions. The role of the steward, joint affairs and skills might form part of a course run by the TUC or the steward's own union.

Some areas can be covered in an in-company or in-service training course. Since the idea of managers having a hand in the training of their own stewards is still often viewed with suspicion, it is sometimes best to bring in a third party, e.g. The Industrial Society, who can advise on the content of the course, take some of the sessions, and act as a 'neutral' chairman. It is worthwhile discussing this with the steward or full-time official to agree who undertakes the training.

Training arrangements

The minimum aim should be as follows.

On election

Newly elected stewards should be taken through agreements, have important conditions of employment outlined to them and be given a brief description of the organisation structure. This should be done within a week of the elections if possible. Explanations should be given by line managers and members of the personnel department. Duration: half a day. if numbers warrant it, e.g. six or more, a more formal course should be arranged, with participation by full-time officials who should help with the explanation and discussion of agreements.

At regular intervals

A course should be arranged for all stewards. If possible, all stewards should be trained together. Management and unions should plan the course jointly, varying the programme according to needs, but concentrating on:

- the role of the steward
- agreements and procedures
- conditions of employment
- company organisation and policies
- employment legislation and codes of practice.

Formal lecturing should be kept to the minimum and the maximum time should be allowed for group work and discussion. Line managers should play a major part. Duration: three days.

According to individual needs, stewards should be encouraged and given time off without loss of earnings to attend union and TUC courses, and other special courses, e.g. to improve skills or to broaden attitudes. Joint sessions with supervisors should be arranged to discuss annual financial resources and financial information to employees.

Communication

Consultation

Although informal consultation between managers and employees, and managers and representatives, obviously plays a big part in the smooth running of any works or company, a great deal can be achieved through formal committees. They can be particularly valuable at section or department level, where the employees and managers concerned can discuss those matters which are most familiar to them and in which they are directly involved.

The purpose of consultative committees is to provide a recognised and regular way of:

- giving employees a voice in decisions that affect them
- making the fullest possible use of their experience and ideas in the efficient running of the enterprise
- giving management and employees the opportunity to understand each other's views and objectives.

Their main function is:

- to discuss, before decisions are taken, any matter affecting the efficiency of the enterprise and the interests of employees to which representatives can contribute.

It is management's responsibility to see that this function is carried out.

The committees should have written terms of reference which allow discussion of the widest possible range of topics. In companies where unions have negotiating rights, management should ensure, if it possibly can, that stewards can represent employees in both consultation and negotiation, and that the consultative and negotiating machinery is directly linked. In this way, there need be no barring of subjects because they are covered by union agreements.

Negotiation, by its nature, tends to take the form of confrontation and compromise. But it can be considerably more productive if it is preceded by effective consultation or discussion. The achievement of change, in particular, requires maximum consultation and exchange of views on all relevant matters, negotiable or otherwise.

Negotiation

Negotiation is the means whereby management and unions settle the issues that arise between them, both collective issues and the grievances of individual union members.

An essential requirement for effective negotiation is a precise, comprehensive, written agreement with a negotiating procedure that aims to settle disputes as near the point of origin as possible. It is important that the procedure should be used not only for matters that are raised by management, e.g. a change in an established work practice, but also by employees' representatives.

The procedure should have clearly defined stages, indicating what types of issue can be raised at each stage and who should be involved. There should be clear time limits between stages.

Many agreements satisfactorily cover both collective issues and individual grievances. The first stage in the grievance procedure must be for an employee to see the supervisor. Only if this fails should the steward be brought in. Friction between supervisor and steward is almost inevitable if this step is omitted from the procedure.

Negotiating skills

All too often, managers, and for that matter union representatives too, come to the negotiating table having taken up an entrenched position, prepared to rely solely on the inspiration of the moment for defending it and with only a very rough idea of how negotiation is likely to go.

Effective negotiation demands careful consideration beforehand of all the facts of the issue, the alternative solutions, and their likely effects in a wider context, e.g. on the wages structure, or other departments. The tactics of the negotiation must be carefully planned with the managers/supervisors concerned. Key points to be settled at the management's pre-meeting are as follows.

- What is the most management can achieve and the least it will accept?

- What are the union's likely reactions to the management's arguments?
- What are the strongest/weakest points in the management's case, and also in the union's case?
- What is the initial statement and what supporting arguments will be left until later in the discussion?

In opening the negotiation, the leader of the management side should get the atmosphere right by setting a standard of reasoned, unemotional, argument. This is very much easier to do if preparations have been thorough and the other members of the management team have been properly briefed. Reaching an acceptable solution depends almost as much on hearing out the union's arguments and controlling emotions as on the strengths of the management case.

Throughout the negotiation, the management team should be looking for proposals which meet the interests of both sides, bearing in mind that *both* sides have got to 'sell' whatever is agreed; the management team to the management concerned, the union representatives to their members. At the end of the negotiation, both what has and has *not* been agreed must be clearly established.

Communicating during negotiations

A negotiation should result in an agreement. An agreement calls for the commitment of both sides, and both sides are, therefore, responsible for seeing that the bargain is carried through. This needs to be understood down the management and the union line.

There are special difficulties about getting news of settlements and negotiations accurately to the right people at the right time, and making sure that both the facts and the reasons behind them are understood. All too often, stewards are not in a position to tell either their own members, or managers, what has been settled and why. This is in nobody's interest – it is bound to cause friction even if the reports are accurate, and worse trouble if they are not.

To avoid this, a drill for producing agreed statements needs to be set up with the unions so that the following can be achieved.

- A brief factual statement saying what stage negotiations have reached is drafted and agreed at the end of each important meeting. As confidence in the system develops, the statements can be extended and the reasons behind claims, offers, or settlements can be explained.
- Copies of the statement are issued down the line to supervisors and stewards as quickly as possible. Copies should be distributed as widely as possible, rather than being circulated from one manager to another, and lists of the people who are to receive copies need to be prepared in advance. These will include managers and supervisors as well as full-time officials and stewards.
- A brief announcement for posting on noticeboards, and the time at which it is to be posted, also need to be agreed. Notices should be posted as soon as possible, but not before managers, supervisors, stewards and officials have received their copies of the statement.

Of course, this drill does not guarantee that the right information gets to the right people in the right sequence, but it does establish a system on which people can rely. It reduces the incentive to be 'first with the news', and the knowledge that an official version is on its way effectively deters people from deliberately distorting the facts. A procedure on these lines is found in practice to be a small price to pay for reliable communication in a vitally important field.

An 'agreed statement' drill obviously is most valuable when issues of organisation- or company-wide significance are being negotiated. When it comes to plant or workshop bargaining, written statements are also useful, particularly if complicated issues are at stake. Difficulties about the timing and accuracy of reporting back can also be overcome if one of the first line supervisors concerned attends the negotiations as part of the management team.

Consultation and communication with full-time officials

More often than not, full-time trade union officials are treated like the fire brigade and only get called in when things have already gone wrong. They cannot be expected to see things in perspective or to do a constructive job if this is their only contact with management. It is as important for managers to establish something more than a negotiating relationship with full-time officials as it is with stewards. A close, informal, relationship is most important but something more is needed.

Managers should hold regular meetings with the full-time officials with whom they normally deal. Meetings should be on a works, departmental, or company basis, depending on the normal pattern of relationships. The meetings should be on the employer's premises and the stewards should know that the meetings are taking place and why.

A senior line manager should take the meeting. Management should be represented primarily by line managers. Members of the personnel department and other departments should also be present, e.g. the commercial departments, to report on sales.

The meetings should be regarded as business, and not purely as social occasions, the objects being:

- to keep full-time officials up to date with the affairs of the organisation, e.g. the company's financial results, the state of the order book, new products, changes in management structure
- to enable union officials to be consulted about forthcoming changes, e.g. promotion or recruitment policy, new shift-working arrangements.

APPENDIX 1

Leadership action cycle

Defining objectives

For the leader to define objectives, it is necessary to consider:

- how they relate to the longer-term objectives of the organisation
- limits of own authority
- financial limits of authority
- time constraints at key stages of the task
- what our competitors are doing
- whether there will be conflict with other departments – if so, how it should be minimised
- the skills available
- whether the physical working conditions (equipment, heat, light, layout) will be appropriate for the job
- how jobs can be designed to encourage the commitment of individuals and the team
- when to hold a team meeting to brief on the objective.

Planning

Gathering information
The leader will need to check the following points:

- any potential gaps in the abilities of the team (including the leader) that are needed in order to achieve any of the tasks. If necessary, identify what steps need to be taken to fill them by training, by additional staff, or by the use of specialists
- availability of necessary resources – staff, money, materials,

methods, machinery, and time
- whether consultation is appropriate. If so, check that the team have been briefed on the objectives and that an agenda has been issued
- what steps can be taken to encourage new ideas from the team (e.g. brainstorming, task group, quality circles)
- what regular opportunities are provided for genuine consultation with the team before taking decisions affecting them (e.g. work plans, output, methods, changing places of work, hours, or reporting lines)
- who outside the immediate team should be involved.

Deciding
The leader should ensure that:

- all the options have been considered within the time-scale set
- everyone knows the time and place of the next team meeting at which decisions are to be communicated
- everyone knows exactly what their job is
- each individual has clearly defined targets and performance standards, set following consultation
- everyone knows by name to whom they are accountable, and will be in teams of four–eight if professional staff, and in any case no more than 15
- arrangements have been made for continuity of leadership in leader's absence
- the degree of delegation (e.g. sign their own letters, write the monthly report, do the next presentation, take the queries on a particular subject, project or profit area) is currently at the maximum
- the decision and plan is recorded in writing.

Briefing

The leader will be identified and 'measured' more by the way he or she communicates, than by any other single factor. It is vital to:

- get all the team together regularly
- explain decisions and gain commitment

- brief those outside your team through their bosses
- put across the plan with enthusiasm
- set objectives for the team that are understood by everyone
- encourage questions and provide feedback for those questions to which the answers are not already known
- listen to people's questions and comments
- read the communication signals from facial expressions and body postures
- confirm the briefing in writing.

Monitoring and supporting

Visible leadership is about:

- regularly walking the job by visiting each person's place of work to observe, listen and praise
- knowing the names and titles of all in the team – and using them
- smiling and saying: 'Good morning' with meaning
- being aware of just how the team and leader are managing time; looking for the best way to do so and ensuring that priorities are right
- ensuring that your own work and behaviour standards set the best possible example to the team
- knowing enough about the members of the team to enable you to have an accurate picture of their aptitudes and attitudes at work
- looking for better ways to design jobs, or arranging work to make the best use of people's aptitudes, skills and interest, in order to involve them and gain their commitment
- giving sufficient time and personal attention to matters of direct concern to the individual – their development, training and, where relevant, social and recreational opportunities
- seeing that the team is clear about the working standards expected from them, e.g. in timekeeping, quality of work, housekeeping, safety. 'Having a go' at those who break them
- looking for opportunities for building teamwork into jobs
- checking that there is a formal and fair grievance procedure understood by all, and that the leader deals with grievances and complaints promptly.

Evaluating

Defining the team's direction, planning and briefing, and leading visibly, is to no avail unless the leader allocates time to thinking and evaluating against the original objectives.

- Are the objectives being achieved? If so, are there any individual or team contributions to acknowledge? If not, do the objectives have to be redefined, or does the plan need revising? What authority do I have in these areas?
- In the event of success, do I acknowledge it and build on it? In the case of failure, do I criticise constructively and give guidance on improving future performance?
- Do I design jobs or arrange work to make the best use of peoples' aptitudes, skills and interest, in order to involve them and gain their commitment?
- Can I remove some controls, while retaining my accountability? E.g. can I cut down on the amount of checking I do by holding subordinates more and more responsible for the quality and accuracy of their work?
- Can I delegate more decisions to individuals?
- Has each individual a continuing list of short-term targets for the improvement of their performance, each with its own maturity date?
- Have I made adequate provision for the training and (where necessary) retraining of each person?
- Is the overall performance of each individual regularly (at least annually) reviewed in face-to-face discussion?
- Do I take action on matters likely to disrupt the team, e.g. unjustified differentials in pay, uneven workloads, availability of information technology, discrepancies in the distribution of overtime?
- Do I care for the well-being of the team and seek to improve their working conditions?
- Am I sure that for each individual, work, capacity, and pay are in balance?
- Does the individual see some pattern of career – and salary – development? And if someone is about to retire, do they need help in meeting the problems of retirement?
- If, after opportunities for training and development, someone is still not meeting the requirements of the job, do I try to

find a position for them more nearly matching their capacity – or see that someone else does?

- Is the human resource planning correct, or will I need to start redefining recruitment, selection, and training needs? Do I really have an equal opportunities policy that is seen to be working?
- Do all team leaders get a minimum of three day's leadership training a year?

APPENDIX 2

Communication complicatrions

Reporting negotiations

The rapid communication of results of negotiations between management and the trade unions on hours, pay and other conditions, presents real difficulties. At present, the usual method in industry, commerce, and the public services is for the trade unions' representatives to tell their members what has happened. At some later date, a notice giving the bare essentials may be put up by management. Such arrangements are not adequate. Inaccurate stories get through, wrong explanations are given, and supervisors and managers hear the result from shop stewards. This is unnecessary, as there are better ways of communicating negotiated matters.

Many managers and trade union officials accept the necessity for supervisors and shop stewards being given the facts about what has been settled and what led up to agreement.

Furthermore, the view has been taken that, as a negotiation ends finally in a joint management–trade union decision to accept a particular settlement, there is then a joint responsibility for seeing that the result is communicated to, and understood by, the employees affected. On the basis of these two principles, a drill for joint communication to employees should be aimed at and discussed with the unions involved.

At the end of each negotiating session – whether a decision is reached or not – a brief statement is agreed by the parties outlining what has taken place. If a decision has been reached, the main considerations advanced by both parties may be briefly added.

This joint statement is duplicated in sufficient quantities to ensure that every manager, supervisor, trade union official and shop steward concerned receives an individual copy within 24 hours of the settlement. In large organisations or industries with scattered units this may involve faxing, telexing, or telephoning the statement to large factories, offices or departments, in order to have it run off locally. In the case of smaller units, it may be possible to send the necessary number of copies by post.

In either of these cases, the managers, supervisors and shop stewards receive their own individual copies by hand delivery in the factory. Trade union officials receive their copies by post in pre-addressed envelopes direct from the centre where negotiations have taken place. *Notices are not placed on boards nor are announcements made to the press until 24 hours after the meeting.* By this time, managers, supervisors and trade union officials should all have received individual notification of what has taken place.

These arrangements will not prevent rumour, nor a possible leak to the press, but they do ensure that all those who are likely to influence opinion – both management and union – receive an identical, authoritative statement from their headquarters officials about what has taken place. Experience has shown that, once most people know that there is an official and reliable way of hearing the result of negotiations quickly, they do not base their judgements and actions on rumour alone.

Explaining management decisions where formal consultation has taken place

This problem arises where management has consulted the consultative committee before taking a decision (e.g. a change in meal times, a change in production planning). Management then takes a decision; in the majority of cases, the usual procedure is to inform the consultative committee, whose members are expected to explain that decision to those they represent. As pointed out this method is inadequate, particularly if management has decided to take action *contrary* to that recommended by the committee.

What should the timing be, bearing in mind the need to inform management and respect the position of the work committee representatives?

The most effective order for informing people in such cases is:

1 top management explains the decision to management, including supervisors
2 management explains the decision to the consultative committee
3 managers and supervisors explain the decision directly to all employees affected

---

Example

A company has consulted its works committee on a matter affecting individual employees, and has taken a decision. The next meeting of the works committee is on a Thursday. Satisfactory communication timing is as follows.

● *Monday to Thursday a.m.* Top managers inform their managers and supervisors by systematic team briefing sessions, and if necessary arrange for the distribution of a manager's brief. Managers and supervisors are instructed not to pass information on to employees until Friday morning.

● *Thursday p.m.* The works committee is informed of management's decision and the reasons for it: if the decision does not agree with the previously expressed view of the works committee, some additional explanation will be needed. The committee is also told that managers and supervisors will explain the decision to all employees and the co-operation of the representatives is sought.

● *Friday a.m.* Junior managers and supervisors explain the decision to their working group in briefing sessions.

● *Friday p.m.* Notices posted and/or news-sheet made available.

Communication in a crisis

In a crisis, and particularly if there is a stoppage, it is very tempting to adopt some new method of communication. This can be dangerous, because if confidence has been lost, the introduction of any new procedure may only make matters worse. It is, however, at the very time of crisis that face-to-face communication through managers and supervisors becomes vitally important. This is a strong argument in favour of getting the system of face-to-face communication by managers accepted beforehand as a normal way of explaining things that matter.

Communication across an organisation

Problems of communicating between departments cause difficulty. Such difficulties become obvious more quickly than problems of upward and downward communication. Actions that can be taken to overcome sideways communication problems are:

- encouraging people to go and see their opposite number and not just to write or telephone
- setting up interdepartmental working parties for particular jobs
- moving staff so that, by the time an individual becomes a head of a department, they have spent some time in another part of the firm
- holding management discussion groups at intervals – management training seminars fill this need as a by-product.

APPENDIX 3

Checklist: action by managers

Action by all managers

Personal example
- Have I sorted out priorities for what must be communicated? Is the definition of the subjects involved acceptable? If not, what is a better one?
- Have I a systematic method for explaining face-to-face all such matters to the next two levels of management or supervision responsible to me?
- Do my supervisors, each month, talk to their working group about these matters?
- Is the noticeboard satisfactory? Is it up to date? Is someone responsible for it? Are immediate and permanent notices separated?
- Have I got a newsletter? Do I need one?

Instruction
- Have I told all managers and supervisors responsible to me what is wanted from them on communication? Is it in their job description? Do they know when they should hold a briefing session and what matters they should talk about?
- Do they require training in order to understand their responsibilities, or training in the practice of effective speaking and running a briefing group or a briefing session?

Check
- Do I periodically check that communication is getting through? Have I a reminder system?

- Do I walk the job to check that what I *think* is happening *is* happening?

Action by managing director or general manager

Check

- Am I satisfied that departmental heads have a drill for face-to-face communication on those matters which cause people to give of their best to their work? Would it help to ask each departmental head to write me a note outlining how they operate such a system and how frequently it is used?
- Do supervisors in the offices and on the shop floor get their people together each month for briefing sessions?
- Are supervisors (including those on shifts) brought together by managers in briefing teams? Are they at least as well informed as the shop stewards?
- Have we a system of representative consultative committees for upward communication covering works, technical and office employees?
- Is there a publication readily available for all to read, which carries essential information affecting employees? A news-letter? Or a newspaper?
- Is there an arrangement whereby a management bulletin can be circulated to managers and supervisors whenever they need to be informed of the background to a decision or a negotiation?
- Is there a brief, written annual report for all employees?
- Is there an annual meeting on each site which employees can attend and ask questions about points in the annual report, or anything else concerned with the progress of the company? Should we appoint, perhaps for a limited period only, a particular person to be responsible for seeing that communication is being carried out adequately in the organisation? Alternatively, would a senior person in the personnel department do it part-time?
- Are there accountability charts available for all in the organisation showing who is accountable for whose performance?

Action by personnel officer

- Am I keeping a check on where communication is failing? Am I watching for evidence of failures from committees, courses, individual discussions, surveys, investigations and walking the job?

- Is appropriate training available for managers and supervisors: in their responsibilities for communication; in the techniques of effective explanation and conducting briefing sessions; in the purpose and practice of consultative committees?
- Should I introduce a system of management bulletins?
- Have I approached the trade unions on ways of rapidly reporting negotiated decisions?
- Is there a drill for communicating management decisions on matters discussed in consultative committees which ensures people are informed of them in the right way?
- Do I act as the board's conscience so that when decisions are taken at senior level the communication aspects of the decision are not overlooked?
- Is there a handbook on conditions of service for office and works? Is it adequate and is there a method for keeping it up-to-date?
- Are there accountability charts that make clear who is the immediate boss of each person?

APPENDIX 4

Subjects covered in team briefings

This is a list of subjects that have been briefed by many companies. It is by no means exhaustive but neither is it suggested that your company use all of them.

Progress

Product sales
Market share
Planning
Trading position
Development of subsidiaries
Financial results
Contracts gained/lost
Circulation figures
Cost comparisons
Export sales
Competitors' products
Quality index

Waste reduction
Safety comparisons
Productivity figures
Safe driving awards
Faults
Holes punched
Budgets
Sales targets
Accident record
Order position
Company achievement

People

Appointments
Resignations
Promotions
Internal vacancies
Selection procedure
Relocation of personnel
Overtime levels
Time-keeping

Labour turnover
Grievance/disciplinary
  procedures
Training courses attendance
Job security
Attendance at union branch
  meetings
Research into foreman

Company visits
Customer visits
Absenteeism
Long service awards

selection
Management development
  programme
Conference plans

Policy

Legislation
Change in procedures
Supervisor development
  programme
Expansion plans
Capital investment
  programme
New committees formed
Advertising policy
Employee purchase plan
Setting up of new division
Industrial relations statement

Factory reorganisation/
  extension plans
Job evaluation exercise
Employee saving scheme
Drivers insurance
Suppliers hold-ups
Short-time working
New product information
Project reports
Long/short-term company
  objectives
Training courses

Points for action

Explanations of efficiency
  monitoring system
Fulfilling orders quickly
Sub-contractors on-site
Emergency procedure
Suggestion scheme
Heating, ventilation system
Accident reporting
Fire prevention
Start up after annual break
Stock shrinkage
Private phone calls

Car parking
Dealing with VAT
Maintenance priorities
Production of invoices
Increased costs
Stock discrepancies
Shortage of raw materials
Dealing with complaints
Non-decisions
Correcting of 'grapevine'
  rumours

APPENDIX 5

Checklist: the selection interview

1 Purpose

To match a person to a job.

2 Preparation

- Study available data, e.g. job description, person specification, school report, application form, test results, etc.
- Make an interview plan – guard against bias.
- Allow adequate time.
- Ensure privacy – ensure room appropriate to job ranking – no interruptions.
- Ensure proper reception of applicant.

3 Conduct

- Put at ease, welcome in a friendly way (don't keep applicant waiting).
- Be sure to give precise details about the job concerned.
- Encourage applicant to talk freely about previous jobs, interests etc. Do this by the type of question used. Don't ask leading questions or those which only require a 'yes' or 'no' answer.
- Listen and observe.
- Check that all relevant ground is covered.
- Advise when an answer can be expected.

4 Follow up

- Decide on suitability of applicant – guard against bias.
- Advise accordingly.

APPENDIX 6

Checklist: the termination interview

1 Purpose

(a) To discover person's true reasons for leaving the company with a view to taking any required action to prevent others leaving for the same reasons. Such reasons could be in respect of:

- poor recruitment
- selection
- inadequate training
- company policy
- salary
- management/supervision.

(b) To secure employee's goodwill and company's reputation.

2 Preparation

- Check resignation letter – reason stated.
- Study employee's records.
- Where necessary check with other appropriate people, e.g. supervisor, etc.
- Ensure privacy and no interruptions.
- Allow adequate time.

3 Conduct

- Put at ease.
- State purpose of interview.

- Encourage and allow employee to talk freely about the job, the company and the people.
- Listen and observe: be alert for clues to underlying reason.
- Thank employee for services rendered and wish him or her well.

4 Follow-up

Decide if any action is necessary in the light of information gained, and implement accordingly.

APPENDIX 7

Guide to employment legislation

The main Acts relating to employment are:

Race Relations 1976; Sex Discrimination 1975; Sex Discrimination Act 1986; Equal Pay 1970; Equal Value (Amendment) Regulations, 1983; Disabled Persons 1944, 1958.

These acts seek to promote equality of opportunity and to ensure that no person is treated less favourably than another person, simply on the grounds of their race, nationality, colour, ethnic origin, sex or disability. Under the acts it is unlawful for employers to discriminate in recruitment, promotion, training or transfer, terms and conditions of employment and dismissal. Employers are also liable for unlawful discriminatory acts carried out by their employees in the course of their employment, unless they can show that they took such steps as were reasonably practicable to prevent them from occurring. Job applicants or employees who believe they have suffered discrimination may take their complaint to an Industrial Tribunal.

Discrimination

The most common types of discrimination are:

- *Direct discrimination* – consists of treating a person less favourably than others
- *Indirect discrimination* – consists of applying a requirement or condition which, whether intentional or not, adversely affects one group rather than another.

Both direct and indirect discrimination are unlawful. The act applys to all employers, their employees and to all employment agencies.

Exceptions to this are in cases of genuine occupation qualification. For *race relations* these are where:

1 If authenticity is required for a dramatic performance, or as a model, or where there is desire for a 'special ambience' where food or drink is served.
2 Where the job-holder provides services and welfare, and those services can be provided most effectively by a person of that racial group. This applies to welfare, social services, etc., and explains why advertisements for 'Bengali waiter' are allowed under the acts.

For sex discrimination they are where:

1 As (1) above.
2 Where the job involves physical contact with the opposite sex, or working in a place where members of the opposite sex are likely to be in a state of undress – for example lavatory attendants and persons who sell clothes and may assist in changing rooms.
3 Work in single sex prisons, hospitals etc.
4 Where the law requires the employee to be of a particular sex.
5 The job involves working outside the UK in a country whose laws and customs are such that the duties could not effectively be performed by a person of the opposite sex.
6 Different height requirements for male and female prison officers and police.
7 Ministers of Religion.
8 The Armed Forces.

The Commission for Racial Equality and the Equal Opportunities Commission promote a *code of practice* to implement equal opportunities policies. The codes of practice do not have the force of the law, but employers who do follow the codes of practice are more likely to ensure they follow the spirit of the acts and are less likely to discriminate unwittingly (indirectly). The codes of practice embody the practical steps employers need to take to move towards equality of opportunity:

- responsibility for the policy should be allocated to a suitably qualified member of senior management
- the extent and implementation of the policy should be discussed and agreed with trade unions and employee representatives
- the policy should be made known to all employees and job applicants
- training and guidance on the law and company policy should be provided for supervisory staff and other relevant decision-makers
- selection procedures and criteria should be examined for indirect discriminatory effects and charged where this is found
- the policy should be monitored through analysis of the ethnic origins and gender of the workforce and job applicants.

Monitoring and review

Through monitoring and gathering statistical data on the shape of the workforce, employers can identify areas of under-representation. Appropriate action can then be taken.

Positive action should not be confused with positive discrimination. Positive discrimination means employing someone simply because of their race, sex etc. This is illegal is this country. Positive action is the term used for measures taken under Sections 37 and 38 of the Race Relations Act and under 7.10–7.20 of the Sex Discrimination Act, which in broad terms enables employers, training bodies and trade unions to:

- encourage applications for job or membership from members of a particular racial group or sex
- provide training to help fit them for particular work or posts where they are under-represented.

These exceptions do not however make it lawful for the employer to discriminate at the point of selection to achieve a balance of gender or race.

Segregation The Race Relations Act states that to separate a person from other persons on racial grounds is seen as less favourable treatment, even if the facilities are equal or better.

Disabled Persons (Employment) Act 1944

The act provides that every employer with 20 or more employees has a duty to employ a quota of registered disabled people. The quota is currently 3 per cent of the workforce.

An employer who is below quota should not engage anyone other than a registered disabled person without first obtaining a permit to do so.

The jobs of lift attendant and car park attendant have been designated for registered disabled people.

Equal Pay Act 1970

The main act came into force in December 1975 and the Equal Pay (Amendment) Regulations 1983 on 1 January 1984.

Scope of the act
The title of the act is misleading as it covers almost all the contractual conditions of service and is not restricted to pay. It gives women the right to an 'equality clause' which means that if any term in their contract is less favourable than that in a man's contract it can be modified to make it the same. Also if there is a clause in a man's contract giving him some benefit which is not in the woman's contract it will be awarded to the woman.

A man is also entitled to equality with a woman.

Who can claim
Men and women are entitled to equal pay and conditions if:

1 they are employed on 'like work', which means that their work is the same or of a broadly similar nature,
2 their jobs have been given equivalent rating under a non-discriminatory job evaluation scheme,
3 if paragraphs (1) and (2) do not apply, if their work is of 'equal value' in terms of the demands made on them (for instance under such headings as effort, skill and decisions).

A woman may establish that her work is similar to a man's under one of these three headings, but she will not be entitled to equal pay if the employer can show that the variation in pay is due to a 'material difference (other than the difference of sex) between her case and his'.

Enforcement of the act

A claim may be made to an industrial tribunal during the period of employment or within six months of leaving. A woman can only claim parity with a fellow male employee and a man with a female employee.

If the claim is successful the tribunal can award the difference in pay between the claimant and the employee selected as the comparator backdated for up to two years before the date when the proceedings were instituted.

This appendix is merely a guide to the acts. The law is interpretive; for a particular query or situation, the following bodies will be able to offer further information:

Commission for Racial Equality
Elliot House
10–12 Allington Street
London SW1E SEH

Equal Opportunities Commission
Overseas House
Quay Street
Manchester M3 3AN
Tel: 061–833 9244

Both provide a range of publications and guides to the acts.

The Industrial Society
Robert Hyde House
48 Bryanston Square
London W1H 7LN
Tel: 071 262 2401

The Industrial Society has a phone-in information service which deals with any matter relating to employment legislation. All enquiries are treated confidentially.

APPENDIX 8

The board or panel interview

Advantages

1 Reduces the bias inherent in the individual interview.
2 Enables different interests to be represented so that candidates are viewed from several aspects.
3 Gives each member a chance to concentrate wholly on listening to the candidate while others are asking questions.
4 Makes a more impressive occasion suitable for senior appointments.
5 Enables inexperienced interviewers to learn from experienced ones.

Disadvantages

1 Takes a great deal of time to organise and involves a lot of highly paid manpower.
2 Creates a formal atmosphere which inhibits some candidates.
3 While it overcomes individual bias, it sometimes creates other problems due to serious differences and disagreements between Board members.

Constitution

Sometimes as many as 20 (generally too large to be effective); three or at the most five is appropriate for industry/commerce. This allows for variety in membership (e.g. status, technical or other interest, sex, age, etc.). It enables all members to participate and share the work of interviewing and assessing.

The chairperson

Usually the senior person in the group or someone in a neutral situation, e.g. the personnel or staff officer. He or she should be someone with a wide knowledge of the company and the jobs available.

The chairperson is responsible for:

- planning the work of the board
- briefing members of the board of requirements of the job and the main points of each candidate
- greeting the candidate, introducing members
- opening the interview with 'formal' questions such as verifying basic details of the job and the candidate
- possibly calling on other members to question the candidate or give further information about the job
- closing the interview and telling the candidate when they can expect to hear the results
- thanking the candidate for attending.

The chairperson conducts the assessment by inviting and summing up opinions of members and formulating an agreed view. As in any office, the chairperson is in control of the proceedings and gets to know the idiosyncrasies of his or her members and how to deal with them tactfully.

Members

Members of the board share the questioning and information – given according to a pre-arranged plan. When not asking questions etc., they must listen to and observe the candidate and make their own assessments. They should avoid repeating questions or comments made by other members, unless seriously dissatisfied with candidate's replies. During the assessment they should state their own opinion and discuss it.

Planning and procedure

Careful planning is essential to avoid wasting time and also to enable the board to give a business-like impression. They should have a plan of campaign and stick to it. For example, a three member panel or board might work as follows:

1 The chairperson welcomes the candidate and introduces members, checks main particulars of job and candidate, and may ask further questions on some specific topic.
2 Technical members may ask questions on technical qualifications and experience.
3 'User Department' (i.e. probably candidate's future boss) asks further questions on type of experience, background, interests, etc.
4 Chairperson asks further information, gathering questions and makes sure candidate has asked all the questions and got all information he or she needs. The chairperson then concludes the interview.

Timing: ten minutes for chairperson, five minutes each member. This may be taken in order – or varied – but too much hopping about confuses both candidate and panel members. The chairperson must make sure all points have been covered (some kind of checklist may be helpful).

Assessment

This may be done by informal discussion of members' overall impressions of the candidate or, more generally, by some rating sheet. A five-point scale (giving two points discrimination above and below average) is a sound basis. This may be an alphabetical or numerical scale – depending on the basis of assessment (e.g. NIIP seven-point-plan) – so various aspects of the job must be 'weighed up'. For example, experience will probably be more important than health and physique. Members mark their own rating sheets and then the chairperson invites comments from members, giving ample opportunity for discussing varying views. As the chairperson is usually a senior person,, his or her views should be stated last or they may unduly influence ratings of individual members. Agreement may be reached by informal discussion or by a vote; if agreement is impossible the chairperson usually has the casting vote. While selection is a great responsibility for all the board members, the wise chairperson will usually be influenced by the wishes of the user department.

Assessment may take place immediately after each interview and while it is obviously advantageous to rate each candidate while they are fresh in mind, there are disadvantages to this in that it takes time (a lot of time if serious differences exist). This sometimes leads to an acrimonious discussion, leaving panel members bad-tempered and irritable and acts unfavourably on the following candidate. It is generally better to allow members just time to mark their own rating sheet and note special points they wish to raise on each available candidate. All candidates are assessed at the end; where only one job is available, candidates are ranked in order of preference.

General

As in all selection interviews, the candidate must be treated courteously and an effort should be made to make the interview as friendly and informal as possible: this is more difficult to achieve within the formal setting of a board interview. Board members need some training in interviewing and in the use of the rating sheet and any other 'aids' – and the chairperson and members must learn to work together as a team.

APPENDIX 9

Performance appraisal

A minimum organisation policy.

1 All employees shall have a discussion at least once a year with their manager about their performance. The discussion should recognise good performance and address weaker areas. Most of the content should relate to the future and should result in a specific plan for targets, training and development to help the individual improve.
2 The immediate line manager is responsible for seeing that this is done.
3 The discussion shall take place AT LEAST once a year.
4 Both parties should prepare for the interview and have an input on previous performance and priorities for the future.
5 The conclusions of the manager AFTER the interview shall be written on the appropriate form and individuals shall have the opportunity to add written comments if they wish.
6 Either during the interview, or soon after, a limited number of important targets shall be set on areas of work where progress is needed during the coming period. The person accountable, the timescale and result required should be clearly indicated.
7 Performance against these targets and key result areas should be reviewed regularly throughout the year.

APPENDIX 10

Appraisal – job-holder's checklist

Job holder's checklist for use in preparation for appraisal and target setting interviews.

Difficulties which hinder effective performance.

1 Are you sure of the exact boundaries of your job?
   - Is there any overlap – two people each believing they are responsible for a certain area of work?
   - Is there any uncertainty – areas where you are not absolutely sure whether this item is your responsibility at all?
   - Are there areas not covered – areas for which no one seems to take any responsibility?
2 Are you sure of your exact authority?
   - What are the limits of authority in each area of work?
   - Are these limits high enough/too high?
   - In what areas are decisions left to your discretion?
   - In what areas do you need more room to use your discretion?
   - In what areas would you like more room to use your discretion?
3 What level of performance have you reached in each of the areas of your accountability and against your targets?
   What restricting factors prevent effective job performance?
   - Money – is the departmental budget reasonable/too high/too low?
   - Admin. resources – is the equipment satisfactory for the job? is the recruitment geared to your needs?
   - Communication – do you have adequate warning of changes? Sufficient information on matters affecting the

work? Communication of management thinking?
- Knowledge – what other knowledge would help you in your work?
- Other departments – is there sufficient liaison with other departments, i.e. those from whom you receive work and those to whom you pass work?
- Other difficulties – any other difficulties which hamper you: lack of space, poor floor planning, awkward access, lack of prompt attention to maintenance of machines, etc?

4 Do you have adequate information on your progress towards targets?
5 What specific assistance can be given to help you?
Invitation to say constructively what:
- you personally need (perhaps training)
- what colleagues can do to help
- what management can do to help.

APPENDIX 11

Target analysis questionnaire

When setting targets it is essential that the following questions are asked.

1 How significant is this target in terms of the known objectives of this organisation?
2 How urgent is this target?
3 To what extent is this target measurable? (Consider the yardsticks you have developed.)
4 How clearly is this target described? Does it precisely describe the end results expected?
5 What should the target completion date be? To what extent does this target statement describe an activity leading to a target as opposed to a real end result?
6 To what extent is this target challenging as opposed to being routine? That is, to what extent does this target stretch the individual?

APPENDIX 12

Counselling and appraisal

Questions for the job holder.

1 Consider your performance in your present job. What have you accomplished and how efficiently was it done?
What difficulties did you encounter?
2 What do you consider to be the most important responsibilities of your present job?
3 Do you feel that your present job fully utilises your abilities, training and interests? If not, which of your abilities could be utilised?
How would your job have to be changed to accomplish this?
4 What aspect of the job interests you:
(a) the most?
(b) the least?
5 Do you feel there are some areas of difficulty in your job performance? If so, what action do you feel might be taken to overcome these by yourself or your manager?
6 What kind of work would you like to be doing two to five years from now?
7 Would any special training or experience be required for you to do such work?

APPENDIX 13

Targets and performance review form

1 Name of job holder

2 Department

3 Title of job

4 Date of commencing job

5 Name of immediate boss

6 Name of boss's boss

7 Date when targets were set

8 Date of revisions, if any

9 Date of performance review

10 Dates of intermediate reviews, if any

11 Proposals, if any, for improving contribution by training, extra experience or promotion

12 Comments by job holder on performance review (**18** & **19**)

Signed ....

Date ....

13 Date of last performance review form
Do comments still stand?

14 Comments in **12** noted

Signature of boss ....

Date ....

15 Comments by boss's boss and proposed action in **11** noted

Signed ....

Date ....

16 Objectives of job

17 Main points job holder should concentrate on

1

2

3

4

5

6

7

18 Performance review

1

2

3

4

5

6

7

19 Other comments on performance

Notes: 1 Ask people for whom you (the boss) are responsible
        for their suggested targets
     2 Discuss with them, set targets, and fill in **16** and **17**
       and complete **1–7**
     3 If targets revised, note in **8**
     4 At date of review, complete **9**, **10**, **11**, **18** and **19**
     5 Discuss reviews with people concerned. They should
       complete **12**
     6 Complete **13** and **14**
     7 Pass to boss's boss to complete **15**, and return to boss
       of job holder

The form can be simplified through the deletion of steps **8**, and
10–16.

APPENDIX 14

Example individual training programme (part of)

Objectives. At the end of this part of your training you should: be familiar with the organisation; know the work of the personnel department; be able to deal competently with the correspondence; be able to type copy to required standard; be competent to arrange meetings and record proceedings; demonstrate a shorthand speed of 120 wpm.

Item	Method	Instructor	Location	Time
Knowledge of the organisation	General induction course	Training Personnel manager	Training centre	½ day
Knowledge of work of personnel department: scope/specific aspects	On-the-job	Manager/deputy	Department	Spread over several weeks
Knowledge of external contacts	On-the-job; visits	Manager	Department	Spread over several weeks
Knowledge of secretarial routines	On-the-job	Senior secretary	Department	Spread over 5 days
Knowledge of meeting arrangements	On-the-job	Manager	Department	2 hours
Knowledge of meeting procedures; skill in reporting, drafting, etc.	External course	Specialist instructor	External centre	1 week
Increase shorthand speed to 120 wpm	Coaching	Specialist instructor	Training centre	1 hour per evening until proficient

APPENDIX 15

Example course training programme

Objective. At the end of the training period supervisors should: know the appraisal scheme; be able to assess an employee against a job description; complete appraisal forms and write reports; conduct appraisal interviews.

Subject	Method	Instructor	Time	Aids
First day				
1 Why we are introducing an appraisal scheme – benefits to supervisor and company	Talk and discussion	Senior manager	1 hour	Chart pad
2 The scheme – what it is and how it operates	Talk and discussion	Trainer	1 hour	Slides or transparencies
3 Preparing job descriptions	Talk and questions	Trainer	½ hour	Chart pad Specimen documents
	Practical exercise: preparing job descriptions		1½ hours	
4 Assessing the person	Talk and questions 'Syndicate' discussion	Trainer	½ hour	Case study Chart pad
Second day				
5 Appraisal reports	Talk and questions	Trainer	½ hour	Slides or transparencies
	Individual exercises – filling up forms, writing reports		1½ hours	Specimen forms
6 The appraisal interview; what to do before, during and after	Filmstrip and discussion	Trainer	1 hour	Sound filmstrip
	Role play exercises (two groups); summary session	Trainer and assistant	2½ hours	Case studies
7 Action session: how the learning is to be applied	Discussion	Senior manager	½ hour	Action notes Chart pad

Note: The 'trainer' could be the departmental manager, the training/personnel officer, or an outside specialist instructor.

APPENDIX 16

Training young people: example schemes

B&Q
National DIY Retail Chain
c. 14,000 employees

The average age of a B&Q employee is 27. They open 40 new stores a year; many of the 2,000 or so new staff joining are young people.

B&Q run three main training schemes.

B&Q trainee scheme (YTS)

About 200 young people are taken onto this two year YTS scheme each year and become full employees from day one. They are paid an additional amount and receive employee benefits. The programme includes on-job training and off-job training from external training consultants and leads to a vocational qualification in retail. B&Q were instrumental in writing a recognised DIY specific retail certificate for levels 1 and 2.

'A' level scheme

It is hoped this new scheme will cater for 30–40 trainees, who will receive 15 months' training leading to Department Manager positions. Trainees can qualify for a Certificate in Supervisory Management. The training is reviewed with field-based training officers every three months.

Graduate trainees

Graduates of any discipline are recruited to undertake 12 months of intensive training leading to their appointment as Assistant Store Manager. The programme involves six months in-store experience on the sales floor learning retail skills, followed by three months as acting Department Manager, and three months as acting Assistant Manager. In addition, the trainee receives off-job training in leadership, interpersonal skills, and finance.

All trainees plus the general store assistants who are recruited directly into positions benefit from:

- an in-store induction programme with an induction work-book
- use of an open learning work station, found in every store. The interactive video and computer based learning pro-grammes cover a range of subjects, from how to deal with solvent abuse, through product knowledge to inventory management. Employees complete relevant open learning workbooks in company or their own time. Certificates are awarded for completion of workbooks
- managers trained in assessment procedures and instructional skills
- training follow-up and evaluation by Store Managers, and Training Co-ordinators in larger stores.

APPENDIX 17

Sample objectives of youth forum/apprentice association

Example 1

1 To establish and perpetuate the corporate identity of trainees at work.
2 To increase job knowledge and company knowledge.
3 To increase knowledge of civic and legal matters.
4 To promote social life among trainees.

Example 2

1 To consider ways in which the personal development of young people may be encouraged.
2 To identify community problems and to plan to alleviate them.
3 To provide a structure through which young people will be able to exchange ideas among themselves and with management.

Example 3

1 To provide a common meeting ground for all members, for social, recreational, and training purposes.
2 To provide the means of collective consideration of mutual and individual problems, and bring these to the manager concerned.

Example 4

The objectives of the Association shall be to provide for its members educational, social, and recreational activities not normally provided by the company.

APPENDIX 18

Sample constitution of youth forum

1 The aim of the youth forum is to establish and perpetuate the corporate identity of trainees at work by increasing job and company knowledge, serving the community and promoting social life among the trainees.

2 The youth forum committees shall consist of a chairperson, a secretary, a treasurer, and six other members.

3 At the discretion of the committee, other members may be co-opted on the committee with the consent of all the other forum members.

4 The committee shall be elected by the members present at half-year general meetings.

5 Each committee member shall hold office for a period of six months (March to August – September to February).

6 No committee member, if re-elected, should hold 'committee' office for more than one year. No person shall be allowed to hold more than one position on the committee.

7 Voting at youth forum meetings shall be by a show of hands.

8 The constitution of the forum and any amendments, rescindments or suspensions of any part of the constitution must be approved by a majority vote of the youth forum members present at a general meeting.

9 Enrolment to the forum shall be by invitation of the committee and by presentation of a valid membership subscription card.

10 Membership subscription cards will remain the property of the forum.

11 Resignation from the forum shall be by completing and signing a resignation form by the resigning member.

12 Should the youth forum committee consider it just to suspend or terminate a person's membership they may, after consultation with the person concerned, suspend for a defined period or terminate completely his membership.

13 A subscription of 50 pence per week will be collected fortnightly from the members.

14 Every matter shall be determined at a committee meeting by a majority vote of committee members.

15 At general meetings, in the case of an equality of votes, the chairman shall have a casting vote.

16 There shall be a quorum of five.

17 Minutes shall be taken at each meeting and distributed to all committee members and other interested persons prior to the next meeting where this is possible.

APPENDIX 19

Industrial Society youth campaigns

The Industrial Society works with young people in schools, colleges, universities, and polytechnics to show them the opportunities that exist in industry and commerce; to encourage them to start acquiring the skills they will need in their working lives; and to keep updating those skills. The Society:

- develops programmes for young employees that encourage them to be self-reliant and enterprising, and to take more individual responsibility for their further development
- works with organisations to help managers and team leaders develop the full potential of young employees
- forges links between the education sector and the business world so those in business appreciate the tasks of education and those in education understand the needs of business and can ensure that their students are prepared for working life.

The Graduate Industrial Society

The GIS is a society of graduates from university, polytechnics, and colleges of higher education. Formed in 1986 by ex-students and Industrial Society members, the GIS aims to:

- improve the effectiveness of graduates in industry and commerce
- encourage companies to use their graduate resources more effectively
- maintain the enthusiasm of new graduate recruits and their belief in the importance of industry and commerce while they

go through the difficult period of learning the ropes
- forge stronger links between education and industry.

The GIS also organises speakers, meetings, development workshops, and industrial visits. The GIS publishes a newsletter and annual magazine.

The Student Industrial Society

Student Industrial Societies exist to increase awareness amongst undergraduates of the importance of industry in society and to stimulate debate on Britain's industrial future.

There are 60 societies with over 12,000 members spread throughout universities, polytechnics, and colleges in Britain. Local societies organise visits to a wide range of organisations, including coal mines, factories, and retail stores and speakers from management, trade unions, and small businesses.

Nationally, the Society runs an annual conference, a business quiz, and a yearly magazine, as well as many other projects with a wide range of companies.

For further information about the Society's work in youth services, contact the principal office at:

Quadrant Court
49 Calthorpe Road
Edgbaston
Birmingham
B15 1TH
Telephone: 021–454 6769

APPENDIX 20

Personal symptoms of under-delegating

Do you need to delegate more?

1 Do you have to take work home almost
every night?   YES/NO
Why? ....
Outline actions you can take to cut this
down ....

2 Do you work longer hours than those you
supervise?   YES/NO
Steps you could take to change this to a
'No' ....

3 Are you frequently interrupted because
others come to you with questions or for
advice or decisions?   YES/NO
Why does this happen? ....
Plans for cutting down these interruptions
....

4 Do you spend some of your working time
doing things for others which they could
do for themselves?   YES/NO
Actions you might take to avoid this
....

5 Do you have unfinished jobs accumulating,
or difficulty meeting deadlines?   YES/NO

6 Do you spend more of your time working
on details than on planning and supervising?   YES/NO

Why? ....
For better balance, you could ....

7 Do you feel you must keep a close watch on
the details if someone is to do a job right?   YES/NO
Examples ....
Different plans for control of results would
be ....

8 Do you work at details because you enjoy
them, although someone else could do them
well enough?   YES/NO
Such as ....
What to do about this ....

9 Do you lack confidence in your staff's
abilities so that you are afraid to risk letting
them take on more responsibility?   YES/NO
Examples ....

10 Are you too conscientious (a perfectionist)
about details that are not important for the
main objectives of the job in hand?   YES/NO
Examples ....
New plans to try for this ....

11 Do you keep job details secret from staff,
so one of them will not be able to displace
you?   YES/NO
Examples ....
New plans for action ....

12 Do you believe that an executive should be
rushed in order to justify his or her salary?   YES/NO
Why? ....
An executive's principal job is ....

13 Do you hesitate to admit that you need
help to keep on top of your job?   YES/NO
Examples of help you could use ....
List those of your staff who could be trained
to give this help ....

14 Do you neglect to ask staff for their ideas
about problems that arise in their work?   YES/NO
Examples ....
To change this you could ....

Adapted from *The Techniques of Delegating*, by Donald and
Eleanor Laird (McGraw-Hill, 1957).

APPENDIX 21

The process of delegation

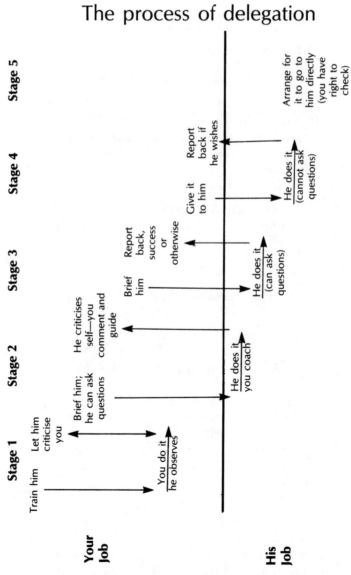

Courtesy of Group Personnel Division, Reed International.

APPENDIX 22

Allocation of time

Activity	Hours per month now	Percentage of total time	Present time spent: + too much ◯ about right − not enough	To which of my objectives does this activity contributes	Could any of this be delegated?	Notes for action
Forward planning						
Liaison with customers, suppliers, etc.						
Regular meetings						
Special meetings						
Budgeting and cost control						
Visiting other department, branches of the organisation						
Reporting back to my manager						
Dealing with problems delegated by my manager						
Dealing with problems brought up by my staff						
Appraisal and training of staff						
Briefing own staff about plans, etc.						
Self-development (courses, visits, etc.)						
Creative thinking						
Travelling						
Breaks (meals, etc.)						
Other						

Notes

1 The above headings are examples only and will vary according to the type of job.

2 When you have marked 'Too much time spent/Not enough time spent', etc. beside each item, some of the headings may need to be broken down into more detail, e.g. if regular meetings are taking too much time, does this apply to all such meetings or only some? The purpose of this chart is thus to point to areas which look out of proportion within the total job.

APPENDIX 23

Example delegation plan

Name:
P. Harding

Task delegated:
Recruitment of staff
for branch office

**Target date for
full acceptance:**
1 October

Section of task	Additional authority needed	Plan for additional training and/or experience	Others to be notified
1 Designing and placing newspaper advertisements	Up to £X per advertisement Total annual limit as per budget	A Course on job advertisements 17–19 June B PH to draft all job ads for head office staff for next two months (I to coach)	KL
2 Preparing short list for interview		A PH to spend three days at branch office with heads of departments. Late July (i.e. holiday period) B PH to redesign application forms by 1 September	BRB MS
3 Initial interviews		Refresher course on interviewing techniques July	
4 Use of special aptitude tests	Access to test result files	PH to be coached by JMR. PH to be self-sufficient by mid-July	AS MDV
5 Letters of appointment	From general manager	PH to study Employment Protection Act	SLP

APPENDIX 24

Company policies: decision taking

A number of organisations have evolved policies on decision taking. These, of course, amount to little more than guidelines – how *can* you legislate for every situation? However, at the same time, they can be enormously helpful once the right sort of environment has been created. They help managers sort out the priorities and make them more consistent people to work for or deal with. Here are two typical policies, written down, after consultation, by chief executives.

Policy 1

- Decisions should be delegated as far down the management chain as practicable.
- Sufficient preparatory work, often by specialists, should be carried out to ensure that a meaningful discussion with employees or their representatives can take place.
- Managers should take the final decision only after considering fairly and fully the facts and the opinions of employees or their representatives.
- Employees or their representatives should be involved as early as possible before any decision is taken on changes which may affect their conditions of employment, their work or their working environment.
- All relevant information should be provided in terms which can be readily understood.
- Many day-to-day decisions can be made without direct employee involvement on every occasion if general parameters are already established.

Policy 2

Delegation
Our policy on decision taking is based upon the principle that the most highly motivated decisions are those that we take ourselves. Therefore, wherever possible, decisions in this organisation should be delegated to whoever has to carry out the action.

Consultation
Where a decision is to be taken that affects either an individual or a number of people, it is the job of the leader of that group to take the decision *after* consulting. Leaders should therefore, first, sincerely seek people's views, except on those few occasions when time prevents. *They will also consult employee representatives, where appropriate.* Having done this, they will then take the decision themselves, basing it upon what they believe to be right, but having taken into account the views expressed, their own experience, and judgement.

Explanation
Deciders will explain *why* they have taken the decision, in order to help people to live with it and enthusiastically carry it out, *even if they don't agree.*

Consistency
Where a decision has been taken at a higher level, and affects people, it is the responsibility of the leaders at *every* level to see that it is implemented energetically, *whether they agree or not.*

Company objectives
When taking decisions, the guiding principle will be the greatest possible achievement of the organisation's objectives. The decision taker will try to be as positive and consistent as possible. If events show that the decision is wrong, the deciders must be prepared to admit that they made a mistake and change the decision accordingly.

Right of appeal
If somebody believes that the decision involves an injustice and not merely a difference of opinion, they must be encouraged to make use of the grievance procedure or, after talking to their immediate boss, go and see the level above.

APPENDIX 25

Time savers' checklist

- Study recurrent crises and find out ways to plan ahead to avoid them.
- Spend more time in future on upward rather than downward communication.
- Think about the boss's problems.
- Keep all your scribbled notes, telephone message slips, and doodles for a period of a month; analyse them and you may find clues to how to save time next month.
- Draw up an occasional 'laundry list' of detailed activities for periods of a half-hour at a time; analyse these and see where the time went.
- Note how long things take.
- Develop a daily/weekly/monthly/annual 'timetable' and encourage others to do the same.
- Learn when to say 'no'.
- Think periodically of what you will do when you retire.
- Get well acquainted with modern mathematical and statistical methods.
- Delegate.
- Ask other people what devices *they* use to save time.
- Schedule active/positive tasks *first*. Build-in interruption allowances and allow time for reactive tasks.
- Avoid lots of short work periods; try to get a continuous stretch.
- Schedule the jobs requiring maximum 'brain capacity' to be carried out when you are at your best.
- Aim to *achieve* something every day.
- Ask yourself regularly: 'What is the best use of my time right now?'

APPENDIX 26

Chairing and leading meetings

Meetings are occasions when a group of people come together to share ideas and experiences. They serve a variety of purposes, e.g. information giving, information gathering, persuading, problem solving. The role of the chairperson is influenced by that purpose.

Preparation and planning

Consider: purpose, membership, size and agenda.

Arrange: venue (quiet, comfortable, everyone able to see and hear)
visual aids and recording of proceedings.

Plan: procedure, including own introductory statement.

Conducting the meeting

- Create 'climate' by treating members with courtesy, respect and impartiality.
- Open by explaining purpose and procedure.
- Start discussion by an 'overhead' or 'direct' question.
- Encourage full participation: remember that maximum participation by the chairperson means minimum participation by the members.
- Assist communication by asking questions, listening to members' contributions, clarifying misunderstandings, correcting errors, rejecting irrelevancies, co-ordinating ideas, giving information, and summarising.
- Aim for systematic progress towards achieving the purpose of the meeting.

- End meeting by summing up and agreeing conclusions with the group.

Controlling the discussion

Questions
- 'Overhead' question: addressed to group as a whole; engages everyone's attention; avoids putting pressure on individuals before they are ready to answer.
- Direct question: brings in individual with special knowledge, or a reticent member; increases tempo.
- Redirected question: aids continuity; involves other individuals.
- Relay question: readdressing a question, directed at the chairperson, to the group for reply.
- Reverse question: get individuals to answer their own questions – polite way of asking them to think again to bring out views they are known to have. (N.B. when addressing a question to individuals, say their name first to engage their full attention.)

Statements
To supply information needed; to stimulate discussion; to clarify or reflect the views of an individual or of the group.

Summaries: interim
Review progress; highlight important points, refocus 'off-track' discussion; change direction; slow down pace of discussion.

Summaries: final
Confirm conclusions; give members a sense of achievement.

Problems

People
- Talkative types: use when relevant and not monopolising conversation – otherwise interrupt, thank for contribution, and redirect question to another member.
- Long-winded types: try and help them express their ideas concisely; be tactful.
- Silent members: encourage and support them – draw them

out by asking questions you know they can answer; try to analyse reason for silence.

- The quibblers: want to concentrate on minor points – ask rest of group if they want to do so, or suggest it be deferred.
- Persistent questioners: return questions to them or group if they are trying to trap chairperson; if they genuinely do not understand, try to help them.
- The objectors: can be quarrelsome – ask for their reasons/ evidence.
- Dominating types: try to hold back their contribution until others have had their say. (N.B. to counter-balance the above types, encourage the positive members, i.e. knowledgeable, experienced people with a commonsense attitude.)

Situations

- Conflict: hold the ring; relieve tension by rephrasing in less emotive terms, by humour, by change of subject; avoid getting personally involved.
- Unpopular decisions: when under attack from group, continue to argue your case and build on any support from individual members.
- Lack of interest: try to illustrate to group how matter might affect them personally; drop topic temporarily and come back later; change approach.
- Off-the-track or irrelevant questions/discussion: may indicate lack of interest; if genuine concern on a vaguely related issue, try to deal with it quickly; ask relevant question; summarise frequently.
- Confidential information: by accident or design chairperson may be asked for this – state clearly that that information cannot be given, and explain why.

APPENDIX 27

Main legislation affecting employment

Data Protection Act 1984
Disabled Persons (Employment) Acts 1944 and 1958
Employment Acts 1980, 1982, and 1988
Employment Protection Act 1975
Employment Protection (Consolidation) Act 1978
Equal Pay Act 1970
Factories Act 1961
Health and Safety at Work, etc. Act 1974
Industrial Training Acts 1964 and 1982
Offices, Shops and Railway Premises Act 1963
Race Relations Act 1976
Rehabilitation of Offenders Act 1974
Sex Discrimination Acts 1975 and 1986
Shops Acts 1950–1965
Social Security Act 1973
Social Security and Housing Benefits Act 1982
Trade Union Act 1984
Trade Union and Labour Relations Act 1974
Transfer of Undertakings Regulations 1978
Transport Act 1968
Wages Act 1986
Young Persons (Employment) Acts 1939 and 1964

APPENDIX 28

Health and Safety at Work

The ways of securing the health and safety of people at work and protection of the public affected by work activities are established in Great Britain by law. In 1974 the Health and Safety at Work Act (HSW Act) set out the relevant responsibilities of employers and of people at work.

The HSW Act put duties on employers, the self-employed, employees, controllers of premises, designers, manufacturers, importers and suppliers. It requires that, so far as is reasonably practicable, premises, equipment, systems of work and articles for use at work are all safe and without risks to health. Supporting Acts and Regulations deal with particular hazards and types of work.

The Health and Safety Executive has a special responsibility to ensure that the HSW Act and other law on health and safety is observed. Its main instruments for this purpose are the Inspectorates listed below.

Through a network of twenty Area Offices throughout Great Britain, HSE inspectors review a wide range of work activities. They work mainly by giving expert advice and guidance, but they will, where necessary, issue enforcement notices and institute prosecutions.

HM Factory Inspectorate: manufacturing and heavy industrial premises and processes, as well as construction activities, local authority undertakings, hospitals, schools, universities and fairgrounds.

HM Agriculture Inspectorate: farms, horticulture and forestry.

HM Explosives Inspectorate: the manufacture, transport, handling and security of explosives.

HM Mines and Quarries Inspectorate: all mines and quarries.

HM Nuclear Installations Inspectorate: which on HSE's behalf licenses nuclear installations ranging from nuclear power stations and nuclear chemical works to research reactors.

Local Authorities: In most commercial undertakings enforcement of the legislation is undertaken by officers of the Local Authority.

All this work depends on close co-operation between field inspectors, policy branches, specialist inspectors, technical and scientific staff involved in research, testing, sampling and measuring activities and the Employment Medical Advisory Service.

Information about HSE and its work can be obtained from enquiry points at:

Baynards House,
1 Chepstow Place,
Westbourne Grove,
London W2 4TF
(Tel: 071–221 0870 Ext 6721/6722)

Broad Lane
Sheffield S3 7HQ
(Tel: 0742 72539 Ext 3113/3114)

St Hugh's House,
Stanley Precinct,
Bootle,
Merseyside L20 3QY
(Tel: 051–951 4381)
Prestel: HSE lead frame No '575'.

APPENDIX 29

Long-term absence through ill-health: procedures

1 The employee should be contacted periodically and, in turn, should maintain regular contact with the employer.
2 The employee should be kept fully informed if employment is at risk.
3 The employee's GP should be asked when a return to work is expected and of what type of work the employee will be capable.
4 On the basis of the GP's report, the employer should consider whether alternative work is available.
5 The employer is not expected to create a special job for the employee concerned, nor be a medical expert, but to take action on the basis of the medical evidence.
6 Where there is reasonable doubt about the nature of the illness or injury, the employee should be asked to agree to be examined by a doctor appointed by the company.
7 Where an employee refuses to co-operate in providing medical evidence or to undergo an independent medical examination, the employee should be told in writing that a decision will be taken on the basis of the information available and that it could result in dismissal.
8 Where an employee is allergic to a product used in the workplace, the employer should consider remedial action or a transfer to alternative work.
9 Where the employee's job can no longer be kept open and no suitable alternative work is available, the employee should be informed of the likelihood of dismissal.

10 Where the dismissal action is taken, the employee should be given the period of notice to which they are entitled and informed of any right of appeal.

See ACAS Advisory Booklet No. 5: *Absence* (1985).

APPENDIX 30

Persistent short-term absence: procedures

1 Absences should be investigated promptly and the employee asked to give an explanation.

2 Where there is no medical advice to support frequent self-certificated absences, the employee should be asked to consult a doctor to establish whether medical treatment is necessary and whether the underlying reason for absence is work related.

3 If, after investigation, it appears that there were no good reasons for the absences, the matter should be dealt with under the disciplinary procedure.

4 Where absences arise from temporary domestic problems, the employer, in deciding appropriate action, should consider whether an improvement in attendance is likely.

5 In all cases, the employee should be told what improvement is required and warned of the likely consequences if this does not happen.

6 If there is no improvement, the employee's age, length of service, performance, the likelihood of a change in attendance, the availability of suitable alternative work and the effect of past and future absences on the business, should all be taken into account when deciding on appropriate action.

7 It is essential that persistent absence is dealt with promptly, firmly, and consistently, in order to show both the employee concerned and other employees, that absence is regarded as a serious matter and may result in dismissal. An examination of records may identify those employees who are regularly absent and may show an absence pattern. In such cases, employers should make sufficient enquiries to determine whether the absence is because of genuine illness or for other reasons.

See ACAS Advisory Booklet No. 5: *Absence* (1985).

APPENDIX 31

Checklist: effective discipline

1 Has a disciplinary code been drawn up in consultation with all levels of the workforce?

2 Are the rules and regulations reviewed annually to keep them in line with the needs of the organisation and limited to a minimum of items?

3 Does a disciplinary procedure exist and is it adhered to logically?

4 Does a system exist whereby *all* employers not only have copies of rules and procedures, but have been trained in their use and thoroughly understand them and their objectives?

5 If there are unions, have they been consulted from the outset; do they understand their part?

6 Is a fair and understood management development plan working in the organisation to enable all employees to benefit from the training and possible promotion?

7 Does a structured appraisal system exist, linked closely to agreed standards of performance?

8 Do all those in charge of others receive basic training on all aspects of discipline, grievance, and work-group maintenance?

9 Does the workforce agree all the concepts upon which the disciplinary code is based? Does the disciplinary code concur with socially desirable items?

10 Is there an appeals procedure that enables those people being disciplined to have every opportunity to put forward all aspects of their case?

11 Is the code accepted as an integral part of the management–union agreement?

APPENDIX 32

Disciplinary code

'Disciplinary rules and procedures are necessary for promoting fairness and order in the treatment of individuals and in the conduct of industrial relations. They also assist an organisation to operate effectively. Rules set standards of conduct at work; procedure helps to ensure that the standards are adhered to and also provides a fair method of dealing with alleged failures to observe them.'

Main provisions

1 Define rules in writing and set standards. Define penalties for serious offences – preferably after discussion with trade union. Make rules known to each employee. Avoid unnecessary rules – review all rules and use of discipline procedure at least every two years.
2 Establish whether there has been an offence and what the circumstances are before deciding appropriate action. What are the facts? Does the behaviour make sense? What is the reason/underlying cause?
3 Ensure individuals understand the standard required. Confront them with their failure and aim to get them to change their ways – first by informal and then by formal warning, indicating the consequences of continued failure to meet the standards.
4 Provide evidence of previous warning/behaviour by a written record/warning. Basic justice requires that the disciplinary action can be substantiated to an 'outsider'.
5 Refer case to someone not directly involved before enforcing sanctions (personnel/establishment officer or more senior manager).

6 Provide means of objection/appeal.
7 Specify limits of authority for supervisors/managers.

Essential features of a disciplinary procedure

It should:

- be in writing
- specify to whom it applies
- provide for matters to be dealt with quickly
- indicate the disciplinary actions which may be taken
- specify the levels of management which have the authority to take the various forms of disciplinary action, ensuring that immediate supervisors do not normally have the power to dismiss without reference to senior management
- provide for individuals to be informed of the complaints against them and to be given an opportunity to state their case before decisions are reached
- give individuals the right to be accompanied by a union representative or by a fellow employee of their choice
- ensure that, except for gross misconduct, no employees are dismissed for a first breach of discipline
- ensure that disciplinary action is not taken until the case has been carefully investigated
- ensure that individuals are given an explanation for any penalty imposed
- provide a right of appeal and specify the procedure to be followed.

When operating disciplinary procedure, management should view the prime objective as encouraging improvements in the employee, rather than the imposition of sanctions. Action must be taken promptly as delay allows facts and recollections to fade, and could be interpreted by individuals as management condoning their actions. Only in serious cases should consideration be given to suspension (with pay) for a limited period to establish facts.

In the main, the first formal step ought to be a formal oral warning, followed by a written warning, followed by a final written warning, followed by discharge. However, the type of warning issued will depend on the magnitude of the offence.

Records are important not only for evidence before a tribunal, but as an indication of what has happened in order that all involved parties are in no doubt as to what the offence was and what corrective action is needed.

APPENDIX 33

Model salary policy

1 Introduction

The aim of this document is to set down the organisation's policy with regard to salary. It is the responsibility of all who apply it to explain it fully to their subordinates.

2 Aims

The aims of the organisation's policy are:

- to recognise the value of all jobs relative to each other within the organisation and in comparison with similar jobs outside
- to recognise the value of the individual to the organisation and to relate this to the salary range applicable to the job.

3 Salary structure

The salary structure will be based on job evaluation. Each job will have declared minimum and maximum salary range and it is the organisation's policy to pay at least the minimum for each job.

4 Job evaluation

It is the policy of the organisation to ensure that staff are fully involved in job evaluation. Moreover, a staff representative will be a member of the job evaluation committee.

Job evaluation is a continuing process and once salary grades have been established, the team will meet regularly to deal with regrading of existing jobs as well as grading new jobs.

5 Initial salary

In determining an individual's salary on appointment, no differentiation is made on the grounds of race, sex or age. In addition, the following features are taken into account:

- the value to the organisation of the relevant experience the individual brings
- the individual's value in the outside market
- the individual's value in comparison to existing staff who hold similar jobs.

6 Performance appraisal

An integral part of salary management is the regular appraisal of staff. This helps to determine training needs and it is the basis upon which management counsels individuals in order that employees have maximum opportunity to develop their own potential. During the appraisal, short- and longer-term targets will be mutually agreed with management for the year ahead.

7 Salary reviews

It is the policy of the organisation to review the salaries of all staff on an annual basis. Those under 18 years of age will be reviewed on a quarterly basis.

8 Promotion

An individual who is promoted to higher-grade work will have a salary increase of 10 per cent or will be paid the minimum for the new grade, whichever is the greater.

If an individual is required by the organisation to take work of a lower grade, there will be no salary decrease. Instead there will be a salary standstill until the rate of the new position equals that of the old.

9 Progression within salary range

Everyone will know the salary range for their job. Those who do their job particularly well will reach the maximum for their salary range within four years.

10 Right of appeal

Anyone who feels unhappy about the application of this

policy has the right to appeal first to their manager and then to the Managing Director, whose decision will be final. The individual has a right to bring along a colleague to help his or her appeal.

APPENDIX 34

Model job description

JOB TITLE: DATE:
Secretary to Chief Project Engineer

DEPARTMENT: AGREED BY:
Project Engineering   Chief Project Engineer

RESPONSIBLE TO: JOB TITLES OF
Chief Project Engineer   SUBORDINATES:
                                        None

OVERALL PURPOSE:
To provide a complete secretarial service to Chief Project Engineer by organising the routine aspects of the work.

Daily tasks:
1 On receipt of mail, sort into order of priority, attach previous correspondence, if any, and type routine letters for signature.
2 Take dictation from Chief Project Engineer and deal with urgent correspondence dictated by senior project engineers.
3 Against a timetable, type complicated statistical tables connected with department's project work.
4 Deal with department's travel arrangements and prepare travel itineraries.
5 Maintain simple time records concerning progress of experimental projects. Ensure that progress charts are kept up-to-date.
6 Act as an assistant to Chief Project Engineer by dealing with the more routine aspects of the work.

7 Act as 'shield' by dealing with callers personally and on the telephone.

Weekly tasks:
Prepare for accountant short summary of expenses incurred by department during previous week, and allocate to individual projects.

Monthly tasks:
Collect brief reports prepared by senior engineers on their respective projects and type draft of progress report for the Project Engineering Director.

Six monthly tasks:
Transfer old files to basement and make out new files for next six months.

Annually:
Type statement of account showing income over expenditure on previous year's projects.

Job requirements and other information:

Minimum age:	21 years.
Educational qualifications:	5 'O' levels (including English language) and secretarial college training.
Experience:	3 years' practical office experience including 1 year in a similar firm.
Induction:	3 months.
Other information:	The Chief Project Engineer is frequently off-site and the secretary is expected to deal with all routine problems arising during these periods.

APPENDIX 35

Model job evaluation questionnaire

Job title: ....

Department: ....

Responsible to: ....

Agreed by: ....Date: ....

---

1 What is the overall purpose of the job?

---

2 Draw up a family tree showing the job in relation to others in the department.

---

3 Give a concise description of the main areas of responsibility in the job. Take it area-by-area and stress the important features.

Daily tasks:

Weekly tasks:

Monthly tasks:

Quarterly tasks:

Half yearly tasks:

Annual tasks:

4 Give the titles of the jobs which you directly supervise.

5 Who do you contact inside and outside the organisation during the course of your job? Is contact by telephone or in person? Comment on the reason for contact.

Internal:

External:

6 Do you handle confidential information? If so, describe.

7 Comment on the qualifications and/or experience necessary to do the job effectively.

8 Other information:

APPENDIX 36

Model job evaluation briefing notes

Introduction

Job evaluation is a method of looking objectively at jobs and ranking them in order of importance. By comparing them one with another, each job will be placed in a grade relative to its worth. However, it must be stressed that it is the *job* which is being examined and *not* the individual.

A job evaluation committee has been formed under the chairmanship of Andrew Brown, the Company Secretary. The other members of the committee are Alan Green and Jill Black. The job evaluation committee will be responsible for carrying out the job evaluation and grading.

The scheme

After a great deal of investigation, the committee has decided to use a classification scheme, a copy of which is attached. All members of staff will be required to provide full details of their jobs using the attached questionnaire.

Completing the questionnaire

1 Overall purpose

One sentence will normally suffice here. It should be concise and give the reason for the job's existence in order that the committee has 'something to hang its cap on' before looking at the job in depth, e.g.

Process all orders ensuring that departmental computer codes are included and that VAT figure is correct.

2 Family tree
A clearer picture of your job is given if you draw up a family tree of your department showing your job in relation to other jobs.

3 Job description
It is always difficult to write one's own job description: consider therefore that you are transferring to another department in the organisation and that you must prepare a note for your successor covering the elements of the job. Describe the job as it is and not how it should be. (If you feel you are going into too much detail, it probably means that you are just about right!)

    Write down the area headings first. For example: correspondence, planning, queries, staff, and describe the responsibility involved under each heading, e.g.

> Correspondence – on receipt of mail, decide what can be delegated to subordinates and retain non-routine letters. Where necessary give instructions regarding the handling of particular letters.

4 Supervisory responsibility
Supervisory responsibility can be assessed fairly only by examining carefully the job description of those jobs under your jurisdiction.

5 Contacts
The strength of the organisation lies in the service given to customers. This does not diminish the value of internal contacts. What is important is the level at which contact is normally made and the reason for contact in the first place.

6 Confidential information
Describe in this section any confidential information which you handle regularly in the job. For example: personnel records, salaries or company plans.

7 Qualifications and/or experience
Comment should be made here regarding the minimum qualifications and/or experience which might be brought to the job before it can be done effectively. It may be possible to state an actual qualification or the job may call for 'an aptitude for figures'. Experience required must be quite specific. For example: six months' practical experience in credit control.

8 Other information
No questionnaire can possibly cover all aspects of a job and

since it is important that all staff have the opportunity to comment on all areas of the job which are important to them, space is provided for this, e.g.

Large proportion of work is concerned with meeting tight time schedules.

These comments should cover features which are an integral part of the job and not temporary difficulties.

Completion date for questionnaires

All questionnaires must be completed and returned to Alan Green by Monday, 29 March.

Completion date for job evaluation exercise

With the co-operation of everyone, the committee hopes to complete the grading exercise by 15 May.

Right of appeal

Any member of staff who feels their job has not been fairly evaluated has the right to appeal to the team through their head of department. They can then expect to be invited, along with the head of department, to discuss the job in detail with the members of the committee. The decision by the committee following the appeal will be final.

APPENDIX 37

Example of job classification scheme

Grade A: Tasks are simple and conform to clearly laid down procedures. All written work and calculations are checked. Up to a few weeks' training required.

Grade B: Tasks are subject to laid down procedures but can involve a limited measure of initiative. Work subject to spot checks. Up to six months' training or experience required.

Grade C: Tasks are carried out and decisions made in accordance with standard procedures, subject to infrequent supervision. Routine contact, external and internal, up to own level to obtain and provide information. Probable minimum of two years' experience or training.

Grade D: After specific direction, plans and arranges work within main work programme with little or no supervision. Only non-routine problems referred to supervisor. May have supervisory responsibility. Can have contact at higher level than own, external, and internal, to obtain and give information which may be of a confidential nature. Specialised knowledge may be required. Probably five years' experience.

Grade E: After general direction, plans and arranges work with little or no supervision. Tasks can involve work of non-routine nature requiring an original approach as to planning and method. Would normally have contact at higher level than own, external and internal, to obtain and give information which may be of confidential nature. Can be required to make decisions as to daily action and direct work of subordinates. More than five years' experience required.

APPENDIX 38

Salary structure

Using a scattergram

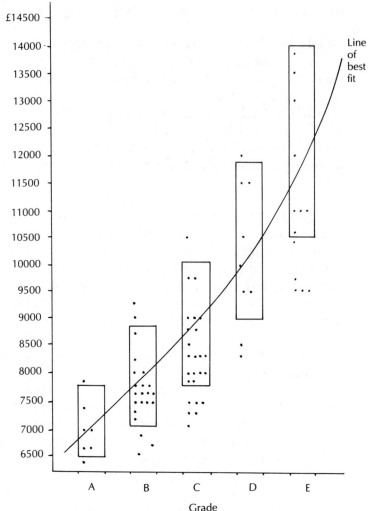

● = Number of people within each grade along with their current salary

Salary structure after a job evaluation exercise

Grade A   £6500–£7850
     B   £7200–£8800
     C   £7850–£10050
     D   £9000–£11750
     E   £10400–£14000

Note that the maximum figures for each grade are between 30 per cent and 45 per cent above the minimum figures and the base for the next grade is at approximately the midpoint of the previous grade. The structure is based on the scattergram above.

Final salary structure after adjustment to match market rates (5 per cent up)

Grade A   £6725–£8142
     B   £7460–£9140
     C   £8142–£10452
     D   £9350–£11237
     E   £10820–£14600

APPENDIX 39

Salary review form

Salary review – 1 April 198

CONFIDENTIAL   **DEPARTMENT** . . . .

1 Name	2 Job title	3 Age at 31/3	4 Service at 31/3	5 Date last perfor- mance increase	6 Amount	7 Present salary	8 Grade	9 Maxi- mum salary	10 Perfor- mance category this year	11 Proposed increase	12 New salary	13 Remark
Total												

APPENDIX 40

Checklists: Trade unions

Union recognition and union membership

1 Is there a written statement of the policy towards the unions, indicating a positive attitude and encouraging employees to join the appropriate unions?
2 Has the policy been carefully explained to supervisors and managers?
3 Do contracts of employment indicate which unions are recognised, and do they encourage employees to belong to the appropriate union? Is the policy also explained to people during recruitment and on appointment?
4 Have all new starters been put in touch with their steward?
5 Have certain noticeboards been set aside for union notices?
6 Have arrangements been made for union meetings to be held on the premises, and where appropriate, for union dues to be deducted from wages?

Stewards

1 Has a minimum period of service before election been agreed with the union?
2 Has the number of stewards to be elected and the area or group they represent been agreed with the union?
3 Have facilities and the arrangements for elections been agreed with the unions?
4 Have elections been given sufficient publicity; is help given with facilities, noticeboards, typing, etc?
5 Have written credentials for stewards been issued jointly by management and the union?

6 If credentials cannot be issued, have stewards been given a formal letter acknowledging their election?

7 Have stewards been given copies of all relevant agreements, rules and schemes by management?

8 Is the steward's responsibility for observing all agreements with the union written into the credentials?

9 Do stewards receive their average hourly rate of earnings while carrying out relevant union duties in working hours?

10 Have the circumstances been defined in which stewards can leave their jobs in order to carry out their duties as stewards?

11 Have agreements, conditions of employment, and organisation structure been explained to newly-elected stewards within a week of their election?

12 Does management discuss the training of stewards regularly with full-time officials?

13 Are stewards encouraged to attend outside training courses, without loss of earnings?

CHAPTER 1

See Chapter 11
   Appendix 1

Further reading:
Adair, J. *The Action-Centred Leader*, London: The Industrial
   Society Press, 1988.
Adair, J. *Effective Leadership*, Aldershot: Gower, 1983.
Henderson, J. *A Guide to the Employment Acts*, London:
   The Industrial Society Press, 1990.
Scott, J. & Rochester, A. *Managing People*, British Institute
   of Management/Sphere.

CHAPTER 2

See Appendices 2, 3, 4

Further reading:
Communication Skills Series, The Industrial Society Press.
Decker, B. *How to Communicate Effectively*, London: Kogan
   Page, 1989.
Scott, B. *The Skills of Communicating*, Aldershot: Gower.

CHAPTER 3

See Chapter 8
   Appendices 5, 6, 7, 8

Further reading:
Henderson, J. *A Guide to the Employment Acts*, London:
   The Industrial Society Press, 1990.

MacKenzie Davey, D. & McDonnell, P. *How to Interview*, Corby: British Institute of Management.
O'Neill, B. *The Manager as an Assessor*, London: The Industrial Society Press, 1990.
Rae, L. *The Skills of Interviewing*, Gower: Aldershot.

CHAPTER 4

See Chapter 7

CHAPTER 5

See Chapter 6
    Appendices 9, 10

Further reading:
Maddux, R. *Effective Performance Appraisals*, London: Kogan Page, 1989.
O'Neill, B. *The Manager as an Assessor*, London: The Industrial Society Press, 1990.
Packard, P. & Slater, J. *The Skills of Appraisal*, Aldershot: Gower.

CHAPTER 6

See Appendices 11, 12, 13

CHAPTER 7

See Chapter 4, 5, 6
  Appendices 14, 15

Further reading:
Honey, P. *The Skills of Training*, Aldershot: Gower.

CHAPTER 8

See Appendices 16, 17, 18, 19

CHAPTER 9

See Chapters 1, 2, 5, 6, 10, 16

Further reading:
Basil, D. C. *Leadership Skills for Executive Action*, New York: AMA.
Brown, M. *The Manager's Guide to the Behavioural Sciences*, London: The Industrial Society Press, 1986.
Dell, T. *How to Motivate People*, London: Kogan Page.
Drucker, P. F. *The Practice of Management*, London: Heinemann.
Herzberg, F. *Work and the Nature of Man*, New York: World Publishing.
Garnett, J. *The Work Challenge*, London: The Industrial Society Press, 1988.
McGregor, D. *The Human Side of Enterprise*, New York: McGraw-Hill.
White, P. *Preparing for the Top*, London: The Industrial Society Press, 1990.

CHAPTER 10

See Chapter 6
    Appendices 20, 21, 22, 23

Further reading:
Adair, J. *How to Manage Your Time*, Guildford: The Talbot
    Adair Press, 1987.
Devery, C. *Working with Management: A Secretary's Guide*,
    London: The Industrial Society Press, 1985.
Devery, C. *Working with a Secretary: A Manager's Guide*,
    London: The Industrial Society Press, 1986.
Garratt, S. *Manage Your Time*, London: Fontana, 1985.
Goodworth, C. T. *Effective Delegation*, London: Business
    Books, 1988.
Holroyde, G. *How to Delegate – a Practical Guide*, Rugby:
    Mantec, 1970.
Jenks, J. & Kelly, J. *Don't Do-Delegate: The Secret Power of
    Successful Managers*, London: Kogan Page, 1986.
Laird, D. & E. *The Techniques of Delegating*, New York:
    McGraw-Hill, 1957.
Townsend, R. *Up the Organisation*, London: Michael
    Joseph, 1970.
Trethowan, D. *Delegation*, London: The Industrial Society
    Press, 1989.
White, P. *Preparing for the Top*, London: The Industrial
    Press, 1990.

CHAPTER 11

See Appendix 24

CHAPTER 12

See Chapters 2, 10
    Appendices 25, 26

Further reading:
Adair, J. *How to Manage Your Time*, Guildford: The Talbot Adair Press, 1987.
Adair, J. *The Effective Communicator*, London: The Industrial Society Press/Kogan Page, 1988.
Devery, C. *Working with Management: A Secretary's Guide*, London: The Industrial Society Press, 1985.
Devery, C. *Working with a Secretary: A Manager's Guide*, London: The Industrial Society Press, 1986.
Haynes, M. *Make Every Minute Count*, London: Kogan Page.
Grummitt, J. *Rapid Reading*, London: The Industrial Society Press, 1977.
Pemberton, M. *Effective Meetings*, London: The Industrial Society Press, 1982.
Vidal-Hall, J. *Report Writing*, London: The Industrial Society Press, 1977.

CHAPTER 13

See Chapter 3, 14
    Appendix 27

Further reading:
Henderson, J. *A Guide to the Employment Acts*, London: The Industrial Society Press, 1990.
Howard, G. *Statutory Sick Pay*, London: The Industrial Society Press, 1990.
Howard, G. *Statutory Maternity Pay and Maternity Rights*, London: The Industrial Society Press, 1990.

CHAPTER 14

See Appendix 28

Further reading:
Carthy, C. *Health and Safety: A Safety Representative's Handbook*, London: The Industrial Society Press, 1990.
Deadly Maintenance: A Study of Fatal Accidents at Work, HMSO, 1985.
Effective Policies for Health and Safety, HMSO, 1986.
Essentials of Health and Safety at Work, HMSO, 1988.
Managing Safety: A Review of the Role of Management in Occupational Health and Safety by the Accident Prevention Advisory Unit of HM Factory Inspectorate, HMSO, 1981.
Morgan, P. & Davies, N. 'Costs of Occupational Accidents and Diseases in GB', *Employment Gazette*, p477, November 1981.
Review Your Occupational Health Needs: Employer's Guide, HMSO, 1988.
Success and Failure in Accident Prevention, HMSO, 1976.

CHAPTER 15

See Chapter 16
Appendices 29, 30

Further reading:
Balcombe, J. *Study of absence rates and control policies*, London: The Industrial Society Press.

CHAPTER 16

See Chapter 13
Appendices 31, 32

Further reading:
Adair, J. *Effective leadership*, London: Gower.
Adair, J. *Training for leadership*, London: Gower, 1978.
Brown, M. *The Manager's Guide to the Behavioural Sciences*,
London: The Industrial Society Press, 1986.
Henderson, J. *A Guide to the Employment Acts*, London: The
Industrial Society Press, 1990.
Herzberg, F. *Work and the Nature of Man*, Cleveland: World
Publishing, 1966.
Maslow, A. H. *Motivation and Personality*, New York:
Harper and Row, 1970.
McGregor, D. *The Human Side of Enterprise*, London:
McGraw-Hill.
Townsend, R. *Up the Organisation*, London: Michael
Joseph, 1970.

CHAPTER 17

See Chapters 2, 5, 6
Appendices 33, 34, 35, 36, 37, 38, 39

Further reading:
Bowey, A. M. (ed.) *Managing Salary and Wage Systems*,
Aldershot: Gower.
McBeath, G. & Rands, D. N. *Salary Administration*,
Business Books Ltd, 1976.
Pearson, S. & Coulthard, D. *Personnel Procedures and
Records*, London: Gower, 1987.
Scott, K. *Clerical Job Grading and Merit Rating*, Institute of
Administrative Management, 1983.

CHAPTER 18

See Appendix 40

Further reading:
Green, G. D. *Industrial Relations*, London: Pitman, 1987.